ESPN
The Making of a
Sports Media Empire

ESPN

The Making of a
Sports Media Empire

TRAVIS VOGAN

UNIVERSITY OF ILLINOIS PRESS

Urbana, Chicago, and Springfield

Library of Congress Cataloging-in-Publication Data
Vogan, Travis.
ESPN : the making of a sports media empire / Travis
Vogan.
    pages   cm
Includes bibliographical references and index.
ISBN 978-0-252-03976-8 (hardcover : alk. paper) —
ISBN 978-0-252-08122-4 (pbk. : alk. paper) —
ISBN 978-0-252-09786-7 (e-book)
1. ESPN (Television network)—History. 2. Television
broadcasting of sports—History. I. Title.
GV742.3.V62   2015
070.4'49796—dc23   2015012600

Contents

Acknowledgments

This book includes a lot of voices. These voices, I think, offer a sense of vitality and even humanity to what is, in the end, a relatively straightforward cultural and industrial analysis. In fact, this book's best and most interesting moments come not from me, but from the many sports media professionals who took the time to teach me about ESPN, the circumstances out of which it emerged, the principles that guide it, and the ever-bulging industry it now so self-assuredly purports to lead. The people with whom I spoke—and who facilitated my correspondences—include Jim Allegro, Michael Antinoro, Jim Bates, Brian Bedol, Bob Beyus, Steve Bornstein, Tommy Craggs, John Dahl, Amanda DeCastro, Mark Durand, Stuart Evey, Steve Fainaru, Mark Fainaru-Wada, Nathaniel Friedman, Libby Geist, Laura Gentile, Jonathan Hock, Steve Isenberg, Nick Kastner, Peter King, Josh Krulewitz, John Lack, Chris LaPlaca, Will Leitch, Shari Leventhal, Robert Lipsyte, Tina Pagano, Bill Rasmussen, Don Rasmussen, Scott Rasmussen, Steve Rotfeld, David Roth, Erik Rydholm, Connor Schell, Ron Semiao, Mark Shapiro, Dan Silver, John Skipper, Alfred Slote, Erik Smetana, Glenn Stout, John Walsh, Jess Walter, Royce Webb, Ron Wechsler, and Norby Williamson. Others opted to remain anonymous (though I did not include any quotations from "off the record" sources in the manuscript). Thanks to all who agreed to be interviewed—your memories, perspectives, and observations improved this book immeasurably.

Big thanks to Mo Smith for making some introductions that got the ball rolling on my interviews—and wound up convincing me to take my research for this project in a more interesting direction. Julian Rubinstein also connected me with some vital sources. Dan Nathan read and provided very helpful comments on an early draft of what became chapter 2. Seth Friedman read the entire draft and provided suggestions that tightened the final manuscript. Thanks to Aaron Baker, Dick Crepeau, and Vicky Johnson for their careful feedback and suggestions for revision. Special thanks go to Vicky for being so encouraging, enthusiastic, and generous over the years. Finally, I want to acknowledge my colleague Dave Dowling for coauthoring an article on *Grantland.com* that helped me to work through a handful of ideas that are sprinkled about this manuscript. It is an honor to have the fingerprints of so many scholars whom I admire on the finished product.

I had the great fortune of research assistance from a bright cast of now former University of Iowa undergraduates: Tom Clos, Bria Davis, Mallory Miranda, and Brady Starnes. Thanks also to the good people at Columbia University's Rare Book & Manuscript Library for facilitating my research trip to peruse Roone Arledge's papers. My research assistance and trips were funded in part by much-appreciated start-up funds and an Old Gold Summer Fellowship from the University of Iowa College of Arts & Sciences. The University of Iowa School of Journalism & Mass Communication's Becky Kick and the Department of American Studies' Laura Kastens were commendably patient in helping me to organize and pay for these ventures.

Thanks are due to several journals—*Convergence: The International Journal for Research into New Media Technologies*, the *International Journal of Sport Communication*, and the *Journal of Sport History*—that granted me the privilege of piloting some ideas that show up in this book in dramatically revised and expanded form.

It is a unique luxury to be able to spend one's professional life doing something enjoyable. It is even sweeter when that life is filled with enjoyable people. I am so fortunate to be surrounded by good-humored colleagues here in the University of Iowa's School of Journalism & Mass Communication and Department of American Studies.

As with all big tasks, it helps to be in the company of clever, experienced, and easygoing folks. I had such a positive experience working with the University of Illinois Press—and Danny Nasset in particular—for my first book that I decided to give it another go with them. Danny, Bill Regier, Tad Ringo, Steve Fast, Kevin Cunningham, and the rest of the crew at UIP have made the laborious process of transforming an idea into a book seem relatively smooth. Thanks also to Annette Wenda for the copyediting services and to Kristen Fuhs for putting the index together.

Finally—and most important—thanks go out to my friends and family for dealing with me all these years.

ESPN
The Making of a
Sports Media Empire

INTRODUCTION

An ESPN Culture

We believe that the appetite for sports in this country
is insatiable.

—Bill Rasmussen, ESPN cofounder[1]

ESPN has turned sports into a utility. What ESPN did
was to make it possible to turn on your TV and have
sports come out, just like turning on your faucet and
have water come out.

—Robert Thompson, Syracuse University Center
for the Study of Popular Television[2]

Shortly after ESPN's September 7, 1979, launch, the *Washington Post*'s Jane
Leavy asked the new outlet's president, Chet Simmons, how he thought the
public would respond to an all-sports cable TV network. "I guess we'll have to
have a battery of divorce lawyers standing by to handle all the cases," Simmons
quipped. "Did you ever think that a television network would be named as a co-
respondent in a divorce action?"[3] Three years later, a woman in Austin, Texas,
actually did name ESPN in her divorce suit. She claimed it ruined her marriage by offering her apparently addicted husband too much sports coverage.[4]

In 1998 ESPN set up a satellite receiver in Antarctica for eight total viewers. The move transformed it into the only cable outlet that provides service
to every continent on Earth. In the process, it made the network's self-given
title as "The Worldwide Leader in Sports" (also adopted in 1998) seem slightly
less audacious. As then ESPN chair Steve Bornstein remarked, "The sun never
sets on the ESPN empire."[5]

On January 26, 2000, Alisha and Chad Blondeel of Newaygo, Michigan,
named their newborn son Espen—a tribute to Chad's favorite TV channel.

Though the first, Espen Blondeel was not the last of ESPN's honorary progeny. As part of its twenty-fifth anniversary celebration in 2004, ESPN included a segment that featured eleven young Espens (several of which spelled the name Espn). The name is now registered on *Babynames.com*. As silly as it may be to name a child Espn, it is almost unimaginable that an infant would be christened HGTV, VH1, or Comedy Central. This is because these parents named their children not after a cable network, but after a brand, a set of cultural meanings that exceed the institution they represent and serve as a recognizable marker of identity and community.

In 2006 ESPN unveiled Mobile ESPN, a cellular phone that also provided on-demand sports content anywhere its customers roamed.[6] A promotion for the gadget featured *SportsCenter* anchor Trey Wingo claiming—in the popular news program's signature smart-aleck tone—that inventions like the wheel and electricity pale in comparison to the space-age product. He then asks an implied audience of straight men to "imagine if you will a world where you could follow Game 3 of the World Series and get credit for sitting through your girlfriend's cousin's wedding" and promises the innovation will ensure that "life will never get in the way of your sports again." Mobile ESPN proved a spectacular failure and was off the market within a year. This costly experiment, however, illustrates ESPN's monumental ambition and even conceit. With Mobile ESPN, the media outlet not only strove for ubiquity, but also attempted to serve as a sort of utility—a branded circuit through which customers passed any time they checked scores, ordered a pizza, or called a friend. "We wanted a total sports ecosystem," said Mobile ESPN senior vice president Manish Jha of the goals that informed the eventually aborted product's creation.[7]

What could be more popular than ESPN? Not much, according to two 2014 *Forbes* reports that named it the world's most valuable media property and the second most valuable sports brand after Nike.[8] ESPN is popular in two principal ways, both of which illuminate its significance and uses. First of all, ESPN is pervasive. Second, it is utterly ordinary. Sports media—in part because of their ordinariness—are traditionally considered to be less thoughtful and refined than other genres. Though the sports page has long driven newspaper sales, it is known throughout the industry as a "toy department" that is not held to the same journalistic standards as "real" news. This attitude is similar in sports television, which is often critiqued for claiming to report on organizations that TV outlets pay handsomely for the rights to carry games. Moreover, the beer-guzzling, pot-bellied male sports television viewer—Al Bundy, Homer Simpson, and the like—has become a popular symbol of idle masculinity. In these representations, sports TV is a mundane excuse to avoid thinking (along with spouses, kids, and jobs) rather than a site that provokes thought. Sports media have a reputation for not providing much in the way of credibility, complexity, or edification. Those who consume sports media have a reputation for not demanding these qualities.

"If culture," notes sports media scholar David Rowe, "is the 'stuff' of everyday life—the frame through which we experience, interpret, mold, and represent everything that surrounds us—then sport occupies an uncommonly prominent position within it." By extension, if "media," as Robert W. McChesney claims, "made sport," then sports media play a key role in culture.[9] The aesthetic, economic, industrial, and political contexts that inform sport's and mass media's long-standing symbiosis shape sport's cultural meanings and uses. No institution has, or has ever had, a more influential role in this popular milieu than ESPN. We blame our failed relationships on it, name our children after it, and can access it anytime and anywhere—even in Antarctica. If you go to an ESPN Zone restaurant and order enough ESPYs—a cocktail named after ESPN's annual awards show—you can get drunk on ESPN. In short, we live in an ESPN culture.

Raymond Williams cites *culture* as one of the English language's most complex terms. Most generally, it is "the signifying system through which . . . a social order is communicated, reproduced, experienced, and explored." But it is also the "work and practices of intellectual and especially artistic activity"—what nineteenth-century poet and literary critic Matthew Arnold called "the best that has been thought and said."[10] Culture, in this second sense, composes the objects and undertakings that make people and institutions *cultured*.

While sports media are inarguably part of culture, they are not stereotypically cultured. However, over the course of its history, ESPN has strategically engaged practices considered more sophisticated than run-of-the-mill sports media—an effort that intensified after the Walt Disney Company's 1996 acquisition of ESPN and the cable network's resultant transformation into a synergy-driven and multiplatform corporate subconglomerate. ESPN began to produce documentaries, publish books, create fictional series, curate film festivals, sponsor literary writing awards, and employ Pulitzer Prize–winning journalists. These activities construct what sociologist Pierre Bourdieu calls "symbolic capital," or contextual value that gives certain objects, practices, people, and institutions greater prestige than others. This book examines ESPN's unlikely development of symbolic capital and probes the ends that inform this effort. It considers and critiques how ESPN's cultural ambitions aid its larger attempts to build authority within and beyond sports media. In the process, it explains how these brand-driven activities illuminate and expand sports media's meanings while asserting ESPN's centrality to this environment.

ESPN's multiplatform efforts to cultivate sophistication illustrate how contemporary media convergence, in Henry Jenkins's words, "alters the relationships between existing technologies, industries, markets, genres, and audiences."[11] Along these lines, ESPN exploits common attitudes that give meaning to the media it uses and the content they deliver. Media ethnographer Ilana Gershon terms these attitudes media ideologies, or "sets of beliefs about communicative technologies with which users and designers explain perceived media structure and meaning."[12] Gershon argues that media's social meanings are relational: attitudes about one medium shape perspectives on others. ESPN's expansion into different media capitalizes on their relative value. For example, its forays into film use the medium's stereotypical status as more artful than television and the Internet to brand its TV and online content as exceptional. ESPN also exploits media genres' ideologically constituted value. For instance, it frequently produces and programs documentary content, a variety of TV that discourses surrounding the medium—what we might call generic ideologies— suggest is extraordinarily enriching. Like its reliance on film's popular meaning, it uses documentary's relative symbolic capital to cultivate respectability that is rare in sports media. In addition to engaging these high-toned media practices, ESPN builds alliances with other powerful symbols—from canonical filmmakers to independent book publishers—that signal refinement. By the time ESPN began these efforts, it had already established itself as a multifaceted culture, a framework through which sport is known, experienced, and represented that, in former company president George Bodenheimer's words, endeavored to "deliver a fully branded experience at every consumer touch point."[13] These activities work to inflect this ESPN culture with culture.

Beyond cultivating sophistication, Bourdieu claims symbolic capital is "economic or political capital that is disavowed, misrecognized and thereby recognized, hence legitimate, a credit which, under certain conditions, and always in the long run, guarantees economic profits."[14] Though it often markets them as such, ESPN's ambitions to create prestige are not motivated by disinterested aesthetic goals. They instead drive a shrewd effort to distinguish ESPN from other sports media outlets, compete for market share, expand its demographic reach, promote its content, and even cut costs.

Importantly, these engagements do not affect an elitist style that derides or dismisses popular forms—far from it. Rather, they cultivate a middlebrow sensibility that satisfies audiences seeking more urbane content without alienating those who simply want to know what is happening in the world of sports.[15] ESPN, in fact, unrelentingly tests how far its brand will extend in virtually any direction that might lead to revenue or positive exposure. As part of its twenty-fifth anniversary, for example, the media outlet licensed a series of McDonald's Happy Meal toys, commemorative cans of Bud Light, and its own Gatorade flavor. The following year, it signed a fifteen-year, $850 million contract that allowed the sports video game company EA Sports to use its brand.[16] Though not always as visible as the beer cans and video games that bear its name, ESPN's more stereotypically refined offerings help to build the branded authority that compels companies like EA Sports to pay such enormous prices to commingle with the Worldwide Leader.

ESPN Culture in Context

This is an exciting time for the study of sports media—a topic long neglected in academe partly because of its low cultural associations that is now gaining currency in the humanities and social sciences. Most scholarship on sports media unsurprisingly focuses on event coverage and popular news programs.[17] This work typically points out and critiques sports media representations' ideological implications and tendency to reinforce dominant hegemonies. But commercial sports media never merely depict sport. They also, for instance, help media outlets to build brands, promote content, and vie for sponsors, clients, and customers. These factors impact the shape sports media representations take and, consequently, are vital to understanding the meaning they make.

Extant scholarship and commentary on ESPN seldom consider the intersecting economic, industrial, institutional, historical, and cultural contexts that inform the content it produces.[18] Journalistic accounts, such as Michael Freeman's *ESPN: An Uncensored History* and James Andrew Miller and Tom Shales's best-selling *Those Guys Have All the Fun: Inside the World of ESPN*, provide behind-the-scenes glimpses that outline and expose the company's history, policies, and practices. While they deliver instructive critiques and entertaining historical tidbits—particularly through their interviews with industry professionals—these popular accounts often privilege recounting ESPN's interoffice scandals and its executives' corporate war stories over explaining the company's place in and impact on sports media and popular culture.

This scholarly and journalistic work can consequently benefit from humanistic media studies, which tends carefully to the contexts that inform media's creation and circulation. "Production practices," Amanda Lotz reminds, "inordinately affect the stories, images, and ideas" that media create and sell. But "stories, images, and audience interpretation," Lynn Spigel adds, "are never strictly ruled by the logic of the market."[19] Media, these scholars indicate, are produced, distributed, and consumed through a sometimes slippery matrix of cultural and commercial forces. They can therefore be properly understood only when considered in relation to these interweaving circumstances. Accordingly, this study considers how ESPN engages a range of practices beyond event coverage and news to construct distinction in sports media and popular culture. It traces the media outlet's development into the so-called Worldwide Leader in Sports and considers how its efforts to establish and maintain this status build on, reconfigure, and enforce contemporary sports media's significance and uses. More broadly, it uses ESPN as a lens through which to consider how contemporary media industries fashion cultural value and to explore the industrial, institutional, commercial, and political purposes this painstakingly manufactured meaning serves over time and in different milieu.

To situate ESPN within the contexts that inform its practices, the chapters that follow consider the company's products across platforms, the discourses and marketing it generates, and commentary on the organization. They do so through considering a combination of texts, popular and trade discourses, archived material, and interviews with ESPN employees and other relevant sports media professionals. The interviews enliven the textual, discursive, and archival research while bringing to light new information and perspectives. The texts, popular and trade commentary, and archival sources corroborate, expand on, and contextualize the interviews, which sometimes reflect individuals' selective memories and self-interests more so than ESPN's actual history and practices.

Chapter 1 offers a brief history of ESPN that outlines its growth from the obscure cable TV upstart Entertainment and Sports Programming Network into a pervasive, corporate-funded media entity. It focuses on ESPN's efforts to establish a visible, credible, and fashionable brand leading up to 1998—the point when the increasingly diversified and persistently self-aggrandizing media outlet nicknamed itself the Worldwide Leader in Sports and undertook the prestige-driven array of activities that compose this book's principal focus.

In September 1998, ESPN unveiled *SportsCentury*, a multiplatform media event that centered on a series of documentary profiles that counted down the twentieth century's top-fifty North American athletes. Beyond chronicling sport history, ESPN used the *SportsCentury* documentaries to brand itself as a public historian. Shortly after its initial run, *SportsCentury* expanded into the ESPN subsidiary channel ESPN Classic's featured prime-time series. While the rebooted series maintained *SportsCentury*'s style and ostensible commitment to recounting sport's heritage, it was primarily used to promote ESPN's other content. Moreover, *SportsCentury*'s development complemented ESPN's larger effort to acquire historical footage and, in the process, to build and govern an archive of sport's visual history. Chapter 2 uses *SportsCentury* to explain how ESPN brands itself as a reliable historiographer, asserts its centrality to sport history, and attempts to control the production of visual narratives about sport's past.

In 1996 *Sports Illustrated* and CNN—both of which are owned by Disney rival Time Warner—collaborated to launch the sports-news cable TV channel CNN/SI. Partly in response to this threat, ESPN premiered *ESPN the Magazine* in 1998. It marketed the magazine as a youthful contrast to *Sports Illustrated* that borrows from ESPN's televisual style. ESPN turned to the Internet—a technological milieu traditionally reputed to produce lower-quality content than print—to establish a connection to more stereotypically serious sports-writing. In 2000 *ESPN.com* formed *Page 2*, an offshoot designed to provide culturally aware opinion and analysis. It crafted a respectable identity for the website by hiring a roster of prominent print journalists that included David Halberstam, Hunter S. Thompson, and Ralph Wiley. In addition to these recognizable authors, *Page 2* hired up-and-coming Web-based writers, most notably blogger Bill Simmons, whose populist and conversational style was native to and designed for the Internet. While many of *Page 2*'s writers lacked Halberstam's, Thompson's, and Wiley's stature, ESPN situated the website's content as exceptional by suggesting it grows out of the print tradition they represent. Chapter 3 considers how ESPN used *ESPN the Magazine* and *Page 2* to establish a symbolically and economically valuable relationship to print that spans multiple platforms.

In 2001 ESPN formed the subsidiary ESPN Original Entertainment (EOE), which produced a variety of content that included reality programs, talk shows, feature-length docudramas, and scripted series. It principally engaged these new genres to expand its viewership beyond adult male sports fans, enrich established customers' connection to its brand, and publicize its other programming. Additionally, these ESPN Original Entertainment productions—specifically the docudramas and scripted series—routinely emphasized ESPN's and its corporate sibling ABC's significance to American sport history. They built realism, for instance, by integrating archived ESPN and ABC footage and including the companies' trademarks and personalities. Chapter 4 examines how ESPN Original Entertainment's productions engaged new generic horizons in ways that reinforce the media outlet's import.

In 2007 ESPN teamed with New York City's Tribeca Film Festival to establish the Tribeca/ESPN Sport Film Festival. The following year, ESPN launched ESPN Films, which specializes in feature-length documentary films. ESPN Films' most ambitious and aggressively publicized project thus far is *30 for 30* (2009–10), a series of thirty documentaries made by thirty commissioned filmmakers to celebrate ESPN's thirtieth anniversary. Spearheaded by Bill Simmons, the series covered a range of topics on sport's history since 1979 and recruited a diverse roster of celebrated directors. ESPN markets *30 for 30* through emphasizing three primary qualities that distinguish the series, and, by extension, ESPN, from other sports media: the use of documentary, the productions' status as films that offer cinematic experiences, and the filmmakers' position as prominent artists. Moreover, ESPN Films extended *30 for 30* after its initial run into a permanent series of documentaries and launched several offshoots. Chapter 5 examines how ESPN Films expands on *SportsCentury*'s use of the documentary genre, *Page 2*'s conscription of respected authors, and ESPN Original Entertainment's long-form productions to situate ESPN as part of cinema culture.

Perhaps even more surprising than its partnership with Tribeca, ESPN joined the PEN American Center in 2010 to create the PEN/ESPN Literary Sports Writing Award for an outstanding nonfiction book about sports. The following year, Bill Simmons leveraged his rising celebrity to create the sports and popular culture website *Grantland.com*. Taking inspiration from magazines like *GQ* and mimicking the strategy by which *30 for 30* created a refined image, the website specializes in long-form journalism, boasts a roster of noteworthy writers and editors who established their renown in print, and is named after the canonical sportswriter Grantland Rice. Moreover, *Grantland* teamed with the independent publisher McSweeney's to produce *Grantland Quarterly*, a collection of the website's best works repackaged as hardcover books. Complementing *Page 2*'s adventurous content and extending ESPN's strategic partnership with PEN, *Grantland* and *Grantland Quarterly* use print's cultural meanings to situate ESPN's online content as literary. *Grantland* eventually morphed into a boutique multimedia hub that hosts a variety of complementary content. Chapter 6 examines how ESPN uses *Grantland* to create a multiplatform subnetwork devoted entirely to building cachet.

In 2012 ESPN partnered with the PBS documentary series *Frontline* to produce *League of Denial: The NFL's Concussion Crisis*. The documentary, based on ESPN investigative journalists Mark Fainaru-Wada and Steve Fainaru's book of the same title, interrogated the NFL's failure to adequately protect its players from concussions' health risks and exposed the league's efforts to discredit research that discovered links between concussions and brain damage. ESPN's alliance with a credible documentary series like *Frontline* extended *SportsCentury* and ESPN Films' documentary practices as well as ESPN's collaborations with Tribeca, PEN, and McSweeney's. ESPN, however, removed its brand from the documentary shortly before its fall 2013 premiere. Although ESPN claimed it separated its brand from the project for editorial reasons, critics charged that the NFL—ESPN's most valued client—pressured the media outlet to do so. I end this book by using ESPN's involvement with *League of Denial* to explain how the organization balances its cultural ambitions and institutional priorities and to explain how these priorities shift in response to changes in the sports media ecology.

During his tenure at ESPN, Steve Bornstein reportedly displayed a framed quote in his office that read: "Kill the ones that will eat us. Eat the ones we kill." ESPN, as Bornstein's interior decor indicates, stops at nothing (except perhaps offending the NFL) to control every potentially profitable revenue stream that flows through the sports media landscape. This corporate mission is fueled in part by ESPN's wide-ranging efforts to build sophistication. These practices compose an important strain in ESPN's institutional DNA that showcases how sports media's cultural status is built and illuminates the motives that inform this process.

It would take an enormous book to discuss ESPN's entire history, the full range of its practices, and the many forces that influence them. This is not that book. There are numerous important factors that this project's scope will allow me to consider only in brief. I focus, for instance, almost entirely on ESPN's work for the U.S. market, and I do not provide detailed analyses of its event coverage and news programs. Additionally, while I take into account critical and industrial responses to ESPN, I pay little attention to how everyday audiences—the so-called sports junkies to which ESPN so attentively caters—receive it and put it to use. Despite these limitations, this study does show how ESPN's efforts to build refinement augment its global activities, event coverage, and news programming. Moreover, my focus on ESPN's institutional operations—and its brand management in particular—demonstrates how the company urges consumers to understand it. While this may be the first academic book on ESPN, it surely will not be the last. It leaves much for those who may wish to examine further the Worldwide Leader's history and practices and will hopefully prove useful as they proceed.

From the Entertainment and Sports Programming Network to ESPN

ESPN may become the biggest thing in TV sports since *Monday Night Football* and night-time World Series games.

—William O. Johnson, *Sports Illustrated*[1]

Like hamburgers and French fries, [ESPN] is one of the emblems of America.

—Tom Knott, *Washington Times*[2]

On Memorial Day weekend 1978, Bill Rasmussen, the exuberant forty-five-year-old director of communications for the World Hockey Association's (WHA) Hartford Whalers, received word that his employment was terminated. This did not come as much of a surprise—or even a disappointment, really—to the former entrepreneur and broadcaster who had bounced around the New England sports media scene since selling his interests in an advertising service business to join Amherst, Massachusetts's WTTT radio in 1962. The Whalers, like most franchises in the upstart WHA, were in financial trouble and desperately needed to free up some capital.

Despite his firing, Rasmussen kept an already scheduled appointment with Ed Eagan, an Aetna Insurance agent by day who was producing a TV show on Connecticut-area sports for cable distribution on the side with Bob Beyus, a telecommunications contractor who kept an office at Plainville, Connecticut's

United Cable and owned production equipment. Eagan initially contacted Rasmussen to gauge the Whalers' interest in the program, for which he and Beyus had thus far made only a pilot on hot-air balloons. Rasmussen figured he might use the meeting to workshop some ideas regarding his next professional move. He brought along his twenty-two-year-old son, Scott, who was still working as the Whalers' public address announcer, to help out. While chatting about Eagan and Beyus's program—an idea both Bill and Scott thought had legs—the possibility of a subscription cable channel devoted entirely to Connecticut-area sports arose. Though none of the meeting's attendees had any experience creating a cable network, they considered it a possibility worth exploring. For the interim, they settled on the name Entertainment and Sports Programming Network, or ESP Network for short. They liked the double entendre and assumed any shifts to their idea would likely still fall within the entertainment and sports categories.

Shortly after its first gathering, the invigorated group arranged a meeting for Connecticut-area cable operators in United Cable's conference room to drum up interest (see appendix A). They even parked a rented state-of-the-art production truck near United Cable's entrance to let the visiting operators know that ESP aimed to provide top-of-the-line productions. The presentation was sparsely attended, and those who did show thought the idea of a sports channel to be foolhardy and did not believe the inexperienced speculators possessed the know-how to pull it off. Moreover, the ESP group quickly realized that its plan would be far more expensive than anticipated because the regional cable providers received their content from several multiple-system operators (MSOs) instead of a single centralized source into which ESP could easily tap. All was not completely lost, however. United Cable vice president Jim Doby recommended that the group consider satellite distribution, a relatively new model that provided networks greater geographic range than terrestrial cable.

Though by no means a success, the meeting was encouraging enough to compel the entrepreneurs to rent a spare office at United Cable to set up a temporary base of operations while they researched the project's feasibility and solicited investors. They then staged a press conference, which yielded just four attendees from thirty-five invitations, where they unveiled their plan: ESP would be a cable network focusing on the University of Connecticut and other area sports. It would cost subscribers $18 and run approximately five hours daily during the nine-month school year. Beyus exited the group shortly after. "He thought we were crazy and left," Rasmussen chuckled thirty-five years later. Beyus, however, asserts that Eagan and the Rasmussens exploited his financial and technological resources to keep the nascent project afloat. He claims to have left only because his partners were "conning" him.[3] Interpersonal discord aside, the ESP quartet became a trio just a little more than a month after forming.

Still undaunted, Eagan and the Rasmussens forked over the $91 fee to incorporate ESP one week later. The business license listed Eagan, whose attorney drew up the paperwork, as the company's president, with Bill and Scott as vice presidents. With Doby's assistance, the group scheduled a meeting with RCA's Al Parinello, who was in charge of marketing and selling transponder space on the company's SATCOM 1 satellite. Parinello was having a surprisingly difficult time renting the transponder's channels, as satellite distribution was still uncommon in the United States. After Parinello explained RCA's rates for five hours per evening (which amounted to $1,250 per day), the group realized it would be less expensive to rent space for twenty-four hours a day, a service for which RCA charged $35,000 monthly. They couldn't afford either deal, recalls Scott Rasmussen, so they figured they might as well reserve space for twenty-four hours.[4] The only catch was that their lease required a five-year commitment and would carry a termination fee. RCA—which rented its transponder space on a first-come, first-served basis—did not require payment for ninety days after the satellite's first use. The grace period provided a necessary buffer for the ESP group to get its financial act together. Furthermore, the transponder rights gave ESP a way to entice investors, or at least to prove it was slightly more than an idea. In fact, the rights became far more valuable after a front-page *Wall Street Journal* article trumpeting satellite cable as the wave of the future prompted corporate communication outlets to gobble up the rest of RCA's available slots.[5]

In his memoir about ESPN's development, Bill Rasmussen suggests the transponder rights set in motion "a series of events that no scriptwriter worth his salt could concoct." In doing so, the charismatic businessman reinforces a storybook, ex nihilo creation myth for ESPN that situates him and his colleagues as the prescient visionaries who conceptualized the revolutionary—and now commonplace—practice of twenty-four-hour sports TV. Though certainly innovative, their idea was not as groundbreaking as Rasmussen—an infamous yarn spinner whose tales most commentators have reproduced without scrutiny—suggests. By the late 1970s, sports television was at an all-time high in the United States. The previous two decades saw ABC Sports redefine sports TV's aesthetic ambitions and demographic reach with the "up close and personal" approach Roone Arledge developed that informed *Wide World of Sports* (1961–98) and *Monday Night Football* (1970–present). Moreover, syndicated programs such as *NFL Game of the Week* (1965–86, 2003–9) and *This Week in Baseball* (1977–98, 2000–2011) appeared outside of the weekend and evening time slots to which sports content was traditionally confined. Sport media scholar Garry Whannel suggests the 1970s set the stage for sports TV to "reach its mature form."[6] During this era, average American households had their television sets turned on for approximately six hours a day and devoted roughly 20 percent of that time to sports programming—a figure that jumped to about 25 percent among male viewers.[7] "Television," as a 1979 *New York Times* report puts it, "became America's Big Daddy of sports during the 1970s, buying recognition and respectability for the Olympics, bankrolling pro football, basketball and baseball, building its own games and names, rebuilding boxing, and tantalizing viewers with sophisticated space-age toys like mini-cameras and video tape machines."[8] ESP grew in large part out of the fertile ground its broadcast predecessors cultivated.

ESP also emerged as cable TV was gaining momentum. Though only about 20 percent of American television households received cable when ESP was forming, these numbers—in combination with satellite technology's expanded distributional breadth—were enough to justify pursuing a national service. Originally called community antenna television (CATV), cable developed as a locally oriented service designed to provide access to communities that could not get over-the-air broadcast TV. Like many new technologies, cable was accompanied by utopian discourses that championed its potential to deliver different types of content to underserved and underrepresented groups. The 1971 Sloan Commission on Cable Communications—an independent research group—dubbed cable the "television of abundance," and journalist Ralph Lee Smith optimistically called it "an electronic highway." "The faith [in cable]," explained journalist Brenda Maddox in 1972, "is religious in that it begins with something that was once despised—a crude makeshift way of bringing television to remote areas—and sees it transformed . . . into a cure for the ills of modern urban American society."[9]

This moment of optimism, which TV historian Megan Mullen calls cable television's "blue sky period," was accompanied by the increased deregulation of the communications industry. These implementations, in particular the 1972 Cable Television Report and Order, were ostensibly designed to realize cable TV's democratic potential. Mullen, however, observes that they actually aided a broader free-market, neoliberal trend in Federal Communications Commission (FCC) policy making. Neoliberalism, as Robert W. McChesney outlines, "is almost always intertwined with a deep belief in the ability of markets to use new technologies to solve social problems far better than any alternative course. The centerpiece of neoliberal policies is invariably a call for commercial media and communication markets to be deregulated. What this means in practice is that they are 're-regulated' to serve corporate interests."[10] In contrast to its terrestrial predecessor, satellite cable had the potential to serve niche audiences on a national scale. Within this market-driven environment, however, the new technology became a tool only the wealthiest could afford, resulting in outlets such as the Turner Broadcasting System WTBS "superstation" (originally named WTCG for Turner Communications Group) that media mogul Ted Turner launched in 1976 and the Christian Broadcasting Network that evangelist Pat Robertson started in 1977.

Though ESP would become the first all-sports network—a status it flaunted with its initial slogan, "The Total Sports Network"—sports content found a welcome home in early satellite cable. The Madison Square Garden Network, which launched in 1971 and became the USA Network in 1979, provided a national service with a schedule dominated by sports.[11] Home Box Office (HBO) started in 1972 as a subscription-based terrestrial service and switched to satellite in 1975. It employed sporting events like the Wimbledon tennis tournament, which it carried from 1975 to 1999, and Muhammad Ali and Joe Frazier's 1975 "Thrilla in Manila" heavyweight championship boxing match to develop a national audience.[12] Ted Turner used his Atlanta Braves and Atlanta Hawks sports franchises to fuel his advertiser-supported superstation. The Braves, in fact, are sometimes referred to as "America's Team" because the consistent national exposure TBS provides makes the franchise more visible than nearby teams in certain markets.[13] The surge of network sports television during the 1970s created the robust market these cable outlets exploited, and these nascent channels generated even greater demand for spectator sports. The notion of a twenty-four-hour sports network still seemed outlandish; however, if it made sense for a cable outlet to devote itself entirely to a single genre, sport certainly stood among the most reasonable candidates.

The ESP group had a license for twenty-four hours' worth of satellite distribution but was still unsure as to precisely how to use it. One thing had become abundantly clear: programming that focused on Connecticut—hardly a hotbed of sport—would not attract a national audience. The entrepreneurs consequently set out to rethink their model by considering ways to augment their sports material with syndicated reruns, old movies, or anything else that might inexpensively attract a steady stream of advertisers and eyeballs. They also shifted their original plan to operate as a subscription service to an advertiser-supported model that would capitalize on the many national companies eager to reach the adult male demographic that sports content so effectively delivered. Bill and Scott were kicking around ideas on a muggy August road trip from Connecticut to Ocean Grove, New Jersey. The humidity and brainstorming eventually wore on Scott, who exasperatedly attempted to bring the long conversation (and his loquacious father) to a momentary pause by exclaiming, "Play football all day, for all I care!"[14] Bill liked the idea—a lot. He realized that only a tiny fraction of the hundreds of college football games played on autumn weekends were featured on TV and that many less prominent sports—even with the presence of *Wide World of Sports* and the similar network anthology programs *CBS Sports Spectacular* (1960–present) and *NBC Sportsworld* (1978–92)—received hardly any exposure.

Eagan also liked the idea (or at least had not thought of anything better), and the group began in earnest its search for investors to augment Bill's $9,000 in maxed-out credit cards and the roughly $30,000 he had collected from various family members.[15] Through one of Bill's many business contacts, the group established interest from K. S. Sweet Associates, an investment firm that was actually more attracted to the value of the transponder space than how ESP would fill it. After a daylong meeting at K. S. Sweet's King of Prussia, Pennsylvania, headquarters, the firm agreed to provide ESP $75,000 in seed money—a contribution that eventually ballooned to $275,000—and to help it compose a business plan for potential clients and investors. The ESP group primarily used the investment to traverse the country in search of financial backing, content providers, and MSOs willing to give them space. They focused most of their attention on the National Collegiate Athletic Association, an organization they accessed through Bill's relationship with University of Connecticut athletic director John Toner, a member of the organization's powerful television committee. Their proposal promised to "complement rather than compete with NCAA television contractual engagements" and claimed the new network would "televise nationally a minimum of 500 NCAA Division I, II, and III men's and women's athletic events," with "each event . . . broadcast at least twice to maximize exposure."[16] The NCAA was understandably reticent, however, as ESP's proposal conspicuously gave no inkling as to how the upstart would fund its endeavor. NCAA president Walter Byers rightly worried the group was using his organization to get a "hunting license" that would help it to entice other investors and clients.

Meanwhile, J. B. Doherty, the K. S. Sweet associate who handled ESP's account, had shopped the network to six potential buyers with no luck. The seventh meeting he organized, with Getty Oil Company vice president of diversified operations Stuart Evey, initially seemed a long shot. Though Evey's division handled Getty's nonoil interests, it mostly focused on luxury real estate and had never before ventured into cable TV or any part of the communications industry. The Los Angeles–based Evey, however, was a devoted sports fan who always wanted to be part of the comparatively glamorous entertainment business. After consulting with attorney Ed Hookstratten, who represented several prominent sportscasters, Evey became convinced that ESP had the potential to serve as a "major lift" network that would enhance cable subscriptions and provide operators greater potential to sell their more lucrative pay channels like HBO and Showtime.[17] Evey was further motivated by the interest Anheuser-Busch expressed in ESP. The brewing company, a staple in sports media, rightly speculated that although ESP might not immediately attract large total audience numbers, the viewers who did tune in would likely fall within its target market of adult men. Given the combination of Evey's successful track record and Anheuser-Busch's interest, Getty's board green-lighted the effort.[18] Getty's initial $10 million investment gave it 85 percent ownership of ESP and prevented the original ownership group from selling its stock without its new parent's permission. Though the terms of the agreement were stacked heavily in Getty's favor, ESP had no other options. K. S. Sweet, both Evey and Bill Rasmussen recount, would have likely discontinued its funding had Getty passed on ESP.[19]

Bill and Scott Rasmussen describe the ESP group as "jugglers" who were simultaneously maintaining the NCAA's interest by claiming its deal with Getty was almost finished, banking that Anheuser-Busch would officially agree to an advertising deal after it signed the NCAA, and hoping cable operators would give the new channel space once they realized it had secured financial backing, a prominent content provider, and advertising.[20] In fact, Bill Rasmussen received confirmation that Getty was officially joining the project while in a meeting with Walter Byers at the NCAA's suburban Kansas City headquarters. Getty's high-profile support made the NCAA confident enough to sign a contract with the cable outlet on March 1, 1979. The NCAA had other reasons for teaming with ESP. The organization had undergone scrutiny since the 1972 passage of Title IX, which guaranteed equal opportunities for men's and women's collegiate sports at publicly funded schools. Byers and the NCAA hoped the positive publicity ESP's programming provided their women's athletics would temper backlash against Title IX as well as criticism that the NCAA had not given women's sports adequate support since the legislation passed.[21]

Still juggling—though with two fewer items in the air—Bill Rasmussen unveiled the NCAA agreement at the Texas Cable Show in San Antonio to entice cable operators.[22] While ESP aimed to give women's sports unprecedented attention, its potential to attract men composed the principal selling point it used to court advertisers and cable providers. A full-page ad it ran in the trade magazine *Broadcasting* claimed the new network's seven-days-a-week devotion to sports programming provided advertisers "seven ways to be an agency

ESPN advertised its contract with Anheuser-Busch, the largest in cable TV history, to lure other clients.

hero" by using the channel to reach "18–34 year old men."[23] This promise was enough to convince Anheuser-Busch to sign a $1.38 million agreement, the largest ever in cable TV. ESP's focused marketing strategy was on the front wave of cable's narrowcasting trend, anticipating the development of other advertiser-supported niche outfits such as CNN (1980), BET (1980), and MTV (1982).

With a marquee content provider, a deep-pocketed sponsor, and an expanding roster of cable operators in place, Evey, his finance manager, George Connor, and the original ESP group (sans Eagan, who took a buyout after butting heads with Doherty and Evey) bought a one-acre parcel of land in Bristol, Connecticut—a short drive from Plainville—and took to staffing the network in preparation for its ambitiously scheduled September 1979 launch. They first changed the ESP Network's name to ESPN, or Entertainment and Sports Programming Network. Evey sought a prominent and experienced staff that would drive viewership and have the industrial clout necessary to help ESPN secure TV rights, attract advertisers, and recruit other employees. His first major hire, brokered by Hookstratten, was NBC Sports' Jim Simpson, a gentlemanly and recognizable senior sportscaster who had worked alongside Walter Cronkite earlier in his career. He also looked to NBC to hire ESPN's first president, Chet Simmons, an industry icon who helped Roone Arledge develop *Wide World of Sports* before leaving ABC to join, and eventually run,

NBC Sports. ESPN introduced Simmons as its first president on July 18, 1979. Immediately afterward, Simmons began poaching his old staff at NBC Sports, most notably operations executive Scotty Connal. This wave of industrial migration prompted the novice company to jokingly dub its budding Connecticut headquarters "NBC North." Ironically, RCA—the corporation from which ESPN leased its transponder space—was NBC's parent company at the time. The communications conglomerate was indirectly helping ESPN to pilfer one of its key assets' most popular and successful divisions.

ESPN's aggressive maneuverings began to generate considerable buzz in the trade and sports press. Most of this attention focused on Bill Rasmussen. *Adweek* called him "one of the 12 biggest headline makers of the year," and *Connecticut Magazine* ran a cover story that featured a photo of Rasmussen smiling complacently with his foot resting atop a TV and the title "Why Are ABC, CBS, and NBC Afraid of This Man?"[24] The attention he received bruised Evey's and Simmons's substantial egos and escalated the already sharp tensions brewing among the burgeoning network's three most powerful personalities.

Like most cable networks at the time, ESPN adopted a funding model inspired by broadcast networks' payment of affiliates for carriage. Simmons negotiated a combination of per-subscriber rates and advertising incentives with cable operators to get ESPN on the air.[25] While he imitated the broadcast networks' funding model, Simmons described ESPN's projected relationship

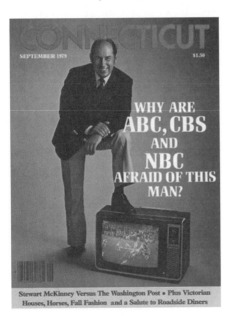

Connecticut Magazine published a profile on Bill Rasmussen and ESPN shortly after the cable channel's September 1979 launch.

to the networks as more cooperative than adversarial. "During the [1979] U.S. Open, CBS broadcast two Saturdays and two Sundays," he explained. "There were matches the first week like [Ilie] Năstase vs. [John] McEnroe, that weren't on. What's wrong with us carrying early round matches? I could live with that role."[26] Simmons even suggested ESPN's supplementary coverage would provide valuable promotion for the networks' featured broadcasts, most of which aired on weekends. Though it did not initially promote itself as comparable to the networks, ESPN did work to place itself into association with them. In late 1979 the cheeky outlet bid for the rights to carry the 1984 Summer Olympic Games. ESPN management realized the company could never afford to purchase the rights, which consistently stand among the most expensive in sports TV. However, they ponied up the $750,000 deposit required to place a bid in order to drum up publicity.[27] "The networks recognize our presence," Simmons remarked. "We're like a fly buzzing around their head. They think if they can just brush it away, it will go somewhere else."[28] By the time of its launch, the young company had gathered the financial support, personnel, programming contracts, and sponsors to be far more than a mere blip on the networks' radar.

Opening the Gates of Sports Heaven

In a *Sports Illustrated* article published less than two months before ESPN's launch, Scott Rasmussen—who shared his father's charisma and media savvy—provided a comment that would become the embryonic channel's mission statement. "What we're creating here is a network for sports junkies. This is not programming for soft-core sports fans who like to watch an NFL game and then switch to the news. This is a network for people who like to watch a college football game, then a wrestling match, a gymnastics meet, and a soccer game, followed by an hour-long talk show—on sports."[29] ESPN's first broadcast on September 7, 1979—produced despite the network's unfinished production facilities, which required staff to use portable toilets and to hop over mud holes while en route from production facilities to sets—reinforced this attitude. It opened with host Lee Leonard's voice along with stock footage of sports fans wildly cheering: "If you're a fan, *if you're a fan*, what you'll see in the next minutes, hours, and days that follow may convince you you've gone to sports heaven. Beyond that blue horizon," Leonard explains as the image track cuts to a shot of the sky, "is a limitless world of sport, and right now you're standing on the edge of tomorrow, with sports twenty-four hours a day and seven days a week with ESPN."[30] The introduction then transitions to a fast-paced montage of exciting sports moments not unlike *Wide World of Sports*' iconic introductory package and an upbeat, disco-infused song wherein a chorus of voices urges viewers to "hook us up and check us out / 'cuz we're the one worth watching."

Leonard reemerges after the introduction, on a set decorated in Getty Oil's red and orange corporate color scheme, to explain the largely unfamiliar technological means by which ESPN planned to create this sports Eden. "And note the stars of the show," he states as the network's two satellite dishes appear. "These H. G. Wells invaders of the quiet countryside. These two dishes are each ten meters or thirty-three feet across, and they're eight feet deep at the center. And what they are are a pair of eyes peering up at RCA SATCOM 1, 22,300 miles up in the sky near the equator south of Hawaii. ESPN extends from New York to Los Angeles, from Miami to Point Barrow [Alaska], and from New England to Texas," he proclaims with the aid of a graphic diagram. Leonard then hands off to Bill Rasmussen, who stands alongside the dishes to emphasize their enormity as he explains further how satellite TV works.

> Years ago tales of Jules Verne and Buck Rogers were made of dreams and bits of wild imagination. Today modern technology has taken those dreams and that imagination and turned it into a reality that allows us to bring a television picture into your home via satellite. The pictures you're watching right now have been taken by a camera sent through some sophisticated equipment to this transmitting station, which in turn feeds a satellite. . . . The satellite receives the picture, sends it to an earth station near your home, which in turn sends the picture over cable into your living room set. Total elapsed time: one-fifth of one second.

As with Leonard's discussion, crude graphics accompany Rasmussen's comments that sketch the satellite transmission process and, in doing so, endorse a utopian vision of cable's miraculous potential to transcend time and space.

The segment then unveils the *SportsCenter* desk, where Leonard's younger counterpart, George Grande, outlines the show's purpose. "It goes without saying that we'll be bringing you highlights of the action. But we'll go beyond the highlights; we'll go beyond the scores. We'll try to answer some of the questions that some people will leave unanswered." To deliver on this promise, Grande offers a brief update of a Billie Jean King and Chris Evert tennis match, which Evert won in straight sets. With cutting frankness, he suggests King is a washed-up has-been who should retire with some dignity rather than continue to embarrass herself against superior competition. Grande's brief remarks combine with Leonard's and Rasmussen's introductory comments to bill ESPN as an innovative media outlet that pulls no editorial punches.

Though the introduction manifests a clear vision for ESPN, the network's opening hours were not without hiccups. Its first event footage showcased a softball game between the Kentucky Bourbons and the Milwaukee Schlitzes—a team sponsored by one of Anheuser-Busch's main competitors. Not long afterward, it presented a live interview with University of Colorado football coach Chuck Fairbanks that ran without audio. While these glitches mortified ESPN's new production staff, Scott Rasmussen claims the network's administrators remained calm. "We told them not to worry," he laughed. "Nobody was watching anyhow."[31]

ESPN originally ran from 3:00 p.m. to about 4:00 a.m. Monday afternoon through Thursday morning and continuously from Friday afternoon through early Monday morning.[32] It showed a wheel of promotional messages and its upcoming schedule after sign-off until transitioning entirely to a twenty-four-hour format on September 1, 1980. The network's earliest programming notoriously featured obscure sports—the rights to which cost ESPN very little—that took *Wide World of Sports*' promise to showcase sport's "constant variety" to esoteric new heights. It featured nonlive telecasts of Australian rules football, hurling, darts, table tennis, hydroplane boat races, and even model boat races. An overwhelming 65 percent of the network's footage during its first years revolved around the NCAA—content that included games, news reports, and instructional programs.[33] The few prominent college contests it did showcase were typically limited to tape-delayed presentations. In fact, NCAA rules would only allow the weekend football games ESPN carried to air nonlive in order to protect its network agreements. Other scheduled productions would be postponed or canceled based on when tapes arrived in Bristol, and some programs were run multiple times when content was lean. ESPN also enjoyed little support from the major networks it originally set out to augment. "We couldn't even get clips at first," Bill Rasmussen complained. "CBS was going to sue us at one point because we used some of their coverage."[34] Rasmussen also claims the networks threatened to stop covering certain sports organizations if they sold content to ESPN, pressured the Nielsen Company to exclude the cable channel from its ratings, and strong-armed *TV Guide* into not publishing ESPN's schedule until readers finally demanded its inclusion.[35]

Critics responded to ESPN's emergence with a combination of excitement and dystopian skepticism. The *Sporting News*, for instance, named the network's development "the biggest [sports] story of the year," and the *New York Times'* legendary sportswriter Red Smith wryly claimed the cable TV experiment would "represent the ghastliest threat to the social fabric of America since the invention of the automobile." *Sports Illustrated'*s Stan Isaacs even used ESPN's launch as the backdrop for a *Clockwork Orange*–inspired journalistic stunt where he tested whether he could withstand watching the new channel for twenty-four hours straight.[36]

As ESPN struggled to find its stride, tensions flared among its leaders, all of whom felt justified in flexing their authority based on their resources (Evey), experience (Simmons), or vision (Bill and Scott Rasmussen). Evey forced Scott Rasmussen to resign just days after the network's launch by demoting him and cutting his salary by 75 percent. Bill followed in December 1980, but only after Getty gave him a sizable severance and allowed him to keep his stock.[37] While its behind-the-scenes leaders battled it out, ESPN was cultivating appealing—and almost exclusively white and male—new personalities in front of the camera. Aside from polished and conventional anchors like Simpson, Leonard, and Grande, it hired fresh faces such as Chris Berman, Greg Gumbel, Bob Ley, and Dick Vitale, the former NCAA and National Basketball Association (NBA) coach whose raspy effusiveness (which he initially provided for only $150 a game) became a network hallmark. ESPN also opened a New York City office in early 1980 to handle its broadening portfolio of advertising accounts, which included orders from Chevrolet, Datsun, Toyota, Hertz, Gillette, Hilton, Sony, and even Tampax.

ESPN continued to lose money despite its slowly growing popularity. Between its production costs and the fees it paid MSOs for carriage, the network was burning through roughly 1.5 million of Getty Oil's dollars monthly. Evey put his continual requests to the Getty board for additional support in a parlance its members would understand: "Gentlemen, I would like to equate ESPN with an oil well," he would say. "Seismic indicated there was a reservoir, and we determined that was true. Experience has shown that the reservoir is there and is a hell of a lot bigger than we originally thought. Unfortunately, it is also deeper than we thought. So I need more pipe." Beyond using the extra funds to keep ESPN afloat, Evey invested it in communications infrastructure to offset the network's eventual losses.[38]

Partly because it had such difficulty securing rights to telecast noteworthy games, ESPN started to create its own events—several of which have become popular sports media traditions. Capitalizing on the success of the 1979 NCAA men's basketball tournament, which featured a now famous championship match between Earvin "Magic" Johnson's Michigan State University Spartans and Larry Bird's Indiana State University Sycamores, ESPN began to air early-round games, contests the networks did not previously schedule. It enhanced its coverage with live cut-ins to whatever game happened to be most exciting at a given time. This practice set the stage for the NCAA's eventual rebranding of the tournament as "March Madness" and the CBS TV contracts that now compose more than 90 percent of the NCAA's total annual revenue. ESPN also made programming from seemingly staid events such as Major League Baseball's (MLB) annual Hall of Fame induction ceremony in Cooperstown, New York, and, more notably, the National Football League draft. Though the NFL draft was "an occasion people thought was one step above reading the Yellow Pages," the affair provided ESPN with a valuable connection to the United States' most popular sports organization.[39] The network trumpeted this new relationship by purchasing a full-page *New York Times* advertisement for the event that stressed its unprecedented live coverage while explaining to readers how they could subscribe to ESPN.[40] Moreover, since no other media outlets had ever thought to televise the draft, ESPN did not have to bid against any competitors. It became the "channel of record" for the event and, as journalist Michael Weinreb notes, transformed it "from a glorified insurance seminar into a televised happening"—a must-see spectacle around which ESPN organized its spring lineup.[41] In doing so, it set the stage for the development of year-round discussions of the draft and ESPN's eventual hiring of full-time NFL draft experts such as Mel Kiper Jr. The promise these original programs demonstrated compelled Anheuser-Busch to sign a new contract with ESPN for five years and $25 million. The agreement eclipsed its previous contract's position as cable's largest-ever advertising deal.

Beyond its original made-for-TV events, ESPN suggested its programming capacity and complete devotion to sports enabled it to offer more careful and detailed coverage than its competitors. "I used to get tired of those short sports

ESPN's decision to air early-round games from the NCAA Men's Basketball Tournament precipitated "March Madness."

programs on the nightly news," claimed Simmons. "We can go much deeper." Along these lines, in 1981 ESPN provided the first start-to-finish coverage of a NASCAR race, and in 1982 it showcased a Davis Cup tennis match between John McEnroe and Mats Wilander that ran six and a half hours, the longest-ever continuous sports telecast. Some critics pointed out, however, that ESPN's commitment to quantity came at the cost of quality. "With that kind of time to fill, or kill," chided Jane Leavy, "you can't always have caviar. ESPN is the fast food of sports broadcasting. The rights to the gourmet dishes, the World Series, the heavyweight championship fights, belong to the networks." Slowly, though, ESPN inched into closer association with the major broadcast networks. When Simmons left the channel in early 1982 to become commissioner of the United States Football League, he immediately negotiated a deal with his successor, Bill Grimes, wherein ESPN would share rights to the organization's games with ABC. The two-year contract was ESPN's first deal with a major professional sports league, and its initial USFL telecasts shattered the network's previous viewing records. "More than any other event," Grimes noted, "our fortunes are tied to the success of the USFL."[42] Later that year, ESPN added a contract with the NBA and struck an agreement with ABC that allowed the cable channel to supplement some of the network's event coverage and gave it access to taped content that did not make *Wide World of Sports'* final cut.[43]

While ESPN filled its early schedule with a diverse slate of content, its women's programming—which ranged from live events to the independently produced magazine show *SportsWoman*—rarely appeared during peak time slots. In 1981 the *Pittsburgh Courier* pointed out that ESPN seldom covered historically black colleges or universities (HBCUs).[44] Instead, it focused its energies on catering to the presumed interests of the prosperous white male audience its main advertisers craved. A 1979 ad in *Broadcasting* titled "Pitch the Rich" promised to deliver "affluent 18–34 year old men," and a 1980 ad that focused on ESPN's tennis coverage asked programmers to "imagine what a big percentage of your potential subscribers play tennis," suggesting the channel could effectively attract the country club set.[45] Another ad in the *Wall Street Journal* claimed "men who don't watch TV watch ESPN," implying that ESPN satisfies cultured men who might sneer at "regular" TV and operates as a marker of distinction for those viewers who tune in. "Cable subscribers," Chet Simmons noted, "have a bit more money, are a bit more educated, buy bigger cars and take longer vacations than the average network sports viewer." ESPN's earlier claims to offer an outlet for content the networks passed over were made more out of budgetary necessity than an effort to broaden sports television's conventional boundaries. These revenue-driven activities illustrate the politics of cable TV narrowcasting. While cable provides the potential to

ESPN assured potential advertisers that it could effectively attract young men with disposable income.

serve underrepresented groups, the deregulated industry—as media critics including Patricia Aufderheide, Thomas Streeter, and Brian Winston point out—typically opts to serve more lucrative, corporate-driven interests.[46] In this case, advertisers used ESPN to reach prosperous men. In the process, ESPN programmed content that reinforced long-standing assumptions regarding which audiences matter most in sports media.

By 1983 ESPN surpassed TBS as the United States' most popular cable TV service. Cable operators could no longer sell their packages without including the "Total Sports Network." Meanwhile, the advertiser-supported network continued to hemorrhage money.[47] To climb out of the red, ESPN boldly decided to leverage its popularity and demand that cable operators pay it 10 cents per subscriber. The new model inverted ESPN's original relationship with cable providers to give it another revenue stream and drastically cut costs. The arrangement, which ESPN chroniclers James A. Miller and Tom Shales liken to "selling cake and getting paid to eat it," is now standard practice throughout the cable industry.[48]

A Network within a Network

In January 1984, after investing a total of $67 million in the cable venture without turning a profit, Getty Oil sold ABC a 15 percent stake in ESPN along with options for the later purchase of up to 49 percent and the right of first refusal should the network be sold entirely.[49] Texaco purchased Getty the following month for $10 billion. To defray the costs of its mammoth acquisition, Texaco sought to sell the nonoil holdings Evey spent his career collecting and managing. As a result, ABC purchased ESPN's remaining 85 percent—including the satellite transmission facilities it had developed and the shares Rasmussen's original group still owned—in June 1984 for $227 million. The already sports-heavy network, which owned the cable channels Lifetime and A&E, sought to enhance its presence in the rapidly expanding and increasingly influential cable industry. Just as important, it wanted to prevent Ted Turner, who expressed interest in purchasing ESPN, from acquiring the popular network. The ABC purchase also occurred shortly after the U.S. Supreme Court, in *NCAA v. Board of Regents of the University of Oklahoma*, ruled that the NCAA's regulation of its college football telecasts violated antitrust laws and, in doing so, allowed "football schools" to sell the rights to as many games as they could. The ruling opened the door for cable outlets like ESPN to televise live college games.[50]

To offset its substantial investment in ESPN—along with the debt it incurred after purchasing the rights to televise the 1984 Olympic Games—ABC sold 20 percent of the cable outlet to RJR Nabisco for $60 million. Ohlmeyer Communications Company's Don Ohlmeyer and John Martin, both of whom began their careers at ABC under Arledge's tutelage, partnered with Nabisco to manage its acquisition and to represent the company on ESPN's board of directors.[51] ESPN maintained its separate brand and continued to use less expensive, nonunion labor. Though its production practices and personnel differed from ABC's, ESPN integrated into its new parent's programming and promotional practices by airing select content ABC did not have the space to include.[52]

ABC's purchase—and Capital Cities Communications' acquisition of ABC the following year—was aided by the 1984 Cable Communications Act, which allowed cable operators to set rates and let the market decide their feasibility. As a result of the legislation, which the *New York Times* likened to "allowing telephone companies to decide who may use the phone and what they may say," the *Christian Science Monitor* named cable TV the "largest unregulated monopoly in the country."[53] To be sure, the deregulation exemplified Ronald Reagan's neoliberal mantra that "government is not the solution to our problem," but rather "is the problem." ABC, and then Capital Cities, took full advantage of this environment by increasing ESPN's per-subscriber fee from 10 to 13 cents in 1984 and hiking it again to 19 cents in 1985. Cable operators, because of ESPN's growing popularity, were constrained to acquiesce and passed along the costs to their customers. Not coincidentally, ESPN finally turned a profit in 1985.

ABC was as interested in enhancing ESPN's already resonant brand as it was in exploiting its programming capabilities. "ESPN has done a good job in building brand awareness," remarked ABC executive Herb Granath shortly after the acquisition. "What we need to do now is tell [consumers] what it stands for." The parent company set out to help its new property develop an image that would more clearly distinguish it from competitors like USA and TBS. Branding emerged as a dominant and crucially important business practice alongside corporations' increasingly prominent and unfettered presence in 1980s global culture. Naomi Klein claims that "successful corporations must primarily produce brands, as opposed to products," and that the "real work" for these organizations "lay not in manufacturing but marketing." More broadly, Scott Lash and John Urry argue that contemporary culture is lived and negotiated through branded symbols that constitute what John Sherry calls a corporatized "brandscape."[54] The organizations that own and manage brands strategically sculpt their properties' cultural meanings to exploit target audiences. Consumers, in turn, use brands to build identity and community, which often—though certainly not always—reinforce the brand's intended significance.[55]

As the cable TV industry crowded during the 1980s—a shift impelled partly by ESPN's success—the development of recognizable brands became increasingly important.[56] A&E vice president Michael Cascio claimed, "The most important thing for a young cable network is for people to get a handle on who you are."[57] Though ESPN and ABC were not as integrated as they would become during the 1990s, ABC Sports' brand, contracts to air big-ticket events such as NFL games and the Olympics, and sporadic willingness to share content inflected ESPN with legitimacy and prestige—a marketable "network quality"—that few other cable outlets possessed at the time. By 1985 ESPN had gained enough recognition to change its official name from Entertainment Sports and Programming Network to ESPN, confirming the acronym's transformation into a brand that signifies cable sports TV.

From Beer to Champagne

Despite finally turning a profit, ESPN still struggled to attract consistent audience numbers. To expand its viewership, the network began incorporating daytime fitness programming geared toward women, most notably *Bodies in Motion* (1985–96). The same year, it aired performances of the stage productions *The Babe*, a one-man play based on Babe Ruth, and *Lombardi: I Am Not a Hero*, a two-man drama, as "trial vehicle[s]" to appease viewers who longed for "higher human interest content."[58] ESPN strayed from sports entirely with *Business Times*, a morning business news show produced by Business Times, Inc., and scheduled against the similar male-focused programs on CNN and the short-lived Financial News Network (FNN). A 1985 *Wall Street Journal* ad

This *Wall Street Journal* advertisement for ESPN's morning business news program, *Business Times*, makes no mention of sport.

for *Business Times* made no mention of sports and even branded ESPN simply as a "cable television network" rather than using the "Total Sports Network" slogan that accompanied its other promotional materials.[59] Though these efforts worked to expand ESPN's audience and round out its schedule with relatively inexpensive content, they did little to cultivate the brand distinction and coherence that had become so important in cable TV. In fact, they ran the risk of confusing consumers while alienating the core viewership ESPN had established.

A watershed moment in ESPN's attempts to build a respectable brand that both satisfied its target demographic and attracted a crossover audience occurred with its coverage of the 1987 America's Cup yacht races between the United States and Australia. The United States had lost the previous America's Cup challenge to Australia for the first time since 1870. The 1987 race, which took place in the Indian Ocean off Australia's western coast, consequently took on a nationalistic tenor, with U.S. captain Dennis Conner's *Stars & Stripes* boat vying against the Australian team's *Kookaburra III*. ESPN dramatized the event by incorporating cameras on helicopters and blimps and including minicameras on the yachts that showcased crew members' frenzied maneuverings. When Conner demanded $100,000 to include a camera onboard *Stars & Stripes*, ESPN convinced Anheuser-Busch to foot the bill in exchange for naming the gadget the "Bud-cam."

Even though the competition took place on the other side of the world, ESPN opted to display the America's Cup's final rounds live to bill it as a must-see TV event. The telecasts, which started at 11:00 p.m. EST and sometimes ran past 3:00 a.m., amazingly attracted audience numbers that rivaled, and at times exceeded, the network's most popular prime-time programming. Nationally syndicated sports columnist Ira Berkow called the race "one of the great studio sports of all time" and claimed that ESPN's coverage "made insomniacs out of about 1.5 million Americans."[60] In fact, the *New York Times* published two front-page articles on the America's Cup as well as a glossary of sailing terms to educate the unfamiliar before they tuned in—a testament to the ESPN coverage's event status.[61] The America's Cup also attracted upscale advertisers that included Cadillac, Atlantic Financial, Quantas, and Domain Chandon champagne. George Bodenheimer, ESPN's fifth president, said the event put ESPN "on the map" and was "the first time [the network] got into the psyche of America." More bluntly, Bodenheimer's predecessor, Steve Bornstein, locates it as the "first time that a group of people looked at us as other than a chickenshit operation."[62] ESPN's $2 million investment in the 1987 America's Cup yielded $4 million in revenue to make it one of the outlet's most profitable endeavors to date. The coverage, however, was as organized around the effort to prove, in Bill Grimes's words, that ESPN "could do a complex production and provide intelligent commentary."[63]

ESPN used this newfound respectability to help persuade the National Football League to sign its first cable TV contract in July 1987. "The critical acclaim for our America's Cup coverage," Grimes insisted, "did more than anything in our history in making us perceived as television, not just cable TV.... I remember a conversation with [NFL commissioner Pete] Rozelle, telling him we'd finally arrived."[64] The initial contract gave ESPN four preseason games, eight regular-season contests, and the Pro Bowl. The network branded its regular-season games, which took place during the season's second half on Sunday evenings, as *Sunday Night Football* and adopted a stylish, entertainment-driven format inspired by ABC's *Monday Night Football*. For instance, it initially included three commentators in the broadcast booth, one of whom was a rotating celebrity "guest host" with some connection to the city where the contest was held. It recruited actor and former college football player Burt Reynolds to fulfill the role at a Los Angeles Rams game and brought in Chicago Bears legend Dick Butkus to provide analysis for one of his former team's games. While *Washington Post* columnist Norman Chad, who later joined ESPN, criticized *Sunday Night Football*'s showy excesses, likening watching it to "sitting in a crowded singles bar trying to concentrate on a William Faulkner novel with Janis Joplin on the jukebox," he praised the production as "network quality." Though only a preseason game, ESPN's first NFL telecast received the network's highest-ever rating. "Next to getting on the air," noted Chris Berman, "getting the NFL is the biggest thing to happen to ESPN." Grimes claimed the contract finally made ESPN "legitimate in the eyes of the sports establishment."[65]

ESPN financed the three-year, $135 million NFL contract—by far its largest programming investment up to that point—by increasing its subscriber fees by 9.5 cents. Taking advantage of the Cable Communications Act's leniency, ESPN rightly bet that the NFL's monumental popularity would force cable providers to accept the increase for fear of losing their football-loving subscribers. More than 90 percent of the network's clients cleared the NFL package without incident, and the bigger fees more than compensated for the minor losses ESPN suffered. Despite the increases, Grimes asserts that ESPN's deal ultimately did not generate much revenue. Like many big-ticket TV sports, ESPN's NFL package operated as a loss leader, or programming that loses—or comes close to losing—money but generates enough exposure for the programming that surrounds it and prestige for the outlet that produces it to be worthwhile. Beyond attracting new viewers, Grimes claims the NFL contract was motivated by an effort to cultivate increased credibility among audiences, potential clients, and advertisers.[66] The 1987 America's Cup and the NFL contract, in other words, transformed ESPN from what Jane Leavy called the sports TV equivalent to fast food into an outlet that would satisfy the gourmand. ESPN still happily shilled Budweisers and Chevrolets, but it also hawked champagne and Cadillacs.

The year 1987 also marked the point when ESPN became the first cable TV outlet to achieve 50 percent penetration in television households. This unprecedented success prompted increased competition. Both USA and TBS still had vast portfolios of live event coverage, and FNN carried SCORE, a news-driven sports subchannel that ran on weekends. While CNN did not air live events, its evening news program *Sports Tonight* (1980–2001) consistently outrated *SportsCenter*. Bornstein even claims *Sports Tonight* was at the time "more credible" and polished than *SportsCenter*. To ward off these formidable rivals, ESPN hired John A. Walsh—founder of the literary monthly sports magazine *Inside Sports* and a former editor at *Rolling Stone*, *U.S. News & World Report*, and the *Washington Post*—as a consultant. After observing the network's practices, Walsh suggested ESPN should devote greater resources to *SportsCenter* and use the flagship program as the main platform to grow and promote its brand. "I made the recommendation," remarked Walsh, "that the NFL [contract] is going to come and go; college football is going to come and go. The only thing you have permanently here on a 365-day basis is *SportsCenter*. So why not invest resources in *SportsCenter* and make it the nightly gathering place for sports fans?" Bornstein agreed, though for more pragmatic reasons: "I looked at ESPN as a sort of department store. We were televising all different sports—some were important, some were curiosities—and that was getting people into our store. Ultimately, where we were going to make a lot of money and fans would be the *SportsCenter* franchise."[67] As Bornstein indicates, *SportsCenter* was far less expensive to produce than live events—even the novelties.

Walsh, who joined ESPN full-time in 1988 as executive vice president and editor, was particularly interested in using *SportsCenter* to enhance ESPN's journalistic respectability. The network's most famous on-air personalities up to that point, such as Dick Vitale and Chris Berman, heavily—and unapologetically—privileged entertainment over analysis. As Vitale bellowed in a 1984 *Sports Illustrated* profile: "I'm Hollywood, I'm shtick, I'm mustard, I'm hot dog." He was not, however, a journalist. Along these lines, an ESPN colleague claimed Chris Berman—who had established himself as a cable TV star by assigning players goofy nicknames like Frank Tanana "Daiquiri" and Oddibe "Young Again" McDowell—"likes the game and the players" but "doesn't care much for the newsy part of the sport."[68] To balance Vitale's and Berman's marketable styles, Walsh hired practiced reporters with established expertise on specific sports, such as Peter Gammons, Andrea Kremer, and Charley Steiner. He also created news bureaus to foster enterprise reporting that would allow ESPN to break stories and feed *SportsCenter* original and exclusive content. Moreover, and building upon his background in print, Walsh retooled *SportsCenter* to mimic the format of a newspaper's sports section. Rather than giving rundowns of each sport, he arranged the most newsworthy items first. For Sundays, he developed a longer edition meant to mirror the meatier format of a Sunday paper. Walsh also incorporated more storytelling into the *SportsCenter* highlights' then straightforward and linear format by experimenting with nonchronological recaps.

Riding these shifts, ESPN became a more aggressive presence in TV sports news. When Cincinnati Reds manager and retired baseball star Pete Rose was banned for gambling in 1989, ESPN posted reporters at the Baseball Hall of Fame in Cooperstown, Rose's home in Cincinnati, and Major League Baseball's New York City headquarters to ensure no outlet beat it to any aspect of the story or matched its reportage's depth. That same year, ESPN was the only organization to report on the World Series after the San Francisco Bay Area's Loma Prieto earthquake interrupted it. None of the several other outlets present at the event had brought backup generators. By virtue of its equipment, then, ESPN owned the story of how the World Series was affected by the natural disaster—a key thread in national news coverage of the earthquake—for more than a day. ESPN and *SportsCenter* expanded on these journalistic achievements to situate themselves at the forefront of sport's most important stories, such as Loyola Marymount University basketball player Hank Gathers's 1990 death on the court, professional basketball player Magic Johnson's 1991 announcement that he was HIV positive, heavyweight boxer Mike Tyson's 1992 rape trial and conviction, and retired football player O. J. Simpson's 1994–95 murder trial. Though ESPN had the space to give these stories more attention than mainstream outlets, Walsh took measures to ensure it would be recognized as a site that skillfully uncovered and reliably illuminated sport's biggest news.

The changes Walsh instituted compelled the *Washington Post*'s Leonard Shapiro to cite *SportsCenter* as the "foundation of [ESPN's] vaunted status in the psyche of American sports fans." "A couple sports editors told me," Walsh claims, "that they watched the early [6:00 p.m.] *SportsCenter* show because it helped them with their decision-making for the next day's front page. . . . That was the first indication that we were having some impact beyond what we were doing." ESPN, however, still faced—and continues to face—criticism for its journalistic integrity, much of which understandably focuses on the conflicts of interest that arise from its claims to report objectively on clients it pays for the rights to televise. ESPN defends itself against such claims by maintaining that its news division and programming department are completely separate. "The programming guys who manage those relationships," vows ESPN's sixth president, John Skipper, "have no say in news and information. Those lines do not cross."[69]

Aside from covering and generating news, *SportsCenter* came to serve a function ESPN producer Bill Shanahan likened to "spackle": it is an economical way to fill the gaps between live event coverage while sustaining consistent audience numbers during nonpeak hours. In 1991, for instance, Walsh replaced ESPN's morning business news program with reruns of the previous evening's *SportsCenter* that would run on a partially updated wheel into the afternoon. Walsh's shifts maintained *SportsCenter*'s status as the embodiment of ESPN's brand that enhanced and maintained the respectability that the network's America's Cup coverage and NFL contract established. "Our viewers are not couch potatoes," *SportsCenter* anchor Keith Olbermann claimed. "People who watch . . . are engaged. They're like readers." Moreover, the program created a journalistic foundation upon which ESPN would expand with programs like *The Sports Reporters* (1988–present), a Sunday-morning sports talk show scheduled against the many similar cable TV news programs, and *Outside the Lines* (1990–present), an hour-long investigative program that, as its title indicates, situates sport within its broader sociocultural contexts. By the 1990s, ESPN had become, in media mogul Peter Barton's words, one of cable TV's "untouchables." It was, in fact, more profitable than the network that purchased it in 1984.[70] With the help of ESPN International—a global family of ESPN-branded networks launched in 1989—it was also more pervasive.

An ESPN Lifestyle

Bornstein claims that ESPN's continued success into the 1990s was in large part a consequence of the media outlet ceasing to be simply a network. Instead, he notes, ESPN "had to be a way of life for people, with as many angles into their lives as possible. I wanted ESPN to replace the word 'sport' in the dictionary. And the only way to do this was to be everywhere." "Our position," asserts senior vice president of marketing Lee Ann Daily regarding ESPN's diversified branding strategy, "is that ESPN is not a huge network, but rather it is a huge sports fan. Everything we do comes from that perspective." An extension of its original claim to provide a fix for sports junkies, ESPN builds a branded way of relating to everyday life through the consumption of sports media. It fosters a culture for the community of addicts it created that the Associated Press's John Nelson describes as "more of a hangout than a TV channel."[71] *SportsCenter* became the primary instrument through which ESPN built and vocalized this culture. Spearheaded by telegenic, wisecracking, and almost exclusively male anchors such as Craig Kilborn, Keith Olbermann, and Dan Patrick, the news program morphed into a clever, self-referencing, and irony-laden daily dose of sports commentary that combined trenchant analysis with frat-house shtick. To mention one example, Olbermann and Patrick—who cohosted the late-night edition of *SportsCenter* from 1992 to 1997 and immodestly (though not without self-conscious sarcasm) referred to their segment as "The Big Show"—would mention where the unfortunately named race car driver Dick Trickle finished no matter how well he performed that day.[72] The juvenile gag became a common joke among sports fans that amplified Trickle's modest fame. Moreover, the catchphrases they coined when narrating highlights—such as "en fuego," "nothing but the bottom of the net," and "putting the biscuit in the basket"—quickly became sports media clichés. Like any culture, then, ESPN had its daily ritual of *SportsCenter* along with the shared language, customs, and points of reference it articulated. *SportsCenter* also became the basis of additional brand extensions through which ESPN pursued new angles into consumers' lives. Olbermann, for instance, hosted ESPN Radio's first-ever broadcast on January 1, 2002, and ESPNews, which launched in 1996, is an entire channel spun off from *SportsCenter*.

To emphasize *SportsCenter*'s position as the locus of ESPN's sports-centric culture, the network hired the advertising agency Weiden + Kennedy to create a marketing campaign organized around the show. Most of ESPN's channel identifications and promotional spots prior to the early 1990s straightforwardly reminded viewers to tune in at a certain time to see featured programs, perhaps along with a brief live shot of the location where the event was about to take place. ESPN conscripted Weiden + Kennedy in hopes that it would have an impact on the sports media outlet similar to its iconic "Just Do It" campaign's transformation of Nike into a marker of coolness.[73] Building upon ESPN's identification as a sports fan, Weiden + Kennedy's "This is *SportsCenter*" commercials situated the network's headquarters as the center of the sports world by offering comedic behind-the-scenes glimpses into ESPN's headquarters wherein *SportsCenter* personalities interacted with the athletes they covered. The ads literally depict ESPN as a hangout where basketball player Grant Hill plays piano for tips in the lobby and pitcher Roger Clemens uses the photocopier. One ad features Olbermann and Patrick applying their stage makeup as they casually talk sports before taping. With the program's characteristic self-awareness and deadpan sarcasm, Olbermann interrupts Patrick to say, "You need some more rouge." Patrick welcomes his advice and graciously replies, "You know, your foundation has been looking great lately," as they slide back into a more conventionally macho discussion and the "This is *SportsCenter*" caption emerges to close the commercial.

Taking influence from and referencing the mockumentary *This Is Spinal Tap* (1984), the "This is *SportsCenter*" campaign provided the already popular *SportsCenter* anchors an added degree of celebrity, making them, in Dan Patrick's words, "more than just a talking hairdo."[74] The commercials affirm and justify the sports-obsessed culture ESPN fosters—a sensibility the media outlet has built upon with the similar Weiden + Kennedy–produced campaign "It's Not Crazy, It's Sports," which rationalizes sports customs that seem pathological in other contexts by chalking them up to fandom.[75] The "This is *SportsCenter*" spots, which now number in the hundreds, eventually became so popular that ESPN produced stand-alone specials devoted to them entirely. The promotions, in effect, became programming.

Despite *SportsCenter*'s newfound trendiness, MTV was still the United States' most popular cable channel among younger viewers. Moreover, MTV was expanding into sports content with *MTV Sports* (1992–97), an anthology program loosely based on *Wide World of Sports* that focused on "lifestyle" sports such as skateboarding, disc golf, and windsurfing. It also began to produce specials like the *Rock 'n' Jock* basketball and softball games that brought together athletes and entertainers. John Lack, ESPN vice president of marketing who helped to create MTV and Nickelodeon earlier in his career, reasoned that in order for ESPN to compete for MTV's audience, it would need to borrow from the music channel's style. Along with marketing executive Harriet Seitler, another former MTV employee, Lack sought to expand into these new demographic horizons through developing the youth-oriented sister channel ESPN2. Originally branded as "the Deuce," ESPN2's October 1, 1993, launch in ten million homes was the largest in cable TV history.[76] The new network adopted a graffiti-style variation of ESPN's main logo, and its programming initially focused on extreme sports to capitalize on the then fashionable "alternative" market. "Think of it as ESPN with a transfusion of MTV blood," explained *New York Times* sports media critic Richard Sandomir.[77] To this end, ESPN2 hired former MTV host "Downtown" Julie Brown as a studio personality and included the program *Jock 'n' Roll*, which transformed sports highlights into music videos. "We were trying to respond to the advertising community with differentiated product," Bornstein notes. "We knew we wouldn't get distribution from our cable partners if we just put more of the same stuff on there. It became pretty smart to differentiate it by calling it hipper and younger and cooler."[78] Expanding further upon ESPN2's MTV-inspired efforts, in 1995 ESPN teamed with Tommy Boy Records to launch the series of sports arena–friendly song compilations *Jock Jams*. If MTV was brazen enough to produce sports programming, then ESPN would try its hand in the music business.

Headlined by Olbermann, the Deuce's *SportsNight* offered a "less structured" alternative to *SportsCenter* that placed greater emphasis on gossip and popular culture—what Lack described as a sort of *New York Post* to *SportsCenter*'s *New York Times*. Reflecting this informal style, its anchors wore street clothes. Olbermann, for example, donned a leather jacket over print shirts with jeans. "Anyone who wears a jacket and tie," the outspoken anchor claimed of the new channel's aesthetic, "will look like a narc."[79] ESPN2 contrasted—and even defied—the conventional journalistic rigor Walsh developed. Lack, in fact, unapologetically claims that journalism was secondary to the marketing and programming concerns that drove ESPN2's development. This contrast in style and philosophy was best illustrated by Lack's decision to hire Jim Rome, a shit-talking radio shock jock out of San Diego, to host *Talk2*. While Walsh adamantly opposed the move, Lack argued that Rome possessed greater street cred than ESPN's typical personalities—even the newly leather-clad Olbermann—a quality ESPN2 sorely needed if it was to compete with the youthful authenticity MTV had so firmly established. Rome generated national news shortly after he joined the network when he provoked New Orleans Saints quarterback Jim Everett—whom Rome continually called "Chris Evert" in an attempt to attack his manliness—to shove him to the ground while live on the air. The confrontation, which Walsh called an embarrassment, garnered the Deuce unprecedented publicity and, albeit unintentionally, personified its colorful and irreverent brand. *USA Today* sports media critic Michael Hiestand even sarcastically named Everett ESPN2's MVP, or "most valuable promoter."[80] With the Everett-Rome incident, ESPN2 became an MTV-infused ESPN channel with a dash of *The Jerry Springer Show*. Though only moderate at first, ESPN2's success motivated other cable networks to create comparable offshoots, such as MTV's MTV2 (1996) and Nickelodeon's TV Land (1996), and set the stage for ESPN's continued creation of new sports cable TV niches with ESPNews (1996), ESPN Classic (1997), ESPN Deportes (2004), and ESPNU (2005). Moreover, ESPN2's relatively edgy marketing strategy composed a model that sports organizations like the NFL began to employ to solicit younger fans they worried might shift their allegiance to extreme sports.[81]

ESPN complemented its youth-oriented branding efforts by establishing the ESPY (Excellence in Sports Performed Yearly) Awards in 1993 and the Extreme Games in 1995, which it renamed the X Games in 1996 and augmented with the Winter X Games in 1997. Modeled after MTV's annual Video Music Awards, the ESPYs advertise ESPN's relationship to entertainment culture by providing a made-for-TV event wherein athletes and celebrities hobnob. Just as important, the ESPYs suggest ESPN has the authority to decide which athletes deserve recognition—a distinction previously identified primarily with outlets like *Sports Illustrated* and the Associated Press. Similarly, the X Games, a development attributed to ESPN programming director Ron Semiao, created a championship for extreme sports that marketed ESPN and ESPN2 as their principal home.[82] The X Games, claimed the *Rocky Mountain News'* Mark Wolf, "is what would happen if Pearl Jam ran the Olympics." Unlike the NFL draft, ESPN wholly owns the ESPYs and the X Games. While the National Football League—which has allowed its NFL Network to televise the draft in competition with ESPN since 2006—may someday decide not to let ESPN televise its draft, no other outlet can air the ESPYs or the X Games. "No one could ever take it away from us by simply writing a larger rights-fee check," said Semiao.[83] These now popular annual events' very existence is bound—legally as well as culturally—to ESPN.

ESPN2 eventually scaled back its exclusive focus on the youth demographic and extreme sports to operate as a secondary outlet for ESPN's increasing live event coverage. While ESPN continued the ESPYs and X Games and certainly did not stop courting younger viewers, it canceled gimmicky ESPN2 shows like *Jock 'n' Roll*, *SportsNight*, and the sports-memorabilia home-shopping program *Power2Shop* in favor of more traditional programs that either recycled ESPN's commentary or showcased events it did not have the space to schedule. These efforts, however, demonstrated ESPN's ability to fashion a brand that accommodates both the sports establishment and the counterculture.

A "Magic Name" in the Magic Kingdom

Media critic Timothy J. Lukes suggests ESPN's penchant for humor and persistent self-promotion cheapen the sports it covers. "The ESPN approach," he complains, "is too cool, too smart, too important to elevate the game.... ESPN commentators believe they are as important as the athletes they observe."[84] Lukes's pointed observations overlook the fact that sports media representations are always—to greater and lesser degrees—invested in building and marketing images for the media outlets that produce them. Before it turned its attention to sports programming in the 1960s, ABC was jokingly known throughout the industry as the "Almost Broadcasting Company." The network's innovative sports coverage was deeply informed by an effort to build respectability, and it transformed ABC into the United States' most popular major network by the mid-1970s. Similarly, NBC, which has held the rights to televise the Olympics since 1988, often includes the Olympics' five-ring logo under its network icon throughout all of its programming—sports or not—to cultivate renown. Though Lukes's complaint rests on overly idealistic grounds, he is right to suggest ESPN is driven by an effort to build its brand. Indeed, this self-serving mission unites ESPN's policies and practices.

The ESPN brand's value and potential, in fact, motivated the Walt Disney Company to acquire Capital Cities Communications in 1996 for nineteen billion dollars, the second-largest corporate takeover ever.[85] Disney chief executive officer (CEO) Michael Eisner called ESPN the "crown jewel" in Capital Cities' portfolio and referred to it as a "magic name" with brand recognition comparable to Coca-Cola or Kodak.[86] Beyond collecting ESPN's substantial revenues, Disney would use the network to foster synergy and vertical integration. "There are synergies under every rock we turn over," Eisner crowed as Disney began negotiations to purchase Capital Cities.[87] With this acquisition came shifts like *SportsCenter* segments taped from Disneyland, incessant promotions for Disney's sports-themed films, and suspicion that the Disney-owned Anaheim Mighty Ducks and Los Angeles Angels received more attention than other sports franchises.[88]

A testament to ESPN's brand power, soon after Disney bought Capital Cities it installed ESPN president Steve Bornstein as head of ABC Sports, a move designed to enhance the properties' integration. This transition also marked the beginning of Disney's decision to phase out ABC Sports. It canceled *Wide*

World of Sports in 1998 after thirty-seven years on the air. In 2006 it rebranded ABC Sports as "ESPN on ABC" and moved *Monday Night Football* to ESPN. The cable network had eclipsed what was arguably the most storied brand in sports television history. It was more popular than ABC Sports and because of its insistence on using nonunion labor—a practice it continues—could produce content less expensively. In fact, journalist Michael Freeman claims that by the twentieth century's end, ESPN had established itself as Disney's most valuable asset and was effectively "carrying Mickey Mouse on its shoulders."[89]

Although ESPN had already ventured into radio, the Disney purchase propelled its metamorphosis into a multiplatform media outlet. "Once upon a time," claimed George Bodenheimer shortly after Disney acquired his employer, "our company was our network and our network was our company. Those days are done. We are selling and creating all the time."[90] Like its parent company's myriad offshoots, ESPN's brand extensions began to saturate popular culture, finding novel ways to intensify established fans' relationship to the organization while attracting new consumers beyond cable TV and radio. In 1997 it established the ESPN Store in Glendale, California's Glendale Mall—the same shopping center where Disney launched its Disney Store franchise in 1987. In 1998 ESPN opened the ESPN SportsZone in Baltimore's Inner Harbor—a themed sports bar and restaurant chain that later expanded to New York City, Chicago, Las Vegas, Orlando, Los Angeles, Anaheim, and Washington, D.C.[91] The same year, ESPN erected its Antarctic receiver and officially changed its slogan to "The Worldwide Leader in Sports." Consumers—from Southern California mall-goers to Antarctic researchers—no longer simply watched ESPN. They wore it, walked around in it, and ate it. Like all media, then, ESPN is something people do—a communication-driven phenomenon inseparable from culture. However, its diversified activities provide consumers considerably more to do than many of its competitors.

The year 1998 also marked a point when ESPN began to receive widespread recognition that reinforced its prominence in and beyond sports media. Corporate sibling ABC launched the prime-time "dramedy" *Sports Night* (1998–2000), a critically acclaimed workplace sitcom loosely based on *SportsCenter* and produced by Aaron Sorkin. Though short-lived, *Sports Night* demonstrated that ESPN was renowned enough to compose the backdrop for a prime-time network program. Perhaps an even greater testament to ESPN's rising prominence was President Bill Clinton's decision to use it to televise an April 1998 town hall meeting as part of his initiative to "create a national conversation about race." Entitled "Race & Sports: Running in Place" and held at the University of Houston, the meeting featured Clinton and a collection of athletes, coaches, and executives discussing race and sport's politically charged relationship.[92] While the president likely could have compelled a more stereotypically serious outlet like PBS or CNN to air the meeting, he decided ESPN was the most suitable mouthpiece for his civic endeavor. ESPN received another state-sponsored endorsement one month after Clinton's town hall meeting when the Smithsonian Institution honored *SportsCenter*'s twenty thousandth segment, a milestone wherein the news show eclipsed *Star Trek* as the most aired TV program in U.S. history.[93]

The Kleenex of Sports

When asked to comment on the significance of ESPN's brand, John Walsh flippantly claimed, "Names are names. If you were starting a sports network today, you wouldn't call it ESPN—it's a pretty terrible name. Names don't mean anything until they're attached to what the name stands for." ESPN has spent its history sculpting its name into a powerful and ubiquitous signifier for sports media. This brand-driven effort fuels its stylistic practices, contracts with popular sports organizations, invention of original events, and expansion onto different platforms. "The letters ESPN," claims senior vice president Vince Doria, "have become synonymous with sports the way Kleenex means tissues." Like Kleenex, ESPN works to secure its name's prevalence and, just as important, its authenticity within the ever-expanding market it played such a significant role in establishing. ESPN, as Walsh asserts, is not a great name in and of itself. Dick Vitale admits he thought it sounded like a disease when the network first asked him to work its college basketball games. But the meaning ESPN built has turned the clunky acronym into the best possible name for a sports media outlet—a status ESPN's consistent decision to affix the label to its steady flow of brand extensions confirms and kindles. Aside from a media outlet, then, ESPN is a privately owned public symbol through which consumers fashion status as fans and around which they commune through watching *SportsCenter*, visiting an ESPN Zone, or participating in the fantasy sports leagues *ESPN.com* hosts. "Like hamburgers and French fries," asserts the *Washington Times'* Tom Knott, ESPN "is one of the emblems of America."[94]

When reporting on ESPN just prior to its 1979 launch, *Sports Illustrated*'s William O. Johnson speculated that the cable network may someday "become the biggest thing in TV sports since *Monday Night Football* and night-time World Series games."[95] ESPN has exceeded Johnson's grandiose conjecture. It not only now carries *Monday Night Football*, but also brands the sports TV franchise as *ESPN Monday Night Football*. What's more, ESPN's presentations of *Monday*

Night Football routinely yield larger audience numbers than the World Series games sometimes scheduled against them. Gone are the days when twenty-four-hour sports coverage simply provided a fix for a crazed subculture of sports junkies jonesing for something to watch. ESPN has normalized—and ritualized—practices once considered pathetic symptoms of sports addiction. Indeed, the continual launch of niche cable channels and websites organized around specific sports, regions, and even teams makes ESPN's original intention to target sports fans seem quaint.

ESPN, as *Bloomberg*'s Karl Taro Greenfeld puts it, "no longer covers sports. It controls sports."[96] This power is largely created and flexed on the symbolic terrain of branding. While ESPN's event coverage and news compose its most visible and lucrative content, it also strategically crafts its authority through practices that deliver authenticity, prestige, and credibility that set it apart from other sports media organizations. These practices simultaneously expand sports media's horizons and situate ESPN as the institution that builds and polices those boundaries.

2

SportsCentury

Programming Public Sport History

SportsCentury is not just a retrospective, it's an opportunity for us to educate our viewers on the significant events and athletes of the past 100 years.
—Mark Shapiro, *SportsCentury* coordinating producer[1]

No memory is possible outside frameworks used by people living in society to determine and retrieve their recollections.
—Maurice Halbwachs[2]

Alongside the Y2K-driven frenzy to protect our collective future was a wave of activities designed to sum up and celebrate our past. *Time* published "*Time's* 100 Most Influential People of the Century," the American Film Institute released "AFI's 100 Years . . . 100 Movies," and Random House's Modern Library imprint compiled the "Best Books of the Century." Though contested—and designed in part to spark debate—these much-ballyhooed lists serve as public histories. They are conspicuous discursive monuments now used to assess dominant tastes and attitudes in turn-of-the-century America. Just as important, they construct and announce the sponsoring institutions' credibility and authority.

In September 1998, ESPN launched *SportsCentury*, an eighteen-month transmedia event that reflected on the twentieth century's greatest North American sports figures and moments. Described by ESPN vice president of integrated sales and marketing Tom Hagel as the organization's "most ambitious marketing and programming endeavor" to that point, *SportsCentury* commissioned a forty-eight-member expert panel to select and rank the twentieth century's top one hundred athletes (see appendix B). The project centered on a series of weekly documentary profiles that counted down the top fifty. It augmented these thirty-minute segments with a multiplatform assortment of complementary material. The *SportsCentury* project composed a theme across ESPN's content through the century's end that media consultant Anthony Smith claims "provided a how-to manual for leveraging [its] many platforms in an integrated way."[3]

Though *SportsCentury* spanned ESPN's TV channels, ESPN Radio, *ESPN the Magazine*, and *ESPN.com*, it chiefly relied on its featured documentary profiles to brand ESPN as a site that creates enriching content. Documentary, according to film scholar Bill Nichols, is more closely allied with the "discourses of sobriety" (science, law, politics, and so forth) than with media forms organized around the commercially driven effort to amuse. Television outlets, working in a medium often regarded as "aesthetically rather impoverished," strategically exploit documentary's relatively refined social meaning. The common, and problematically essentializing, perception of TV as a superficial "boob tube" is most famously expressed by Federal Communications Commission chair Newton Minow's description of it as a "vast wasteland" of inane dreck in his 1961 address to the National Association of Broadcasters.[4] Minow, however, granted documentary an exemption from television's lowbrow status, locating it as a point of aesthetic and educational potential within the otherwise culturally barren TV mediascape. Television producers and programmers use documentary to cultivate the richness and depth that sitcoms, game shows, and sporting events presumably lack.[5] For instance, Ken Burns's nine-part, eighteen-and-a-half-hour series *Baseball* (1994) allowed PBS to capitalize on sport's popularity while preserving its civic-minded brand. Similarly, HBO subsidiary HBO Sports has long used documentaries to distinguish its content from mainstream sports TV and to complement the premium cable outlet's insistence that it is "not TV," but something driven by more dignified ambitions. Following these respected media outlets' lead, *SportsCentury* used documentary—a genre to which the organization had never before seriously committed its energies beyond sporadic productions made for *Outside the Lines*—to garner unprecedented esteem.[6] The series earned a Peabody Award, the first honor ESPN received that was not limited to recognizing sports media. Beyond chronicling sport history, ESPN used the *SportsCentury* documentaries to brand itself as an institution, like PBS and HBO, with the capacity to create "quality TV."[7]

The majority of extant scholarship on sports documentaries interrogates productions' formal properties en route to critiquing their ideological implications.[8] This textual analysis–driven approach has pointed out the *SportsCentury* profiles' tendency to recycle familiar narratives that perpetuate sport's stereotypical reinforcement of dominant power relations. Sports media scholar Andrew C. Billings, for instance, laments that *SportsCentury*'s list of the top one hundred athletes includes only seven women, and he exasperatedly points out that the racehorse Secretariat (#35) outranked all but three of them (Babe Didrikson Zaharias [#10], Martina Navratilova [#19], and Jackie Joyner-Kersee [#23]).[9] More specifically, sport sociologist Nancy E. Spencer observes that *SportsCentury*'s profiles of tennis players Chris Evert (#50) and Martina Navratilova use "narrative devices, visual imagery, and musical background" to celebrate Evert's heterosexual American identity and to cast Navratilova—despite her athletic brilliance—as a foreign, manly, and lesbian threat to the nationalist normativity her longtime rival embodies.[10] These useful readings, however, overlook the industrial and commercial factors that inform the shapes *SportsCentury*'s profiles take.

Despite his biting critique, Billings acknowledges that *SportsCentury*—for better or worse—"became history." Similarly, although he interrogates *SportsCentury*'s lack of diversity, historian Daniel A. Nathan nevertheless recognizes it as "compelling public history." Historically valuable and influential, the *SportsCentury* profiles are also formally and thematically predictable. Their uniformity reinforces Tristram Hunt's complaint that "history programming on a strict commercial budget has meant exchanging the hard grind of archival research for the stock of recycling of easy images, lazy ideas, and familiar talking heads."[11] Though largely unsurprising, the credibility and expertise the *SportsCentury* profiles built for ESPN are novel. The heavily publicized documentaries suggest ESPN possesses the authority to make sense of twentieth-century American sports.

Shortly after its initial run, *SportsCentury* was rebooted as ESPN Classic's signature prime-time series. While the series maintained *SportsCentury*'s look and ostensible commitment to explaining sport's past, it also produced, scheduled, and recut profiles to publicize ESPN's other content. The repackaged series illustrates a TV industry practice that has emerged alongside the intertwined rise of media convergence and corporate consolidation that John T. Caldwell calls "ancillary textuality," wherein media outlets increasingly invest in programming that can be reused—often in different forms—across platforms.[12] ESPN also uses *SportsCentury* and ESPN Classic to build and preside over an archive of sport's visual past. It lays claim to the stuff out of which this heritage is explained and governs its circulation. ESPN's compilation and regulation of this archive strive to ensure that sport's visual history cannot be constructed without going through the Worldwide Leader.

"We're Not Trying to Rewrite History"

SportsCentury emerged at a time when the sports documentary was gaining unprecedented prominence in American film and television. Steve James's *Hoop Dreams* (1994), which examines the precarious role basketball plays among lower-income urban African American young men, became an independent sensation that gained mainstream theatrical distribution, received the Sundance Film Festival's Audience Award for Best Documentary, earned a Peabody, and was nominated for an Academy Award. Two years later, Leon Gast's *When We Were Kings* (1996)—a reflection on Muhammad Ali and George Foreman's fabled 1974 "Rumble in the Jungle" heavyweight championship bout in Zaire— won the Academy Award for Best Documentary Feature.[13]

Syndicated documentary series like NFL Films' various programs and Berl Rotfeld's *Greatest Sports Legends* had dotted TV schedules across America since the 1960s. Though beloved among devoted sports fans, these productions were not heavily promoted and were typically scheduled either as shoulder program-ming leading into and out of network affiliates' live sports telecasts or as filler in unpopular time slots.[14] The 1990s, however, saw a rise in big-budget and highly publicized television documentary events. In 1991 HBO produced the Peabody Award–winning *When It Was a Game*, a nostalgic documentary on midcentury American baseball composed almost entirely of 8mm and 16mm home movies.[15] Even more notable was *Baseball* (1994), a "blockbuster-size event" that stood as public television's most expensive single-subject program and helped PBS to ward off surging competition from documentary-driven cable outlets such as the Discovery Channel and the History Channel.[16]

Burns and PBS hyped *Baseball*'s significance—and broadened the ways consumers could engage it—by producing and licensing a collection of promo-tional tie-ins that included a coffee-table book, mugs, jackets, T-shirts, compact discs, calendars, and guides to help teachers adopt the series for classroom use. Presenting sponsor General Motors even funded a thirty-minute "making of" special that outlined the film's development and emphasized its importance. These supplementary activities and products helped to make *Baseball* the sec-ond most watched program in public television history after Burns's *The Civil War* (1990). The series' nine-evening prime-time premiere in September 1994 occurred amid Major League Baseball's strike-shortened season, a coincidence that offered an opportune time to reflect on the sport's history and cultural import. Burns's film averaged a 5.5 rating, more than doubling PBS's regular weeknight numbers. "No documentary film in history," observes media scholar Gary R. Edgerton, "has ever been released to the public with quite the level of commercial fanfare as *Baseball*."[17]

ESPN sought to construct a similarly lavish, expansive, and respectable television event with *SportsCentury*, a series *Washington Post* sports columnist Leonard Shapiro lauded as "the most comprehensive sports documentary ever pieced together." Bodenheimer asserted that the media outlet used *SportsCentury* to stake its claim as "the destination for this kind of prestigious programming." These discourses suggest *SportsCentury* helped ESPN to compete with HBO—and to a lesser degree PBS—for market share of the sports television documentary genre. *SportsCentury* coordinating producer Mark Shapiro, the audacious TV industry whiz kid to whom ESPN entrusted the project, claims that ESPN was already on par with broadcast networks with regard to live event coverage and news. Enhancing its documentary programming would allow it to take on HBO. "We had to wrestle the mantle away from [HBO Sports]," he notes. "And there's no reason we shouldn't because HBO Sports is a part-time operation. We are full-time sports, and we should own that area." In fact, *SportsCentury* co-opted the title of HBO Sports' documentary series *Sports of the 20th Century* and used a graphics package similar to the one its more established predecessor employed. Critical reception of *SportsCentury* reinforced its exceptional quality. The *New York Times*' Richard Sandomir, for instance, cited *SportsCentury*'s profile of Baltimore Colts quarterback Johnny Unitas (#32) as more skillful than the hour-long documentary HBO Sports and NFL Films coproduced on him in 1999. Even more enthusiastically, the *New York Daily News*' David Bianculli claimed, "The scope and candidness of the interviews, rivaling those of Ken Burns's *Baseball* miniseries, suggests that [*SportsCentury*] is something not only to watch, but to [video]tape and collect."[18]

Helmed by Shapiro and armed with a budget of twenty-five million dollars, *SportsCentury* began production in 1997 and, like *Baseball*, secured General Motors as its presenting sponsor.[19] Occupying two rented floors of a Westport, Connecticut, warehouse—just fifty miles south of Bristol—Shapiro amassed a thirty-five-person crack team to conduct more than one thousand interviews and to compile roughly 150,000 photos from which it created seventy hours of programming. Despite ESPN's considerable store of archived interviews—many of which featured prominent sports figures who had since died—Shapiro insisted that *SportsCentury* shoot all new interviews with a distinct aesthetic developed by director of photography Peter Franchella. "I wanted one consis-

Former *New York Times* reporter Robert Lipsyte provides commentary for ESPN's *SportsCentury* profile on Babe Ruth. *SportsCentury* coordinating producer Mark Shapiro insisted that the series shoot every interviewee with the same style.

tent, slick, warm, intimate feel to permeate the series," he notes. "I wasn't simply going to have a potpourri of different looks and ugly sit-down interviews messing with the tone."[20] This look—which lights interviewees with a golden hue, frames them in medium close-up, and captions them with a signature *SportsCentury* graphic—fashions a sober, scholarly historical register ESPN has maintained beyond the project's initial run. The series' opening sequence balances this historicity with a nostalgic montage of iconic sports moments and broadcast calls set atop an orchestral score.

Also like Burns's opus—which enlisted a group of expert consultants and featured dozens of prominent interviewees—*SportsCentury* curated a high-profile collection of commentators to nominate, rank, and discuss the individuals it showcases. *SportsCentury* host Dan Patrick described ESPN's panel as "the most perceptive sports observers and journalists ever assembled," implying it is even more learned than the roster Burns put together (though many of the people Burns used in *Baseball* also worked on and were included in *SportsCentury*). Additionally, and expanding on Billings's and Spencer's critiques of the project's gender politics, only six of the ESPN panel's forty-eight members were women, a disparity that reflects and likely informs its top one hundred list's overwhelming male bias (see appendix C).

Beyond compiling a prominent group of expert panelists and interviewees, *SportsCentury* incorporates their voices under ESPN's institutional banner. It emphasizes interviewees' credibility by captioning them according to their affiliations: Robert Lipsyte represents the *New York Times*, Frank Deford speaks for *Sports Illustrated*, Arnold Rampersad is Jackie Robinson's authoritative biographer, and David Remnick's insights carry the *New Yorker's* gravitas. While it advertises interviewees' credentials, its inclusion of them also indicates that they endorse ESPN's ability to synthesize and contextualize their comments. *SportsCentury* enriches their astuteness. For instance, *SportsCentury* included historian and journalist Bert Sugar, author of *The 100 Greatest Athletes of All*

Time (1995), as an interviewee and panelist. In doing so, the project casts itself as an update and enhancement of Sugar's study—an ambition that Sugar, by virtue of his participation, presumably supports. Moreover, the project features many ESPN employees—Chris Berman, Peter Gammons, Bob Ley, Dan Patrick, Robin Roberts, Dick Schaap, John Walsh, and others—as panelists and commentators.[21] It positions these company representatives—whether erudite, experienced, or just entertaining—as possessing knowledge and credibility comparable to its other interviewees.

Along these lines, *SportsCentury* accentuates ESPN's and ABC's importance to sport's visual past by repeatedly using their footage as historical evidence. Its profile on Muhammad Ali (#3) outlines the importance of ABC Sports—and its famous sportscaster Howard Cosell, in particular—to building the boxer's celebrity and mystique. The Michael Jordan (#1) segment is littered with ABC and ESPN footage of his many feats. From a practical and budgetary standpoint, inserting ABC and ESPN content into the *SportsCentury* profiles allows ESPN to avoid paying to license outside footage. But it also emphasizes these media outlets' significance to sport history while reducing (though not eliminating) the presence of competitors like CBS, NBC, and *Sports Illustrated*.

ESPN built *SportsCentury* into a media event—an excessive and highly publicized point around which its content was organized—in part by designing it to provoke public debate that would span beyond its televised presentation.[22] Even the criteria ESPN instructed panelists to use when ranking athletes— based solely on athletic accomplishment without any consideration for social or political import—were designed to be disputed. Athletes' sociopolitical significance, complained panelist and *Boston Globe* columnist Bob Ryan, "was impossible to ignore," particularly with trailblazers like Billie Jean King (#59) and Jackie Robinson (#15). The project elicited the most debate by including three horses (Secretariat, Man o' War [#84], and Citation [#97]) among its top one hundred, prompting a bewildered Frank Deford to ask, "How can you possibly compare horses, even great ones, with humans?" In contrast, the *Washington Post*'s Tony Kornheiser—a *SportsCentury* panelist who began contributing to *ESPN the Magazine* in 1998 and became cohost of the talk show *Pardon the Interruption* in 2001—supported the inclusion of equine athletes. "There are no right or wrong answers," explained ESPN and ABC's Robin Roberts. "The fact that we've caused this great debate is what it's all about."[23]

Beyond the list, *SportsCentury*'s weekly countdown format facilitated speculation regarding which athlete would come next in the rankings and, ultimately, who would be named number one. Excluding the final four, each of the top-fifty profiles was scheduled on Friday evening during prime time. The week's featured athlete was unveiled on *SportsCenter*'s Sunday-night edition—a cross-promotion-fueled programming decision that drove viewers to the program—and was publicized until the profile's premiere the following Friday. New York City bars, according to Bert Sugar, capitalized on the familiar arguments *SportsCentury* triggered by "posting pools and taking bets on whom ESPN will proclaim the greatest athlete of the century." While *SportsCentury* may have intended to incite public debate, "what cannot be argued," observed journalist George Kimball as the project came to a close, "is that ESPN got just what it wanted out of this exercise. People speculated about this list all year long and now that it is over, they are still talking about it."[24]

ESPN adopted a multiplatform design for *SportsCentury* inspired by *Baseball*'s diversified publicity and event status. Though the project did not officially launch until January 22, 1999, its promotional activities began on September 7, 1998—not coincidentally, ESPN's nineteenth birthday—with *Classic Moments*, a series of nostalgic vignettes recounting memorable sporting instances that ran several times daily throughout the project's duration. ESPN also publicized *SportsCentury* via spots on ESPN Radio, articles in *ESPN the Magazine*, and content on *ESPN.com*—synergy-minded distribution channels that were all still relatively new at the time. It released the athletes ranked fifty-one through one hundred on *ESPN.com* prior to the weekly top-fifty series' premiere and allowed website users to build and compare their own rankings. Aside from working to intensify consumers' relationship to ESPN's brand, this transmedia promotion fostered convergence among the company's expanding—though still nascent—palette of platforms. It suggested ESPN did not merely provide content for passive consumption, but offered participatory material fans could affirm, augment, and contest.[25] The integrated project composed a starting point from which *ESPN.com* eventually created *SportsNation*, a poll-based section that ESPN Radio and ESPN2 developed into stand-alone programs.

SportsCentury's weekly profiles were rerun continually on ESPN's other channels, and each of *SportsCenter*'s daily installments devoted sixty seconds to promoting the project. Beyond the featured profiles, ESPN produced four *SportsCentury* documentary offshoots that counted down the ten greatest coaches, games, dynasties, and most influential nonathletes or coaches—groups selected by the same panel that ranked the top one hundred athletes. Finally, it created five *SportsCenter of the Decade* specials that remembered past decades' significant sports moments through melding *SportsCenter*'s format with music, sets, and costumes that reflected the era they covered. The first special commented on 1900–1949. Shot in black-and-white to mimic early TV news broadcasts, it featured a collection of senior anchors—Jim McKay, Dick Schaap, and Jack Whitaker—reporting on Jack Johnson's 1910 heavyweight

One of many *SportsCentury* offshoots produced between September 1999 and December 2000, *SportsCenter of the Decade* presented the top stories from the twentieth century's different decades in a caricatured style of the times. Here, Rich Eisen and Stuart Scott host the special on the 1970s.

title defense against Jim Jeffries, Jack Dempsey and Gene Tunney's 1927 "long count," Jesse Owens's performance at the 1936 Olympics, and other iconic moments. The subsequent *SportsCenter of the Decade* specials focused on individual decades. The 1970s segment presented a mod set along with anchors Stuart Scott and Rich Eisen donning mutton chops and loud polyester suits with butterfly collars while commenting on events such as Curt Flood challenging Major League Baseball's reserve clause, the massacre at the 1972 Munich Olympics, and Billie Jean King and Bobby Riggs's 1973 "Battle of the Sexes."

Moreover, ESPN used *SportsCentury*'s countdown format to create several synergistic subevents. To celebrate the countdown's halfway point in July, ESPN scheduled both Joe Montana's (#25) and Sugar Ray Robinson's (#24) profiles back-to-back on the same evening. It used the occasion of reaching *SportsCentury*'s top twenty in September to publicize the opening of an ESPN Zone restaurant in New York City's Times Square. The event unveiled *SportsCentury*'s top twenty athletes (though not their rankings) and counted several of them— including Jim Brown, Wayne Gretzky, Carl Lewis, and Bill Russell—among its attendees.

SportsCentury's four final profiles were packaged as two hour-long primetime ABC specials on December 24 and 26. ESPN purchased full-page advertisements in major newspapers that asked, "Who Is the Greatest Athlete of the Century?" The ads featured images of the four remaining sports legends—Muhammad Ali, Jim Brown, Michael Jordan, and Babe Ruth—above a list of the forty-six already profiled athletes with blank slots in the spaces they would soon occupy. To milk the last drop of suspense out of the countdown, the final special included the profiles on Jordan and Ruth but did not announce their rankings until the show's end. Shapiro did not even tell John Dahl—the producer who directly oversaw both the Jordan and the Ruth documentaries—the final two athletes' respective rankings. Like everyone else, Dahl found out by watching the special when it aired.[26] After the countdown's completion, ESPN reran each of the *SportsCentury* profiles, finally bringing the extravagant project to an end on New Year's Eve with a melodramatic seven-minute montage of classic sports moments paired with Aerosmith's rock ballad "Dream On," a song used to emphasize sport's mythic reputation as a site where seemingly impossible aspirations are realized.

Aside from its TV documentaries, ESPN built *SportsCentury*'s event status by publishing a coffee-table book edited by sport historian Michael MacCambridge with an introduction by eminent journalist David Halberstam. The book, which enjoyed several weeks as a *New York Times* best seller in the hardcover nonfiction category, features prominent writers reflecting on each decade by discussing an athlete who embodies that moment. Babe Ruth biographer and *Sports Illustrated* staffer Robert W. Creamer, for instance, outlines how the indulgent "Bambino" personified the excesses of 1920s America, and *On Boxing* (1987) author Joyce Carol Oates explains Muhammad Ali's controversial relationship to the politically turbulent 1970s. The book's cover further reinforces the cultural authority *SportsCentury* crafts by adopting the appearance of an engraved golden trophy, a choice that suggests the volume consecrates the people and events it mentions as historically significant.

Perhaps *SportsCentury*'s most inventive promotional tactic was its General Motors–funded thirty-city mall tour and exhibit, which traversed the United States in a *SportsCentury*-themed 18-wheeler. The mobile exhibit featured *SportsCenter of the Decade* walls, short films in a *SportsCentury Theatre*, memorabilia, a sportscasting booth where visitors could record play-by-play, and a life-size animatronic figure of New York Yankees first baseman Lou Gehrig giving his tear-jerking 1939 "Luckiest Man" speech. "While sports fans are able to see, hear, and read about ESPN *SportsCentury* through our television networks, ESPN Radio, *ESPN The Magazine*, and more," claimed ESPN's Tom Hagel, "they can experience it through this dynamic tour."[27] Like the coffee-table book, the tour cultivated ESPN's expertise by positioning it as a populist museum curator. It also increased the branded "touch points" through which *SportsCentury* engaged consumers while broadening its demographic reach—an effort ESPN extended by purchasing inserts in major newspapers to reach older audiences less likely to be cable subscribers and by licensing trading cards and board games to attract children. The mall tour ensured that anyone who visited or worked at the selected locations—a demographic far more diverse than ESPN's standard audience—would be privy to *SportsCentury*.

SportsCentury's wide-ranging efforts to position ESPN as a producer of respectable content were monumentally successful. Sandomir praised the series as "ESPN's most creative work in its 20-year history," and Bob Costas called it one of the decade's "best pieces of television." Roone Arledge sent Shapiro a note of congratulations that claimed *SportsCentury* "added a distinguished dimension to ESPN and made us all proud."[28]

Shapiro advertised *SportsCentury's* quality and scholarly rigor by asserting that "research has been the root of the project." Aside from interviews and photographs, Shapiro and his team—particularly senior producer of research Mark Durand—scoured university film archives, the libraries at most major sports halls of fame, and the newsreel holdings of Fox Movietone, Warner Pathé, Hearst, Universal, and Metronome. They even unearthed some never-before-seen material, such as a 16mm home movie of Babe Ruth's 1932 "called shot"—an artifact that not even HBO's *When It Was a Game* located. Despite the meticulous research that Shapiro claims fueled *SportsCentury*, its profiles favor building entertaining narratives over carefully outlining athletes' lives and significance. "We're not trying to rewrite history with any of this," Shapiro claimed. "We want to give people a fresh look and give them some vision on things they've never heard or seen before."[29]

Although ESPN directed *SportsCentury* panelists to select and rank athletes based entirely on their sporting ability, the profiles often dwell on their imperfections and personal travails. The segment on Michael Jordan discusses at length his gambling and much-maligned unwillingness to take a political stand for fear of compromising his marketability, the Larry Bird (#30) profile exposes the Boston Celtics star as a deadbeat father, and the installment on New York Yankees center fielder Mickey Mantle (#37) outlines his alcoholism and womanizing. Ultimately, however, these biographical warts are recuperated within reverential narratives. *SportsCentury* uses them to humanize the oft-mythologized athletes it profiles and to create obstacles that lend their stories dramatic force rather than treating them as opportunities to critique sport's meanings or the circumstances that inform them.

In this way, the *SportsCentury* segments are mostly quite traditional, and even derivative, within the context of the sports documentary genre. The profile on Babe Ruth was the fifth major American television documentary produced on him in five years, following A&E's *Babe Ruth* (1994); Burns's *Baseball*, which devotes an entire two-hour section to Ruth entitled "A National Heirloom"; HBO's *Babe Ruth: The Life of a Legend* (1998); and ESPN's own *Babe Ruth's Larger than Life Legacy* (1998), a sixty-minute special produced for *Outside the Lines*. Its combination of voice-over narration, archive footage, and talking-head interviews—practices all *SportsCentury* profiles share—mirrors the Burns, HBO, and *Outside the Lines* pieces.[30] Beyond adopting similar conventions, it uses many of the same interviewees and footage included in the other documentaries; its interviews, though stylistically distinctive, are lit and framed very similarly to those in Burns's and HBO's productions; and it repeatedly employs a variation of the "Ken Burns effect," a panning and zooming technique Burns pioneered that isolates a portion of a still image.[31]

SportsCentury's profile on Ruth does provide some information its predecessors do not. It showcases, for example, a letter Ruth sent the Yankees organization shortly after his retirement in which he pleaded to be considered for a managerial position—a request the franchise declined. The profile's antecedents all note Ruth was saddened by the Yankees' unwillingness to let him manage his former team. *SportsCentury*, however, includes interview footage with Ruth's granddaughter that indicates the denial drove him to threaten committing suicide, a tidbit none of the other profiles mention. Although this brief point—which was no doubt incorporated to spice up Ruth's very familiar story—suggests ESPN exposes never-before-discussed elements of the Yankees slugger's life, the overwhelming majority of the profile simply recapitulates the narrative its forerunners built in a form nearly identical to those they adopted. Similarly, Robert Creamer's discussion of Ruth in the *SportsCentury* book does not deviate substantially from his biography *Babe: The Legend Comes to Life* (1974) or the many other volumes that chronicle the baseball icon's life story.[32]

There was no urgent historical need in 1999 for yet another account of Babe Ruth's life. But *SportsCentury*'s generic profile indicates that the documentary is not principally designed to shed new light on Ruth. Instead, it places ESPN in dialogue with A&E, PBS, and HBO as a site that produces documentary content—an association the segment's utter lack of originality actually aids by situating it more comfortably within the genre's typical aesthetic framework. Similar industrial goals informed *Outside the Lines'* special on Ruth, a production that critics panned as "jerry-built" and more motivated by an effort to compete with HBO's Ruth documentary than to explain the ballplayer's legacy. Although very little was fresh about *SportsCentury*'s profiles, ESPN's constructed position as a historian and producer of documentaries was unprecedented. "Money aside," Shapiro claims, *SportsCentury* "is something from a brand perspective that we had to do."[33]

Amid the deluge of content ESPN produced for *SportsCentury*, other media outlets sponsored productions and events to commemorate, piece together, and claim sport's past. The Associated Press—which has been chronicling American sport since the nineteenth century and conducted a widely publicized 1950 poll that ranked the half century's fifty greatest athletes—published *The Sports 100: The Greatest Athletes of the 20th Century*, a volume that registers (but does not rank) the world's best athletes. *Sports Illustrated*—the United States' longest-running and highest-circulating sports magazine—also created a slate of content that included a special issue, a coffee-table book full of its best photographs, and a two-hour prime-time awards show aired on CBS that it marketed as "the most anticipated, exciting, and memorable sports tribute of the year."[34] Like ESPN, *Sports Illustrated* publicized the celebration throughout 1999 in its magazine, on its nascent cable TV channel CNN/SI, and online. Beyond mimicking *SportsCentury*'s transmedia format, the logo *Sports Illustrated* fashioned for its awards show—two hands victoriously lifting a laurel wreath—is strikingly similar to *SportsCentury*'s logo of a male athlete with his hands raised in triumph, an icon it adopted from ESPN Classic (which the channel inherited from Classic Sports Network [CSN]). In some ways brazenly copying *SportsCentury*, much of *Sports Illustrated*'s end-of-the-century content was more inventive than ESPN's comparatively straightforward material. Its special issue, titled "Looking Back: A 20th Century Celebration," included a section wherein staff writers discuss a sporting event they wish they could have witnessed along with an artist's interpretation of it. Kelli Anderson commemorates Gertrude Ederle's 1926 swim across the English Channel with Lauren Ulam's collage representation of the feat, and Josh Gosfield's expressionist painting of the 1919 Black Sox scandal accompanies Frank Deford's discussion of how he might have covered the notorious event.

Despite the Associated Press's and *Sports Illustrated*'s long-standing respectability and regardless of their commemorations' quality, *SportsCentury* overwhelmed and outpublicized their efforts. In doing so, it situated ESPN as the public historian of record for twentieth-century sports. Speaker of the U.S. House of Representatives Dennis Hastert endorsed ESPN's authority by hosting a September 1999 reception to honor the *SportsCentury* athletes, an event more than one hundred members of Congress attended.[35] "You have to hand it to ESPN," noted the *Chicago Tribune*'s Ed Sherman. "Its *SportsCentury* series might have been one of the best television marketing jobs of the century. . . . ESPN actually convinced people it had the final say over who was the best athlete of the 1900s."[36] While *SportsCentury*, as Mark Shapiro asserted, did not strive to "rewrite history," the project did reshape ESPN into a site with the power to organize sport's past through prestigious media events.

Programming Classic Content

Shortly after its initial run, *SportsCentury* was reconfigured as ESPN Classic's featured series. Like ESPN itself, Classic began as an obscure independent upstart, Classic Sports Network, which adopted ESPN's all-sports model and exploited the market for nostalgic sports programming that NFL Films and *Greatest Sports Legends*' syndicated productions created to build a venue devoted entirely to historical sports content. Media entrepreneur Brian Bedol and former Major League Baseball deputy commissioner Steve Greenberg (the son of Detroit Tigers Hall of Fame first baseman Hank Greenberg) launched

Classic Sports Network on May 6, 1995. They hired the flashy former New York Jets quarterback Joe Namath to serve as CSN's national spokesperson and primary on-air personality. They further promoted CSN's launch by conscripting a "Board of Chairmen" that included Ernie Banks, Magic Johnson, Namath, Mary Lou Retton, and Gale Sayers—the types of athletes whose triumphs would presumably be seen on the channel—to endorse it. In an attempt to extend its potential audience beyond older viewers who actually remember the vintage material it would feature, CSN produced a series of six promotional trading cards that featured iconic athletes. The bulk of CSN's initial programming consisted of repackaged sports broadcasts and inexpensive syndicated productions such as *Home Run Derby* (1960), *The Joe Namath Show* (1969), and *Sports Challenge* (1971–79). It also produced several original programs, such as *Sports Court*, which used archival footage to settle sports arguments, and *Those Who Changed the Game*, a biographical series much like *Greatest Sports Legends* that anticipated *SportsCentury*'s profiles.

CSN exemplifies TV scholar Derek Kompare's discussion of "boutique" cable channels that "offer a limited array of products for specialized audiences." This trend, Kompare avers, emerged in concert with cable TV's proliferation and the convergence of content libraries and distribution channels that resulted from the increasingly deregulated media industry's growing corporate consolidation since the 1980s.[37] CSN specifically adopted the model of Nick at Nite, a block of retro programming the children's cable channel Nickelodeon ran during its evening and late-night schedule starting in 1985. Nick at Nite reached out to adult viewers while Nickelodeon's primary audience was presumably asleep without disrupting the channel's wholesome identity. Bedol, in fact, served as Nickelodeon's manager of business development when it launched the boutique subchannel. The industrial recipe he and Greenberg used to concoct CSN rang familiar with audiences and critics already accustomed to both sports and nostalgia programming. *Variety*'s Ray Richmond described the upstart channel as "Nick at Nite with an injection of testosterone, ESPN in a time machine."[38]

"We just started thinking," notes Bedol regarding CSN's development, "how many times have you watched a movie like *Casablanca* or an episode of *The Honeymooners*? There is precedent in entertainment to enjoy the classics again and again even though you know the outcome. . . . All we've done is recognize that same quality in sports."[39] Bedol and Greenberg pitched the channel to cable providers as a supplement to networks and cable sports TV outlets like ESPN that would enhance viewers' appreciation for contemporary sports through offering historical perspective. "We are building a place for sports fans to hang out between games to get to know their heroes better," Bedol claimed. CSN "will serve as a bridge between the past and the present," added Greenberg, "providing context for sports fans of all ages." Bedol even likened the outlet to "graduate school for sports fans" and "a Hall of Fame in your living room."[40] An early CSN channel identification depicted a cigar box—a common repository for keepsakes—slowly opening along with a soft orchestral score to showcase several beloved sports moments. The promo bills CSN as an electronic time capsule that preserves, revives, and explains these artifacts. "The other networks do a fine job of telling viewers who won and lost," Bedol asserts. "Classic Sports is about how they played the game."[41] This statement defines CSN's programming goals by evoking the final lines of sportswriter Grantland Rice's sentimental 1908 poem "Alumnus Football," which idealizes athletic competition by suggesting sport offers a venue wherein humankind's finest virtues are put on display.

Despite rampant audience fragmentation throughout popular media culture, Kompare claims rerun syndication has remained a viable way for network affiliates, independent stations, and cable channels to generate ratings without investing the capital necessary to produce original programs. Moreover, he observes that specialty rerun-driven channels like Nick at Nite and its offshoot TV Land do not merely schedule old productions, but enhance and augment them. "It is increasingly not enough," he notes, "to simply present the familiar over and over again. . . . [T]he familiar must be made unique and remarkable.[42] This is particularly relevant to sports television, since live event coverage and news recaps so dramatically diminish in value after their initial presentation.[43] CSN repackaged these productions to increase their relevance to contemporary audiences. As Greenberg claimed, "Why should we run a two-and-a-half-hour game to get to the last 30 classic minutes. . . . This [programming offers] the story of great events with the perspective of time."[44] CSN added introductions, interspersed interview footage, and created graphics packages inspired by VH1's *Pop-Up Video* that contextualize the featured events and justify their "classic" status.

By 1997 CSN secured exclusivity agreements with the National Football League, National Hockey League (NHL), and Big Fights, Inc., sports film library. The independent outfit, however, struggled to secure carriage from cable operators. Unlike ESPN2 and Time Warner's CNN/SI, CSN could not be bundled with a parent company's other holdings. In particular, it was unable to secure distribution from Cablevision, one of the United States' largest cable providers, after Bedol and Greenberg refused to sell part ownership to its subsidiary Rainbow Media.[45] This tension prompted CSN to file a complaint with the FCC and motivated Cablevision, in cooperation with Fox, to develop a competing channel, American Sports Classics—an extension of Rainbow Media's American Movie Classics channel.[46]

ESPN purchased CSN for $175 million shortly after Cablevision and Fox announced their plans to create American Sports Classics. Originally called ESPN Classic Sports and truncated to ESPN Classic shortly thereafter, the channel adopted CSN's logo, the same image ESPN later used to brand *SportsCentury*. It also initially retained Bedol and Greenberg to assist with the channel's integration into the Disney-ESPN family. "We regard the [Classic Sports] Network as the perfect complement to ESPN," asserted Steve Bornstein, "with many opportunities for cross-promotion."[47] The channel had full access to ESPN's and ABC's vast sports libraries—content ESPN seldom used up to that point—as well as the benefit of being delivered to cable operators along with Disney's other channels. Building on the strategy ESPN used to make ESPN2's 1993 launch the largest in cable TV history, Disney leveraged its more popular channels to persuade (or bully) providers to carry the new boutique outlet. Aside from Classic's promotional potential, the channel aided ESPN's ongoing efforts to compete with Fox, its main rival in cable sports television. Just months before ESPN acquired CSN, Fox purchased a stake in Rainbow Media's regional sports channels. It combined these channels with its extant regional services to build a national network of locally oriented sports programming, Fox Sports Net. While Fox's regional offerings were more expansive and visible than ESPN's at the time, ESPN made sure it would dominate the market for historical content.[48] In fact, its purchase compelled Fox to abandon the development of American Sports Classics.

One year after it incorporated ESPN Classic, and amid the beginnings of *SportsCentury*'s production, Disney purchased Big Fights, Inc.'s library, the world's largest collection of boxing films, which contained footage of more than eighteen thousand fights, dating back to Enoch J. Rector's documentation of James J. Corbett and Bob Fitzsimmons's 1897 heavyweight championship bout.[49] Disney outbid Fox, HBO, the National Basketball Association, and the Madison Square Garden Company for the enormous library, paying a reported $80 million—more than three times *SportsCentury*'s entire budget. Beyond feeding ESPN Classic and *SportsCentury*, the purchase prevented competitors from being able to employ this footage without first licensing it from ESPN and Disney. Fox could persist in developing a nostalgia-driven channel to compete with Classic, but it would have an exceedingly difficult time securing boxing footage.

SportsCentury's historical focus and presentation suggest it was partly designed to build a coherent brand and devoted audience for ESPN Classic. Its adoption of Classic's logo established a connection between the renowned project and the fledgling channel from its inception. Moreover, when Mark Shapiro was promoted to general manager of Classic in December 1999, he immediately organized a relaunch to reinvent the channel's brand. At the time, Classic had little consistency across its schedule. Ron Semiao described it as a "surfer's network" that viewers typically happened upon rather than an outlet that provided appointment viewing. Shapiro rebooted *SportsCentury* as Classic's prime-time centerpiece, recruiting ESPN *College Gameday*'s Chris Fowler to serve as host. The series recut *SportsCentury*'s original fifty profiles for sixty-minute time slots and produced segments on the remaining top one hundred athletes and others that did not make the cut. "What we're doing is destination viewing," Shapiro said. "One of the problems with ESPN Classic is people love the idea, love the concept, but don't know what's on. Now, we're going to educate viewers on how to watch."[50] It did so in part by programming *SportsCentury* profiles as part of themed evenings devoted to specific sports. Classic used *SportsCentury* to fashion its equivalent to A&E's *Biography, E! True Hollywood Story*, and VH1's *Behind the Music*—a stable signature series that typifies the channel's brand and organizes its flow of content. Shapiro even called it "our A&E *Biography*."[51]

Aside from the prominence *SportsCentury* delivered, its profiles were "evergreens" that could be scheduled repeatedly at virtually any time and serve a programming purpose that fulfills Classic's nostalgic mission. To bolster the series' marketability, Classic enhanced the profiles' sensationalism and expanded *SportsCentury*'s original scope beyond the greatest North American athletes to any subject that might attract viewers. Like *Biography* and *Behind the Music*, it privileged juicy and controversial stories over examining the greatest athletes or even limiting itself to the twentieth century. The first *SportsCentury* segment produced after Classic's relaunch examined Moe Berg, a professional baseball player who served as a spy during World War II. Berg's baseball career was unremarkable. However, his unusual and mysterious biography warranted his inclusion in the reimagined series. *SportsCentury*'s 2002 profile of troubled boxer Mike Tyson focused almost entirely on his legal problems, unstable mental health, and drug addiction. In contrast to the original *SportsCentury* profiles' tendency to end on a celebratory note, the Tyson segment closes with *Sports Illustrated* staff writer Richard Hoffer—who also authored a 1998 book on Tyson's struggles—solemnly speculating that the former heavyweight champion will die young if he continues his destructive lifestyle. Demonstrating a similarly tabloidesque spirit, the piece on Russian tennis player turned model Anna Kournikova barely mentions her relatively mediocre athletic career in favor of exploring her status as a global sex symbol.

Classic further broadened *SportsCentury*'s initial scope by including coaches, events, and any other subjects relevant to sport's past. For instance, it profiled Jim Bouton's groundbreaking 1970 memoir, *Ball Four*, which interviewee and *New York Times* columnist Robert Lipsyte calls "the most important sports book ever written" because of the shocking light it shed on professional base-ball's seedy underbelly. The documentary likens *Ball Four* to Bob Woodward and Carl Bernstein's exposure of the Watergate scandal and claims the tome transformed sports journalism from an institution that deified and insulated athletes to one that now seeks out and broadcasts their faults—a shift ESPN hastened and now heartily exploits.

SportsCentury's expanded focus on Classic irked some critics, who com-plained the shift cheapened the series' integrity as reliable public history.[52] The program, however, won the 2001 Sports Emmy for Outstanding Edited Sports Series. Moreover, it propelled Classic's growth from twenty to fifty million homes by mid-2001.[53] In fact, Shapiro claimed *SportsCentury*'s story-driven approach effectively attracted younger viewers and women—demographics all of ESPN's channels had traditionally struggled to draw.[54]

Classic also programmed and produced *SportsCentury* profiles to capital-ize on popular sports and cultural events. It scheduled its piece on former Los Angeles Dodgers pitcher Sandy Koufax shortly after the publication of Jane Leavy's biography on the reclusive ballplayer. In 2001 it produced a profile on college basketball legend Pete Maravich to coincide with its news coverage of the men's NCAA Tournament and to compete with a similar documentary that CBS—the network that owns the rights to carry live broadcasts of the event—was premiering at the same time. Documenting history thus took a backseat to *SportsCentury*'s effort to augment ESPN's other content. Classic, for instance, used the occasion of the New York Yankees' bombastic and dictatorial owner George Steinbrenner's July 2010 death to program three full days of Yankees-themed content that included twenty-two *SportsCentury* segments. Classic also repackages blocks of *SportsCentury* profiles to celebrate related events. In 2013 it organized profiles to commemorate the Super Bowl, Australian Open, Daytona 500, Muhammad Ali's birthday, Black History Month, and Women's History Month. The profiles themselves did not change; Classic simply inserted a graphic that signaled their commemorative purpose. The Wilma Rudolph segment it scheduled in honor of Women's History Month in March 2013 could just as easily have been used for Black History Month a few weeks earlier. In addition to strategically programming profiles to complement other events, then, Classic advertises ESPN as invested in the social causes that Black His-tory Month and Women's History Month champion. Classic and *SportsCentury*, however, also provide inexpensive ways for ESPN to celebrate these socially significant events without sacrificing content on its more visible and profitable flagship channel. In 2012 Classic honored Title IX's fortieth anniversary by scheduling two documentaries about the legislation along with a handful of *SportsCentury* profiles on women. There was surprisingly no special commemorative programming scheduled on ESPN's main channel that day.

Classic Sports Network created similar programming blocks to complement and build anticipation for various events. It showed each of Mike Tyson's professional fights—which it licensed from Big Fights, Inc.—leading up to his 1996 bout against Bruce Seldon. But unlike CSN, ESPN and Disney either owned the rights to carry many of the events Classic packaged the *SportsCentury* profiles to celebrate or was giving them considerable attention on ESPN's news programming. Moreover, Classic does not have to pay to schedule the *SportsCentury* segments, which it can remix in a variety of combinations and use across its parent company's platforms in perpetuity. In fact, Classic updates and augments older *SportsCentury* profiles as the featured subjects' stories continue to evolve. It repackaged the installment on Hank Aaron—which it has also scheduled as part of its Black History Month celebration—to showcase interviewees' responses to Barry Bonds breaking the legendary slugger's all-time home run record in 2007. ESPN also includes snippets of the *SportsCentury* profiles or previously unused interview footage from the project as DVD bonus features along with its ESPN Original Entertainment and ESPN Films productions. It bundled the profile on college football coach Paul "Bear" Bryant along with *The Junction Boys* (2002), ESPN Original Entertainment's telefilm about a grueling summer training camp he conducted while at Texas A&M. The *SportsCentury* materials' frequent recombination and revision embody a broader industrial shift John Caldwell identifies from considering productions as "programming" to conceptualizing them as "content" that is designed to be utilized in various forms over time.[55] "You own the property," says Bornstein of ESPN's evergreen documentaries, "and you can recirculate it, reuse it, and slice it and dice it. That's smart business."[56]

SportsCentury's transformation, programming, and ancillary use since Classic's relaunch suggest the series' primary purpose is to inexpensively aid ESPN's expansion and promotional practices. The series sometimes conspicuously excludes sports ESPN and ABC do not own the rights to cover. For instance, in the spring of 2013, Classic programmed a handful of *SportsCentury* profiles on baseball, auto racing, and basketball to celebrate the start of the Major League Baseball season, the Indianapolis 500, and the NBA playoffs—events ABC and ESPN were carrying. The NHL playoffs—the rights to which NBC owned—were also occurring at this time. Classic, however, did not program a single hockey-themed *SportsCentury* as the playoffs unfolded. In doing so, it resisted—intentionally or not—contributing to the NHL's exposure during a moment when its games were competing with ABC's and ESPN's content. Moreover, this programming decision, by virtue of *SportsCentury*'s constructed position as a historical resource, subtly suggested professional hockey has less historical significance than the sports ABC and ESPN were covering. "Silences," as the anthropologist and historian Michel-Rolph Trouillot observes, "are inherent in the creation of sources."[57] Classic's use of the *SportsCentury* series builds and distributes a history of sport that is shaped by ESPN's ambition to amplify its authority and to mute—or at least muffle—its competitors.

ESPN Classic generates nowhere near the revenue that ESPN or ESPN2 do with their impressive menu of live event coverage. ESPN, however, does not rely on the relatively small revenues Classic creates. Rather, the channel offers opportunities to cross-promote ESPN's other content and to limit competitors' programming potential. In this way, it does important institutional and industrial work for ESPN and the Walt Disney Company. In fact, Classic's relatively small operating costs and potential to augment the sports calendar inspired ESPN International to team with various European partners to create ESPN Classic Sports. Debuting in France in 2002 and eventually spreading to more than twenty countries across Europe, the channel programs historical content that complements current sporting events in different regions. It simultaneously expands ESPN's effort to situate itself as an authority on sport history beyond *SportsCentury*'s North American scope.

Controlling the Classic Archive

In April 2011, an HBO archivist posted a message to the Association for Moving Image Archivists Listserv asking for leads on how the outlet might locate its sports footage from 1972 to 1976, most of which had been discarded or misplaced. This inattention is common in sports television. "Networks and local stations have been terrible archivists," complained Richard Sandomir. "Footage from many games from the 1950s and '60s was destroyed or decomposed."[58] Sandomir enthusiastically endorsed ESPN Classic as an antidote to sports media organizations' often apathetic archival practices.

Beyond its role as a repository, Classic—via ESPN—decides what is included in this collection and oversees its use. "Archives," historians Joan M. Schwartz and Terry Cook explain, "are not passive storehouses of old stuff, but active sites where social power is negotiated, contested, and confirmed." They constitute, notes the philosopher Michel Foucault, "the law of what can be said, the system that governs the appearance of statements as unique events."[59]

Along with the specific protocols that guide their organization, archives both facilitate and constrain the creation of historical narratives. Consequently, the institutions that build, arrange, and control archives possess immense power to shape history and to decide who is authorized to construct it.[60]

ESPN Classic puts on display ESPN's sports archive—a far less mysterious, but still massively valuable, variation of Disney's fabled "vault"—and showcases its command over this abundant collection. The series *Classic Wide World of Sports*, which, like *SportsCentury*, is hosted by Chris Fowler, repackages old episodes of ABC's *Wide World of Sports*. *Classic Wide World* also remixes and enhances the featured episodes. For instance, it excludes the programs' less lively portions, augments them with graphics that offer historical context and explain tidbits contemporary viewers may not understand, adds interview footage (some of which was originally shot for *SportsCentury*) with important ABC Sports figures like Arledge and host Jim McKay, and includes Fowler's studio introductions and commentary. Its episodes end with a short segment titled "Full Circle" that outlines what became of the featured events and their participants since *Wide World* put them on the national stage. These additions stress *Wide World*'s importance to the history of sports media and American popular culture more broadly. The series' first episode, for instance, emphasizes *Wide World*'s political significance by mentioning that the ABC program "made over 70 trips to communist countries closed to most U.S. citizens between 1961 and 1989." Aside from commemorating *Wide World*—and using its old tapes as a relatively inexpensive way to fill ESPN Classic's schedule—the program situates ESPN as a descendant of this important institution and the official keeper of its history. *Classic Wide World* preserves *Wide World of Sports*' memory in ways that avow and fortify ESPN's cultural and historical authority.

While Sandomir praised ESPN Classic for giving "new life" to programming that would otherwise be gathering dust, he critiqued its commercially minded willingness to alter this material. In particular, he derided Classic's insertion of digital ads into footage of old baseball games as a "crass misstep." The ads were used to alert viewers to "Key Play[s] of the Game"—the very instances that presumably warrant the recycled footage's "classic" status. Sandomir, however, argues that integrating these ads diminishes the footage's authenticity and, in doing so, perverts audiences' understanding of the history Classic purports to reveal. Shapiro defended the ads by citing them as an "editorial enhancement that educates viewers by pointing out the seminal moment of the game."[61] Regardless of their ostensibly pedagogical mission, the ads exhibit an overarching goal that guides Classic's programming practices: they reuse and reconfigure content in ways that sculpt ESPN's brand and exploit new revenue streams.

Moreover, and just as important, the control ESPN exerts over its growing store of archived footage limits other media outlets' ability to produce historical films. *Greatest Sports Legends* founder and producer Berl Rotfeld noted that he often had a difficult time securing footage for his low-budget series—which paid each featured "legend" only one thousand dollars to appear—from organizations like NFL Films and Big Fights, Inc., which carefully monitor their materials' circulation.[62] "The only boxer we've done," Rotfeld lamented in a 1983 interview, "is Joe Frazier because we were able to buy films from him."[63] In fact, Rotfeld ended *Greatest Sports Legends* in 1993 because escalating rights fees eventually made it impossible for the series to turn a profit. Wielding a much larger budget than Rotfeld's small independent company, Turner Network Television (TNT) produced *Muhammad Ali: The Whole Story* in 1996. The two-hour documentary used Big Fights, Inc., as its main footage supplier and was lauded for its inclusion of rare archival content to enliven Ali's oft-chronicled career.[64] Disney's acquisition of the Big Fights library two years after the TNT documentary's release ensured ESPN would decide from then on whether and how these treasured artifacts circulate. It prevents competitors from laying claim to the history this footage indexes without licensing it and discourages small-scale independent outlets like Rotfeld's from even attempting to enter this niche programming market.

Despite the tidy sum it paid for Big Fights, ESPN uses only a small fraction of this material. In 2006 Classic produced the series *Classic Ringside* and an accompanying collection of home videos, which featured footage of famous boxers like Jack Dempsey, Joe Louis, and Sugar Ray Robinson. However, most of the content ESPN employs from its Big Fights acquisition depicts either Muhammad Ali or Mike Tyson, the two boxers who still manage to draw a considerable audience at a time when the sport's popularity is waning. Its many other boxing films simply sit somewhere in the bowels of ESPN's headquarters. While this unused content does not directly contribute to ESPN's programming, the organization's ownership of it guarantees that no one else can use it without permission. As artist and critic Allan Sekula notes, "The purchase of reproduction rights under copyright law is also the purchase of a certain semantic license."[65] The boxing footage's dormancy aids ESPN's effort to build and preserve its position as sport history's authoritative voice. Ironically, then, ESPN's ambitious documentation of sport's past is partly organized around an effort to limit the historical content that circulates in popular media culture. This is not to say that ESPN refuses to license footage to its competitors. It routinely supplies content to HBO Sports for its documentaries, such as 2008's *Joe Louis: America's Hero . . . Betrayed* and 2010's *Magic and Bird: A Courtship of Rivals*. However, it typically does so only for projects that do not compete with or otherwise threaten its programming.[66]

In the context of live event coverage, ESPN's competitors have charged that the media outlet "warehouses" games, or purchases contracts to showcase more contests than it has the space to schedule. Though it does not air these events, it also makes certain that no other entity can do so and, as a result, safeguards its industrial dominance. Complaints that this warehousing limits competition—specifically in regards to college football and basketball coverage—drove ESPN to create ESPNU to provide a new space for the scores of live collegiate games it owns the rights to display. ESPN's acquisition and control of archive footage reflect its gluttonous approach to event coverage. The media outlet has escaped the criticism it faces concerning live games, however, because of historical content's comparatively low value and popularity. Though archived footage is less immediately lucrative than event coverage, controlling this content similarly allows media outlets to assert their centrality to sport's cultural meanings and to limit competing outlets' potential to wield comparable authority.

An Ironic Archive

The zany ESPN Classic series *Cheap Seats* (2004–6) perhaps most interestingly illustrates ESPN's use of and control over its archived footage. The program was hosted by the twin brother comic duo Jason and Randy Sklar, who play smart-ass librarians who forgo ESPN talent's typical formalwear in favor of T-shirts, baggy jeans, and sneakers. The Sklars, in fact, host *Cheap Seats* only because its original featured talent, Ron Parker (played by comedian Michael Showalter), was injured by an avalanche of old tapes—a slapstick mishap that gestures toward the archive's enormity. As the program's opening voice-over, delivered by Dan Patrick, announces:

> Deep in the ESPN tape library, the Worldwide Leader in Classic Sports launched a series designed to take a new look at old games. They called it *Cheap Seats: With Ron Parker*. Parker, an anchor with attitude, was helped thanklessly by two librarians, Randy and Jason. The show was slated to go all the way. But moments into the first show, tragedy struck. With Ron on the DL [disabled list], somebody needed to step up—like [Lou] Gehrig for [Wally] Pipp, or [Tom] Brady for [Drew] Bledsoe. Sitting two and three on the hosting depth chart, that someone was Randy and Jason. That is their story, and this is *Cheap Seats: Without Ron Parker*.

The program's title then emerges on a graphic that resembles the labeling tape libraries use to mark their holdings.

Evoking a combination of the cult classics *Mystery Science Theatre 3000* and *Beavis and Butthead*, the Sklars lounge on a couch in the tape library and poke fun at archived sports footage that now seems preposterous, such as Steve Garvey's Celebrity Fishing Tournament, the World Putt-Putt Championships, and the World's Strongest Man Competition.[67] They describe the World Series of Poker, for instance, as "combining the speed and excitement of nursing home shuffleboard with the ability and hand-eye coordination of sleeping." They also include sketches that lampoon the featured events (often with the help of then fledgling indie comics like Aziz Anzari, David Cross, Zach Galifianakis, and Patton Oswalt).

Like many of Nick at Nite's self-consciously campy presentations of retro material, *Cheap Seats* cultivated an ironic viewership that simultaneously commemorates and mocks sports TV's past.[68] Similar to *Classic Wide World, Cheap Seats* provides a highly selective rendering of subject matter that enhances and contextualizes it. While *Classic Wide World*'s various add-ons call attention to materials' importance, *Cheap Seats* points out their absurdity. The Sklars fast-forward through sections they deem unbearably tedious and include a recurring segment titled "Do You Care?" that shares obscure factoids about the footage's decidedly marginal featured events and participants. The implied answer to the question the "Do You Care?" segments pose is an emphatically snarky "No."

For all its sarcasm, *Cheap Seats* still flaunts ESPN's colossal archive. Jason and Randy are awash in a surplus of footage (so much that it actually fell on and injured their old boss) that is unavailable anywhere else. The program's ironic presentation composes yet another way ESPN repurposes its archived content while branding itself as the principal steward of and expert on sport's past. "Control of the archive," Schwartz and Cook claim, "means control of society and thus control of determining history's winners and losers." More ardently, philosopher Jacques Derrida avers, "There is no political power without control of the archive."[69] Along with the other ways ESPN and Disney's archived content is utilized on and beyond ESPN Classic, *Cheap Seats* affirms ESPN's

Paying homage to *Mystery Science Theatre 3000, Cheap Seats* hosts Jason and Randy Sklar play bumbling tape librarians who poke fun at the often bizarre footage in ESPN's enormous archive.

control of sport history and, consequently, advertises and expands the media outlet's authority. Though the short-lived and goofy program seems an unlikely candidate to serve as a politicized instrument of social power, it forcefully advertised ESPN's ownership of this excessive collection and the influence that comes along with its warehoused footage.

After its first season, *Cheap Seats* created a *SportsCentury* parody that playfully emphasized the low-rated program's significance to ESPN and sport history. With a deadpan delivery that mimics the solemnity with which he introduces athletes as revered as Arthur Ashe and Roberto Clemente, Fowler introduces the segment by claiming, "It's hard to imagine a time when Jason and Randy weren't as much a part of our daily lives as the air we breathe. . . . How did this idea become a pop culture phenomenon?" The program situates *Cheap Seats* within the familiar underdog narrative many *SportsCentury* profiles adopt; the obscure production surprisingly rose to heroic and pioneering heights. It includes interviews—lit and captioned with *SportsCentury*'s distinct look—with Jason, Randy, and erstwhile (and presumably recovered) host Ron Parker reflecting on their development of and experience on the show. It also recuts interview footage shot for other *SportsCentury* profiles to make it appear the featured experts and witnesses are remembering *Cheap Seats*' (faux) greatness.

Beyond reaching for easy laughs, the send-up reinforces *SportsCentury*'s identity as a series that reliably illuminates sport's past. Indeed, its humor depends on the program's established image as a prestigious and sober documentary series. It positions the repackaged interview footage as trustworthy historical data and uses its constructed dependability as an ironic foil to generate its gag. In this context, however, the recut materials clearly do not—and are not intended to—shed instructive light on sport's past. Though an exaggerated spoof, the *Cheap Seats* profile illustrates ESPN Classic's production and deployment of historical content to build the ESPN brand and to fuel its programming.

Institutionalizing Cultural Memories of Sport

Regardless of its many problems, *SportsCentury* has become a common resource by which sport's past is now remembered, organized, and debated. Unsurprisingly, ESPN uses the project and its rankings to market more recent ESPN and Disney products. For instance, in 2010 Disney transformed William Nack's 1975 book on racehorse Secretariat—originally titled *Big Red of Meadow Stable: Secretariat, the Making of a Champion*—into the feature film *Secretariat*. That same year, the Disney-owned imprint Hyperion truncated the book's title to *Secretariat* and republished it as a movie tie-in. The volume's back cover uses

SportsCentury to advertise Disney's film and Nack's book: "He [Secretariat] was the only non-human chosen as one of ESPN's '50 Greatest Athletes of the Century.'" With *SportsCentury*, then, ESPN manufactured an accolade Disney later used to promote one of its products.

As *SportsCentury* took inspiration from Ken Burns's *Baseball* and series like A&E's *Biography*, it established a model that several sports cable TV outlets have since adopted to create similar documentary-driven multimedia events that evolved into trademark series. In 2006 the National Football League's NFL Network premiered *America's Game: The Super Bowl Champions*, a series of documentaries on each Super Bowl–winning team made to commemorate the event's fortieth anniversary. Like *SportsCentury*, *America's Game* commissioned a fifty-two-member "blue-ribbon panel" to rank the greatest Super Bowl champions. It counted down the top twenty by airing the documentaries produced on these teams each week during prime time from November 2006 until Super Bowl XLI in February 2007. NFL Network president Steve Bornstein—who served as ESPN's top executive during *SportsCentury*'s development—claimed he wanted *America's Game* to be the NFL Network's "signature show" and to serve a branding and programming function for the channel similar to the role *SportsCentury* performs on ESPN Classic.[70]

The Big Ten Network—in which ESPN and Disney competitor Fox/News Corporation owns a majority stake—followed suit in 2010 with *Big Ten Icons*, a series of profiles hosted by former ABC Sports broadcaster Keith Jackson that counted down the NCAA Big Ten Conference's top fifty players. Mirroring *SportsCentury*'s multiplatform composition, *Big Ten Icons* initially released the athletes ranked twenty-one to fifty online and then counted down the top twenty with weekly profiles scheduled during prime time. Like ESPN Classic, the NFL Network and Big Ten Network use these series to build a supply of productions that can be scheduled to promote their other programming and serve as filler. For instance, they commonly use segments of *America's Game* and *Big Ten Icons* as lead-ins to telecasts featuring the teams they depict. Moreover, they have expanded after their initial premieres with spin-offs such as the NFL Network's *America's Game: Missing Rings*, which chronicles exceptional teams that never won a Super Bowl, and *Big Ten Icons: The Coaches*. *America's Game* and *Big Ten Icons* enable the NFL Network and the Big Ten Network to build and control the National Football League's and the Big Ten Conference's images while situating themselves (and their parent companies) as the official guardians of those organizations' histories—an expertise ESPN claims with its *SportsCentury* profiles on their players. Similar to ESPN Classic, these outlets both put their archival content on display and restrict its circulation.[71]

Sociologist Maurice Halbwachs argues that collective memories—the narratives by which particular groups make sense of the past—are produced through and within matrices of social power. Constructions of the past, in other words, inexorably reflect conditions of the present. Efforts like *SportsCentury* and ESPN Classic foster a media landscape that suggests sport's history cannot be explained—or even remembered—without ESPN's presence, assistance, and permission. As sport historian Richard C. Crepeau claims, "When the history of sport in America is written several decades into the twenty-first century, ESPN may well be regarded as the most important development of the twentieth century."[72] Through *SportsCentury*'s creation, use, and legacy, ESPN works very hard to ensure precisely this result.

ESPN the Magazine and Page 2

Paper and Digital Sports Pages

This [*ESPN the Magazine*] is *Sports Illustrated* for slackers.
—Michael Weinreb, *Akron Beacon Journal*[1]

I can watch a Celtics game from my slingbox on my laptop in a hotel room in Denver. I don't need the newspaper anymore. I can go to ESPN.
—Bill Simmons, *ESPN.com*[2]

In a 2000 installment of his weekly National Public Radio commentary, Frank Deford critiqued ESPN's "This is *SportsCenter*" promotional spots on the grounds that their regular inclusion of famous athletes compromises the network's journalistic integrity. "For a couple of years now," Deford pointed out, "ESPN has been running some delightful commercials praising ESPN that feature the very star athletes that ESPN covers. ESPN and ABC are the same company. Visualize, if you will, [Senators] Tom Daschle and Trent Lott teaming up to do a funny commercial on ABC urging you to watch Peter Jennings's news. Because that's the exact equivalent of ESPN's gambit." Echoing Deford's plaint, the Poynter Institute's Al Tompkins asked, "How would it be if you appear in a promo with an athlete, and then the next day you have to do a difficult story about their cocaine use?"[3]

Deford tempers this charge by acknowledging that sports journalism is traditionally held to less rigorous professional and editorial standards than other genres. Historically known—and ridiculed—as newspapers' "toy department," sports journalism, according to David Rowe, is stereotypically "dedicated to fun and frivolity rather than to the serious functions of the fourth estate."[4] In fact, nineteenth- and early-twentieth-century editors would often avoid sporting topics altogether for fear of compromising their publications' respectability. Regardless, historian Bruce J. Evensen notes that by the 1920s, one of every four readers purchased a paper because of its sports coverage and remarks that sports pages charged advertisers premium rates—a practice that carried over into radio and television. Moreover, these relatively lucrative departments were often allowed to edit their own copy, an allowance that fostered exaggeration that "would not be tolerated on any other page."[5] This tendency toward hyperbole, critics argue, embodies sports journalism's overall propensity to privilege courting moneyed male consumers over producing judiciously written and meticulously vetted content. These appraisals only amplified along with radio's and TV's emergence.

Several of ESPN's "This is *SportsCenter*" spots poke fun at common dismissals of sports journalism—and ESPN's material in particular—as slapdash. A 1995 segment opens with Bob Ley, perhaps ESPN's most trusted journalistic voice, commenting on his employer's commitment to producing credible news. "We can't step over the line between covering a story and possibly becoming part of the story," he sincerely intones. "Like the Jim Harbaugh story; we might have gone over the line there." It cuts to Dan Patrick reporting from the operating room where Indianapolis Colts quarterback Jim Harbaugh is undergoing knee surgery, a procedure that, as it turns out, Keith Olbermann is administering to the half-conscious football star. It then returns to Ley's deadpan commentary: "It just boils down to ethics. People trust us to know where that line is. And that's what journalism is all about." A different "This is *SportsCenter*" from the same year begins with a shot of Ley and fellow anchor Charley Steiner in their cubicles feverishly working the phones to chase leads and fact-check in preparation for that evening's *SportsCenter*. Craig Kilborn interrupts their frenzied labor with a pressing question: "Guys! What do you like better? 'Hurt me' or 'Spank me'?" Ley and Steiner pause from their work to consider which quip would most effectively serve their colleague's journalistic needs. After a moment of careful rumination, the reporters agree that "Spank me" is Kilborn's best bet and promptly return to work. These tongue-in-cheek promos highlight ESPN's joyful disregard for traditional journalism. They indicate that ESPN is not simply a toy department, but a toy store that embraces the frivolousness that gives establishmentarians like Deford and Tompkins pause.

In 1998 ESPN used its playful image to develop a niche in sports magazine publishing, a market *Sports Illustrated* had dominated since 1954. It billed *ESPN the Magazine* as a TV-inspired alternative to *Sports Illustrated*, which had fashioned a respectable status in the traditionally lowbrow context of sports journalism by emphasizing its long-form "bonus" articles that probe sport's sociocultural dimensions.

Two years after *ESPN the Magazine*'s emergence, *ESPN.com* launched *Page 2*, a division that specialized in sport and popular culture. Confronting both sports journalism's vulgar status and online writing's reputation as unregulated and amateurish, *Page 2* compiled a roster of high-profile print journalists that included David Halberstam, Hunter S. Thompson, and Ralph Wiley. It simultaneously hired a collection of up-and-coming online voices, most notably sports blogger Bill Simmons, who emerged as the site's featured columnist by cultivating an intentionally undisciplined, biased, and interactive style designed for and uniquely suited to the Web. While Simmons's work contrasts—and oftentimes overtly critiques—many of print journalism's traditions, he also deliberately positions it as steeped in that heritage. *Page 2* thus builds on common media ideologies to distinguish *ESPN.com*'s content from typical online sportswriting.

Sports Illustrated for Slackers

John Walsh had yearned to develop a magazine since joining ESPN. The media outlet would not indulge the former *Inside Sports* editor's costly ambition, however, until a challenge to its market share of cable sports TV emerged. Shortly after Time Warner and Turner Broadcasting's 1995 merger, *Sports Illustrated* and CNN joined forces to create the twenty-four-hour cable sports news channel CNN/SI, which launched on December 12, 1996.[6] Augmenting the formidable competition CNN's *Sports Tonight* provided *SportsCenter*, CNN/SI melded CNN's and *Sports Illustrated*'s respective identification with hard news and sports.

A contrast to sports journalism's philistine repute, *Sports Illustrated*, according to the magazine's former editor Ray Cave, "legitimized sports. . . . All of a sudden you could read a sports magazine, and still be considered *able to read*." The publication, claims historian Michael MacCambridge, "was for the 'martini' set rather than the 'beer and pretzel' gang," and novelist James A. Michener asserted that "only *The New Yorker*, among contemporary magazines, has been as effective in sponsoring good writing with a certain wry touch."[7] Despite *Sports Illustrated*'s respectability and high circulation, ESPN—which Time Warner incidentally passed on the opportunity to purchase in 1983—composed a significant threat to the magazine. The twenty-four-hour sports news cycle it helped to usher rendered *Sports Illustrated*'s weekly reflections, however insightful, less timely.

Sports Illustrated had some minor forays into television prior to CNN/SI, such as SItv, which launched in 1994 and produced intermittent segments for ABC's *Wide World of Sports*, and several behind-the-scenes specials on the magazine's annual "Swimsuit Issue" made for HBO.[8] CNN/SI marketed itself as a nuanced alternative to ESPN. "We're going to add perspective and depth and point of view to sports news in a way that's not been done before," guaranteed CNN senior vice president Jim Walton just prior to the channel's debut.[9] A print advertisement for CNN/SI depicted a stream of *Sports Illustrated* covers and a stream of images from *Sports Tonight* converging into a television set along with copy that read: "Imagine all the great reasons you read *Sports Illustrated* combined with CNN's unsurpassed ability to cover live events." The ad claims CNN/SI blends *Sports Illustrated*'s expertise with CNN's relevance and ubiquity. The channel featured *Sports Illustrated*'s celebrity journalists and benefited from cross-promotion on CNN, which rebranded *Sports Tonight* as a CNN/SI production and simulcast the nightly program until the channel folded unceremoniously in 2002.[10] While CNN/SI insisted on its stylistic difference from ESPN, it did hire away Emmy Award–winning *Outside the Lines* producer Jean McCormick to oversee its content.

Incensed by CNN/SI's efforts to siphon ESPN's TV audience and staff, Disney CEO Michael Eisner sought revenge. First, his company scrambled to unveil ESPNews—ESPN's third twenty-four-hour channel—prior to CNN/SI's debut.[11] The new channel premiered on November 1, 1996, with a one-hour prime-time simulcast on ESPN's flagship channel that featured a handful of celebrity cameos and an investigative feature. Though primarily a wheel of news updates, ESPNews allowed ESPN to continue covering whatever story was big at the time without cutting away when a given program's time slot expired. In this sense, the channel offers more of the in-depth reporting that CNN/SI contended was lacking from ESPN's standard news coverage.

Eisner claims he called Turner Broadcasting Company's Ted Turner shortly after CNN/SI's announcement and fumed to his competitor: "You're going to do CNN Sports? Well, we're going to bury your flagship. *Sports Illustrated* is old and it's boring." *ESPN the Magazine* was ESPN's most concerted, though not its first, venture into print. In 1988 the company produced Sunday newspaper inserts for distribution to zip codes where average annual household incomes exceeded thirty-five thousand dollars, a solidly middle-class figure at the time. From 1995 to 1997, it published *Total Sports Magazine*, a sporadically released collection of special issues that previewed upcoming seasons. Expanding on its less ambitious predecessors, *ESPN the Magazine* would allow the media outlet to permanently extend its reach into new spaces. "The only place you couldn't take ESPN [before the magazine]," claims Steve Bornstein, "was on the train or in the bathroom." Emphasizing this point, the magazine's first issues included dropout subscriber cards that reminded potential customers that they "can't watch cable in the bathroom." Aside from the new title's mobility, ESPN marketed it as a hip option for younger sports fans. To reach this demographic, ESPN hired John Papanek, a former *Sports Illustrated* managing editor who launched the successful offshoot *Sports Illustrated for Kids* in 1988. "It was clear," Papanek claimed after joining ESPN, "that millions of fans between the ages of maybe 16 and 28 were not being served by *Sports Illustrated*." In fact, when *ESPN the Magazine* debuted in March 1998, the average age of *Sports Illustrated*'s readership was 36.5.[12]

ESPN the Magazine's design reflected its demographic focus. The colorful biweekly deliberately mimicked *Rolling Stone*'s and *Spin*'s oversized formats to suggest it would bring a similar attitude to sports coverage. As executive editor Gary Hoenig claimed, "We feel we can be to athletes what *Rolling Stone* was to musicians in the '70s and what *Vanity Fair* was to celebrities in the '80s."[13] Walsh assured the magazine would compose an energetic contrast to *Sports Illustrated* that emphasizes "bite-sized chunks" instead of longer narratives. Papanek elaborated on the publication's stylistic differences from its competitor in a direct-mail ad prior to its emergence: "*ESPN The Magazine* gives you the good stuff—packaged the way you like it. Bigger pictures, quicker takes. Shorter, snappier stories. Not 10-page yawners about some minor league hockey player growing up on a farm in Manitoba. Or some former world leader stalking bone fish off the Florida Coast." He reinforced this mission statement in an editorial note that appeared in the premiere issue's opening pages: "No rehashes, no game stories, no press-box pontificating, no wistful reminisces about the good old days—none of that. We are not your father's sports magazine."[14] These assertions both insist on *ESPN the Magazine*'s uniqueness and suggest that *Sports Illustrated*'s focus on serious long-form storytelling is out of touch with the youthful sports fans ESPN serves. Along these lines, the magazine initially ended its issues with a visual section titled "0:01" that included cartoonish commentaries comparable to Al Jaffe's *Mad Magazine* "fold-ins" (which themselves were satirical ripostes to *Playboy*'s centerfolds). The section "0:01" thus offered a lighthearted alternative to *Sports Illustrated*'s "Point After," a back-page column that tackles topical issues.

As CNN/SI based its televisual identity around a legacy magazine, *ESPN the Magazine* built its niche in print through mimicking ESPN's TV coverage. The *Toronto Star*'s Garth Woolsey critiqued the title's TV-inspired aesthetic as overly frenetic. "There's no real need to read *ESPN The Magazine* front to back," he observed. "Open it anywhere and there's something to grab your attention. You might say it can be read the same way we watch TV, with our attention spans challenged and our clickers ever posed." *Salon.com*'s James Poniewozik echoed Raissman's comment by writing that the magazine "looks like the cable channel on glossy paper." Walsh, however, cited this design as the publication's distinguishing feature. He described it as "movement on pages" and claimed that "even our long pieces . . . are storytelling done the way we would do it in a good long television piece; they move quickly."[15] The magazine's televisual pace further contrasted *Sports Illustrated*'s focus on narrative storytelling and, in doing so, courted sports fans more accustomed to *SportsCenter*'s highlight packages than to long-form feature articles. It even incorporated ESPN's on-air talent as columnists and included spin-offs like "Outtakes," a regular segment wherein Dan Patrick interviewed sports stars in much the same style he would when hosting *SportsCenter*.

ESPN the Magazine reinforced its position as a cable TV–inspired counter to *Sports Illustrated* by focusing on upcoming events rather than reflecting on those that had recently transpired. "This magazine begins with the assumption that the reader knows what happened," Papanek claimed. "The best action has already been shown on TV, in replays, and slow-motion."[16] Papanek suggests TV game coverage—from live telecasts to highlights—is technically superior to written game reports and has rendered redundant the weekly retrospective print commentary *Sports Illustrated* generates. The publication's first issue exemplified this forward-looking style by adopting the title "Next" and focusing on up-and-coming athletes from the United States' four major sports: Los Angeles Lakers guard Kobe Bryant, Philadelphia Flyers center Eric Lindros, Seattle Mariners shortstop Alex Rodriguez, and Pittsburgh Steelers quarterback Kordell Stewart. The "Next" issue transformed into an annual production that highlights a particularly exciting young athlete. Released at the year's end, "Next" contrasts *Sports Illustrated*'s "Sportsman of the Year" award and accompanying issue, which, like the magazine, reflect on the previous year.

ESPN the Magazine also built distinction by hiring voices from several magazine publishing genres. It recruited *Vibe* president Keith Clinkscales to serve as an editor, *George*'s Peter Keating to write a business column, and the independent San Francisco–based *Might Magazine*'s Dave Eggers and Zev Borow to develop a section of obscure and quirky sports factoids titled "Answer Guy." Well-known columnists that *ESPN the Magazine* brought into the fold included the *Washington Post*'s Tony Kornheiser, the *New York Daily News*' Mike Lupica, and the *Boston Globe*'s Dan Shaughnessy. Like the journalists featured on *The Sports Reporters*, these celebrity sportswriters kept their regular newspaper columns (though often in a scaled-back manner)—a decision that enabled ESPN to profit on their widespread notoriety while strengthening its relationship to their home markets.

Despite Eisner's stated intent to "bury" *Sports Illustrated*, Walsh claims more modest goals guided *ESPN the Magazine*'s development. "Nobody is saying that we're going to unseat anybody. We're just asking for a seat at the table."[17] Be that as it may, the upstart magazine hired away a handful of *Sports Illustrated*'s most popular writers, editors, and production staff—including Curry Kirkpatrick, Rick Telander, and Steve Wulf—prior to its launch. It tried unsuccessfully to lure Deford and, after several failed attempts, acquired popular columnist Rick Reilly in 2007 with a historically lavish contract that the eleven-time National Sportswriter of the Year award winner giddily described as "ballplayer money."[18]

Complementing its position as a forward-thinking alternative to *Sports Illustrated*, *ESPN the Magazine* created a response to the legacy publication's iconic "Swimsuit Issue" in 2009 with "The Body Issue," which depicts nude male and female athletes in a combination of active and sexy poses. Like the "Swimsuit Issue," "The Body Issue" is a highly publicized event around which advertisers plan (and for which certain advertisers build special promotions). Though it would be an overstatement to call "The Body Issue" a progressive indictment of *Sports Illustrated*'s annual issue, it does sometimes present its subjects as more empowered than the exclusively female and most often diminutively arranged bodies that made the "Swimsuit Issue" famous. Furthermore, it routinely features body types that are seldom praised—for example, amputee triathlete Sarah Reinersten, sumo wrestler Byambajav Ulambayar, and seventy-seven-year-old golfer Gary Player. *ESPN the Magazine* uses these exceptional sporting bodies to create an annual publishing event that titillates while sidestepping—and even subtly critiquing—the overt objectification in the "Swimsuit Issue" of conventionally attractive and model-thin women.[19]

As CNN/SI advertised in *Sports Illustrated*, ESPN used its television channels, radio stations, and websites—as well as Disney's many other properties—to promote its new TV-inspired magazine. Just after the magazine's debut, *SportsCenter* included a segment wherein Tom Friend contextualized a feature he penned on heavyweight boxer Tommy Morrison's life after being diagnosed with HIV. Along these lines, ESPN briefly retitled *The Sports Reporters* as *ESPN the Magazine's Sports Reporters* to promote the publication. Beyond ESPN, ABC Sports' play-by-play announcer Brett Musburger plugged the magazine while calling a game, and Peter Jennings praised the title on ABC's *World News Tonight*. *ESPN the Magazine*'s fresh approach and aggressive promotion were rewarded with the National Magazine Award for Design and both *Advertising*

Age's and *AdWeek*'s Best New Magazine awards. Though it has not eclipsed *Sports Illustrated*'s overall circulation volume, *ESPN the Magazine* has firmly established itself as the United States' second most popular sports magazine and the preferred sports title for the younger readers it targets. In 2011 the research firm GfK MRI listed it as the most popular magazine of any genre among eighteen- to thirty-four-year-old males.[20]

The same year as *ESPN the Magazine*'s launch, ESPN extended its presence in print by creating the subsidiary ESPN Books.[21] *Sports Illustrated* had published books since its founding that include instructional guides, spin-offs by its better-known writers, encyclopedias, and almanacs. Following suit, ESPN Books' first title was an almanac with contributions by ESPN staffers. Emerging around the same time as *SportsCentury*, the almanac—which ESPN Books continued to publish annually until 2009—similarly cast the media outlet as an authority on sport history. Other ESPN Books products combined this carefully crafted expertise with ESPN's signature irreverence, such as *23 Ways to Get to First Base: The ESPN Uncyclopedia* (2007), which bundled "totally irrelevant, absolutely essential sports knowledge" into humorous nuggets that mirrored *ESPN the Magazine*'s televisual design. ESPN Books also extended the magazine's reach by repackaging its most popular sections—including "Outtakes," "The Answer Guy," and "0:01"—as stand-alone books and releasing titles written by the publication's staff writers. ESPN Books' diverse catalog capitalizes on new revenue streams and solidifies ESPN's place in print culture. In fact, ESPN briefly teamed with Borders bookstores to create shelves of sports books branded "ESPN-Borders Bestsellers" and "ESPN Instant Classics."[22] These in-store promotions situated ESPN as the principal voice in sports book publishing, even though it entered the industry decades after *Sports Illustrated*.

Like the TV channels on which it is based, *ESPN the Magazine* expanded beyond the United States and the English language. It created a Chinese magazine in 2004 that complemented ESPN's expanding presence in Asia. Its Spanish-language edition, *ESPN Deportes*, emerged one year after ESPN launched the TV channel of the same name, which caters to U.S.-based Hispanic audiences.[23] While developments like ESPN Books' almanacs and "The Body Issue" responded to print traditions that *Sports Illustrated* instituted, *ESPN the Magazine* established an international and multilingual presence before its legacy competitor. In fact, it compelled *Sports Illustrated* to begin publishing Spanish-language special issues in 2005. Though *ESPN the Magazine* used its TV-inspired format to bill itself as a fun and relatively freewheeling alternative to *Sports Illustrated*, this strategy conducts the serious business of establishing a commercially and symbolically valuable niche for ESPN in print.

Magazining *ESPN.com*

Though it came late to magazine publishing, ESPN was an early adopter of on-line media. Paul Allen's Starwave—which the Walt Disney Company purchased in 1998—developed *ESPN.com* in 1995. Like most sports websites at the time, *ESPN.com* specialized in scores, game recaps, and some highlights.[24] Walsh, however, thought *ESPN.com* could also provide commentary that would lure the still-nascent Internet's typically young audience—a rapidly expanding de-mographic that intersected with ESPN and *ESPN the Magazine*'s target market. He consequently developed the division *Page 2* to extend *ESPN the Magazine*'s alternative focus by using sport to examine popular culture.

Though its focus complemented *ESPN the Magazine*'s style, *Page 2* had to confront media ideologies that dismiss online discourse as inelegant. Media critic Nicholas Carr, for instance, claims the Internet fosters "informality and immediacy" that lead to a "narrowing of expressiveness and loss of eloquence."[25] Online media, he and many like-minded commentators suggest, have rendered popular culture and its inhabitants increasingly shallow and incapable of the comparatively deep thinking that print media supposedly demand. This com-mon critique mirrors the charges CNN/SI made about ESPN's superficiality to publicize its launch and build a niche in sports TV.

Online sportswriting is subject to the same gripes, which build on tradi-tional dismissals of sports journalism to charge that it ignores print journalism's professional cornerstones: attending games, gathering quotes, and impartially reporting on events. In his memoir, written as Web-based journalism was gain-ing traction, sportswriter Leonard Koppett romanticizes the press box of old as a "special place" to which "admission could not be purchased." The press box's "unique privileges," Koppett reminisces, "were not available elsewhere, its particular blend of intimacy, visibility, and glamour could not be artificially reproduced." Expanding on Koppett, traditionalists have charged that digital sports journalism—and blogs in particular—lower professional standards by allowing anyone with an Internet connection to disseminate their opinions anonymously and without editorial oversight or access to events.[26] In a 2008 interview with the *Miami Herald*, sportscaster Bob Costas dismissed the sports blogosphere as "a high-tech place for idiots to do what they used to do on bar stools."[27] Less than two months later, Costas hosted a now-infamous panel on his HBO talk show, *Costas Now*, which explored the Internet's impact on sports journalism. His guests included *Friday Night Lights* (1990) author H. G. "Buzz" Bissinger and Will Leitch, founder of the irreverent and sometimes crass Gawker Media–owned sports blog *Deadspin*. Echoing Costas's comments to the *Miami Herald*, Bissinger condemned blogs and bloggers as cruel, dishonest, and sloppy. He then indicted them for "the complete dumbing down of society."

Four years before this altercation, Leitch voiced his critique of the attitudes guiding such dismissals of online writing. "There is a stigma involved in writing on the Internet," he opined. "A piece of journalism that would be at home in *Esquire* or *The New Republic* is somehow, just because it's posted on the Web, lessened. This is a problem of perception that will be corrected in the upcoming years. The future of literature and journalism is right there in your Web browser, if you know where to find it."[28] While Leitch disagrees with Costas's and Bissinger's assessments of digital media, he acknowledges that mediated content's value is shaped by attitudes that cast certain media as more or less sophisticated than others—ideologies that designate venues like *Page 2*, despite the content they produce, as inferior to their print counterparts.

Page 2 editor Kevin Jackson claims the website was principally inspired by *Esquire*, a magazine known for award-winning journalism. ESPN branded *Page 2* as exceptionally thoughtful by recruiting a roster of prominent print journalists to serve as regular columnists that included David Halberstam, Hunter S. Thompson, and Ralph Wiley. These renowned voices reached out to slightly different audiences. Halberstam, a Pulitzer Prize winner for his *New York Times* dispatches from the Vietnam War, wrote from the perspective of a nostalgic old-timer who dearly loves sports but is wary of the many changes they have incurred since his youth. In a praiseful column on the controversial NBA star Allen Iverson, for instance, Halberstam admits, "I own no rap CDs, and by instinct when I hear the name Snoop Dogg, it sounds to me like someone who should be in a comic strip."[29] Though he distances himself from Iverson's generation, he astutely contextualizes the brash point guard's rebelliousness and hip-hop-inflected swagger—traits that many pundits critiqued as alarming symptoms of pampered modern athletes—by comparing him to earlier irascible sports heroes such as Ted Williams and Bill Russell. Thompson was the countercultural father of "Gonzo" journalism who had enjoyed a resurgence in popularity after Terry Gilliam's 1998 film adaptation of his book *Fear and Loathing in Las Vegas* (1971). Like Halberstam, whose *The Breaks of the Game* (1981) stands among the most celebrated sports books ever written, several of Thompson's best-known works centered on sport, such as "The Kentucky Derby Is Decadent and Depraved" (1970) and "Fear and Loathing at the Super Bowl" (1973), which he wrote for *Rolling Stone* while Walsh was at the magazine.[30] Thompson's *Page 2* column, titled "Hey Rube," continued his reckless aesthetic. Specifically, it endeavored to combat what he viewed as an epidemic of "dumbness in America" and to provide a "diary of what it was like to be alive and suffering in the first disastrous days of the George W. Bush administration." Wiley's columns, though less rambling than Thompson's screeds, were similarly polarizing in their interrogation of sport's racial inequities and hypocrisies.[31] While these celebrity columnists focused on different topics and reached out to separate readerships, they were united in their penchant for probing sport's cultural resonances.

Just as important as the columns they wrote were Halberstam's, Thompson's, and Wiley's reputations as respected authors in and beyond the context of sportswriting. The author, Foucault reminds, "is not just a proper name like the rest," but a symbolically potent locus around which a work's meanings are organized.[32] *Page* 2 used its celebrity columnists to inflect itself—and ESPN in general—with a degree of quality seldom associated with sportswriting. Furthermore, it hired these writers at a time when it was rare for prominent journalists to publish online, a strategy that helped to separate *Page* 2 from the Web's stereotypical shallowness. *Sports Illustrated* employed a similar strategy shortly after its 1954 launch to situate itself as superior to most sportswriting by commissioning Nobel laureate William Faulkner to cover the 1955 Kentucky Derby.[33] Faulkner's "Kentucky: May: Saturday" provided a characteristically impressionistic and stream-of-consciousness reflection on the horse race that made up for its lack of straightforward reportage with the authorial prestige it bestowed on the nascent sports magazine.

Halberstam was pegged to edit *The Best American Sports Writing of the Century* one year before *Page* 2 recruited him. This assignment instituted him as the principal authority on American sportswriting's history and canon—a status ESPN fortified by commissioning the writer to pen the introduction to its *SportsCentury* book. Halberstam reinforced Thompson's exceptional status by including "The Kentucky Derby Is Decadent and Depraved" in the anthology. Thompson's ESPN columns also continually insisted on his distinction from everyday sportswriting. At one point, he describes typical sportswriters as "a rude & brainless subculture of fascist drunks," "a gang of monkeys jacking off in a zoo cage," and "more disgusting by nature than maggots oozing out of the carcass of a dead animal." In a later piece, however, he concedes that "the best of sports writing can be as smart and as elegant as any kind of journalism; in the hands of a master, it can sing like a beast in heat."[34] For all his outlandishness, Thompson's implication is clear: he is not a normal sportswriter, and *Page* 2 does not publish common sportswriting.

In fact, "Hey Rube"—Thompson's last regular gig before his 2005 suicide—was not among the Gonzo journalist's finest work. His column appeared only sporadically, and his ramblings sometimes bordered self-parody. Walsh admitted as much in a 2011 interview, but maintained that "even less than perfect Hunter Thompson is still fun to read." ESPN, however, was more interested in capitalizing on Thompson's reputation than the work he produced. His writings, in this sense, were secondary to the cultural value his moniker signified. What's more, Thompson's authorial status enabled him to make controversial comments that ESPN otherwise would not publish. In one column, he called George W. Bush—his favorite target in "Hey Rube"—a "monumentally-failed backwoods politician" and an "egg-sucking weasel." In another, Thompson professed "a soft spot . . . for Ronald Reagan," despite their vast political differences, "if only because he was a sportswriter in his youth, and also because his wife gave the best head in Hollywood."[35] ESPN appended an editor's note to Thompson's raciest columns: "The opinions voiced below are those of the infamous Doctor Thompson and are absolutely not the views of this network or the editors. That is free journalism." The website did, however, later scrub Thompson's reference to Nancy Reagan's apparent sexual expertise. *Page 2* simultaneously used Thompson's established image to suggest it was fostering his Gonzo-style journalism and to absolve itself from assuming responsibility for the unpredictability and inappropriateness that characterize it.

ESPN president John Skipper claims *Page 2*'s conscription of celebrated print journalists "magazine'd ESPN.com."[36] As *ESPN the Magazine* distanced itself from sportswriting traditions to establish a niche in print, *Page 2* invoked this heritage to brand itself as a uniquely thoughtful magazine-style website. It did, however, feature an array of humorous and bite-size segments similar to those in the magazine, such as Jim Caple's travelogues and reports on sporting obscurities and Nick Bakay's "Tale of the Tape," which compared seemingly dissimilar items to comic effect. Moreover, there was frequent crossover between *Page 2*'s and *ESPN the Magazine*'s content and personnel. Like *ESPN the Magazine*, then, *Page 2* enabled ESPN to penetrate new spaces, such as the increasingly wired professional workplace. The website also—as its recruitment of Halberstam, Thompson, and Wiley attests—engaged different cultural sites and groups. This editorial strategy enabled *Page 2* to exploit the Internet's potential as an expansive new revenue stream while distancing itself from the medium's unrefined reputation. It was not a website but a magazine that appeared online.

"The Voice of the Citizenry of Sports Nation"

Although ESPN designed *Page 2* in part as a digital outlet for print-style content, sports blogger Bill Simmons emerged as the website's star contributor.

After earning a master's degree in print journalism from Boston University in 1994, Simmons briefly covered high school sports for the *Boston Herald* and penned freelance pieces for the now defunct independent alternative weekly the *Boston Phoenix*. He quit these low-paying positions to work as a bartender, however, after realizing they would not likely lead to his goal of landing a featured newspaper column. "The only one way to get a column back then was to go through this whole ridiculous minor-league-newspaper system and then kind of hope that other people died," he claims.[37] In 1997 Simmons capitalized on his daily discussions with bar patrons by starting an online column as "The Boston Sports Guy" for Digital City Boston, a service available only to America Online subscribers that paid fifty dollars weekly.

Simmons developed a conversational style that exploited both his ear for the barroom vernacular and the Internet's freedom from traditional print journalism's constraints. As he boasts, "I was one of the first people who realized, 'hey, this is different from newspapers, this is different from magazines, how do I take advantage?'" Unimpeded by strict word counts or close editorial supervision, Simmons wrote sprawling, often sarcastic, and sometimes mildly offensive columns from the perspective of a middle-class straight white male sports fan. "He's the digital version of his newspaper counterparts," wrote *Slate's* Bryan Curtis—who would later join Simmons at *Grantland.com*—"minus the decorum." Simmons, in fact, went out of his way to critique print sportswriting as passé within the continuous sports media news cycle ESPN prompted. "I can watch a Celtics game from my slingbox on my laptop in a hotel room in Denver," he quips. "I don't need the newspaper anymore. I can go to ESPN."[38] Though he represents a medium into which ESPN was just venturing, Simmons situates his craft as a product of the media outlet's impact on sport's delivery and consumption.

While traditional sports journalists are restricted by the commandment "No cheering in the press box," Simmons—who lacked the credentials even to be admitted into a press box—rooted openly for his favorite teams, specifically Boston's major professional franchises. "I had to figure out a way to . . . pull the reader where I was when I wasn't going to locker rooms," Simmons says. "So I wrote about things my friends and I were talking about, arguing about sports movies, talking about players, not in the way reporters were doing it, going into the locker room, getting quotes." The conversations he drew on combined witty banter with sophomoric gibes while borrowing from sports talk radio's bravado, *SportsCenter's* sarcasm and pop cultural awareness, and the Society for American Baseball Research's obsession with arcane statistics. Critics—many of whom represented the profession Simmons built his image by rebelling against—panned his freewheeling style as "slouchy" and "bogged down by self-referential brinksmanship."[39] The journalist turned bartender turned blogger was, quite literally, the brand of barroom "idiot" with which Costas equated sports bloggers. Simmons, however, used his outsider status and idiosyncratic style to fashion a populist image that eschewed and interrogated the journalistic exclusivity on which traditionalists like Costas traded.

Walsh insists that Simmons's writing is not shoddy, but rather is designed for Web discourse's relative immediacy and informality: "The best thing that happened for him is the Internet. I don't know that this form of writing would have come about otherwise." Blogging's personalized and casual style, argues media scholar Geert Lovink, calls into question and even rebels against the objectivity around which traditional journalism is organized. Accordingly, Simmons's work defies journalistic norms and encourages more voices to enter public sports discourse. As Walsh indicates, Simmons reveled in the Internet's function as a forum for sports fans to circulate their opinions, however bizarre. In doing so, he suggested fans do not need conventional journalists. *Sports Illustrated*'s Chris Ballard claims that Simmons's everyman persona and disregard for print journalism's customs embody the online sports community's "prevailing ethos: the empowerment of the fan." Moreover, his grassroots entrepreneurialism illustrates the broader blurring of the line between media producers and consumers that Henry Jenkins and others cite as a characteristic of convergence.[40] While Simmons's work—and the sports blogosphere more generally—certainly gave voice to those beyond the journalism establishment, it did not mark a wholesale democratization of sportswriting. Rather—and as his continual references to macho movies, allusions to wild weekends drinking and gambling with his college buddies in Las Vegas, and casual sexism indicate—it was clearly designed for the middle-class male demographic that ESPN has been chasing since its launch.[41]

Simmons compensated for his inability to access locker rooms by building an unusually familiar relationship with his readers. His improvisational blogging affected a humanized voice that inspired scores of like-minded blogs, such as *Deadspin*, which launched in 2005 and boasts the Simmons-esque motto "Sports News without Access, Favor, or Discretion." Conventional journalism, Simmons complains, "created a void where fans couldn't really identify with many of the visible columnists writing about sports." As Leitch noted shortly after *Deadspin*'s launch, "Before Simmons there was this large disconnect between reporters and their readers. [He] threw all that out the window. . . . It felt like you are all in on a private joke."[42] Taking a cue from sports talk radio's interactivity, Simmons regularly posts "Mailbag" columns wherein he displays and responds to readers' comments. While this interactivity is now standard practice online, Simmons fostered it at a time when many websites—including *ESPN.com*—did not yet include comment sections.

ESPN hired Simmons precisely because of his position as an industry outsider with a fresh perspective and popularity among young readers. In fact, Walsh originally invited Simmons to write three *Page 2* guest columns after reading the Boston Sports Guy's snide real-time commentary—a form now known as a live blog—on the 2001 ESPY Awards, which Simmons likened to a "TV holocaust." Simmons's breakout *Page 2* column, "Is Clemens the Antichrist?," combined personal anecdotes with references to *The Godfather* (1972), *Pulp Fiction* (1994), *The Shining* (1980), and *Star Wars* (1977) to explain and defend Boston fans' disdain for former Red Sox pitcher Roger Clemens. Another of his guest columns, "The Nomar Redemption," used the film *The Shawshank Redemption* (1994)—a Simmons favorite that comes up repeatedly in his work—to outline Red Sox shortstop Nomar Garciaparra's career arc.

Based on the runaway success of his guest columns, ESPN contracted the Boston Sports Guy as a permanent *Page 2* contributor, changing his sobriquet to the less geographically specific, but still familiar, Sports Guy. Though principally an online presence, Simmons's columns also regularly appeared in *ESPN the Magazine* until 2009. ESPN marketed the Sports Guy as a nonconformist outsider while incorporating his subversive voice into its corporate web. For instance, it allowed Simmons to continue his sardonic ESPY commentaries (though he never again likened the event to a holocaust) and permitted him to satirize the *SportsCentury* series' solemn nostalgia by imagining what it would be like if it produced a profile on slasher-film psycho killer Michael Myers. ESPN, however, has briefly suspended Simmons on several occasions—from social media and from his overall duties at the network—when he went too far by criticizing his ESPN colleagues and the National Football League. These slaps on the wrist simultaneously bolster the company's appeals to integrity and Simmons's insurrectionary persona.

Soon after joining *Page 2*, Simmons further codified his trademark blogging style. Expanding on his conversational tone and freedom from word counts, he incorporated footnotes into his columns. While footnotes conventionally demonstrate scholarly rigor by referencing source materials, Simmons used them to augment his already bloated discussions with asides. To be sure, the Sports Guy's purposefully loose and digressive approach would easily accommodate additional remarks. The footnotes, however, signal that Simmons's work is so excessive that it necessitates appendixes. Along these lines, the Sports Guy developed his own pop culture–infused patois by coining phrases like "Alpha

Dog" (a dominant superstar athlete), "The Tyson Zone" (when a celebrity or athlete is commonly recognized as dangerously unpredictable), and "The Ewing Theory" (the notion that certain star players actually, and ironically, harm their team's ability to win). Like *SportsCenter*'s "nothing but the bottom of the net" and "en fuego," these phrases have become part of popular sports discourse.[43]

A contrast to traditional journalists, bloggers, argues Internet scholar Melissa Wall, develop and maintain credibility by asserting their separation from the professional establishment. Many blogs, Wall claims, "turn conventional wisdom upside down—the more personal and more open about opinions a site is, the more trustworthy and credible it will be." To this end, Simmons cultivates authenticity by asserting his nonprofessional status. For instance, in 2001 ESPN sent the Sports Guy to report on a press junket for Michael Mann's Muhammad Ali biopic, *Ali*. Given his well-established preoccupation with sports movies, Simmons was a natural fit for the assignment. While he reported on the event—an experience he likened to "playing journalist"—he focused more on critiquing the "horrifying revelations and realizations about the mainstream media" that it brought to light than talking about the film. In fact, he claims to have left the junket early, "disappointed, exhausted, and ready for home" because of its gross superficiality.[44] His column attacks professional journalism as inauthentic and dehumanized. In doing so, it situates his perspective as reliable and uncompromised, despite the fact that it is housed within the world's largest and most powerful sports media outlet.

Acquiring Simmons gave *Page 2* a connection to both canonical print journalists and what was then online sportswriting's cutting edge. His posts were but a click away from Halberstam's, Thompson's, and Wiley's columns. Walsh, in fact, claims that Simmons's first-person style and tendency to place sport in conversation with culture mirrored these celebrity columnists' approach.[45] But a key difference separated Simmons from his more pedigreed *Page 2* colleagues. While their content was sometimes edgy, Halberstam, Thompson, and Wiley relied upon their professional distance from the common fan. The premise behind Thompson's "Hey Rube" even implied that everyday sports fans were dupes who needed an enlightened voice like his to provide them with a wake-up call. Simmons, by contrast, billed himself as a regular guy. His column on the *Ali* press junket, in fact, had him playing a sort of rube—a homespun and out-of-place fan at a slick professional event whose (performance of) naïveté gives him the perspective to take the establishment to task.

But similar to the way Thompson used his authorial status as license to speak his mind, Simmons employed his constructed amateurism to make comments that professionals might avoid for fear of damaging their relationships with those they cover. The Sports Guy could do things most journalists could not because he was not a journalist and, as a result, was not subject to the profession's codes of conduct. His corporate platform, however, gives him heightened authority over the everyday fan he claims to personify. As the *New York Times Magazine*'s Jonathan Mahler puts it, Simmons is not simply a fan but *"the fan*, the voice of the citizenry of sports nation."[46] Simmons typically ends his "Mailbag" columns, for instance, with a particularly offbeat message from a reader. Rather than replying, he closes the column by joking: "Yup, these are my readers." His sign-off both advertises the fact that he gives regular sports fans—from the insightful to the eccentric—a voice mainstream outlets typically deny and asserts his alliance with them. It also, however, indicates that he maintains a degree of professional distance from the subculture he uses to build his populist credibility.

The Sports Guy quickly became *Page 2*'s most popular writer, doubling the website's audience during his first sixteen months on the job.[47] From 2003 to 2004, he even scaled back his *Page 2* and *ESPN the Magazine* columns to write for the late-night ABC talk show *Jimmy Kimmel Live*. Reflecting ESPN's incessant diversification, Simmons capitalized on his celebrity by expanding his column into two best-selling books—2005's *Now I Can Die in Peace* and 2009's *The Book of Basketball*, both of which were published by ESPN Books—and launching the *B.S. Report* podcast in 2007, a sports and pop culture talk show that extends his column and has featured guests ranging from Larry Bird to Barack Obama.[48] Simmons has become known around ESPN as "the franchise."[49] He is a brand within a brand, the embodiment of a market-tested, Web-driven sensibility to which ESPN devoted an increasing proportion of its resources until his eventual departure in 2015.

ESPN paired Simmons's integration with a broader effort to acquire independent perspectives from online. It hired NCAA basketball tournament prognosticator Joe Lunardi; hosted Paul Lukas's sports uniform column, "Uni Watch," which started at the *Village Voice*; and purchased the NASCAR blog

Bill Simmons hosts President Barack Obama on a 2012 installment of his *B.S. Report* podcast.

Jayski's Silly Season, Chad Ford's *Sportstalk*, Matthew Berry's fantasy sports site *TalentedMrRoto*, and Henry Abbott's NBA blog, *TrueHoop*. As with Simmons, ESPN gave these relatively obscure voices a larger platform. These commentators, in turn, allowed ESPN to penetrate new readerships and build subcultural capital.⁵⁰ In fact, ESPN used Ford's website as the foundation for *Insider*, a premium subscription service that provides information regular users cannot access.

In 2001 ESPN purchased *SportsJones*, a website committed to "cover[ing] sports from a variety of academic and alternative perspectives." Founded in 1998 by University of Iowa graduate student Royce Webb, *SportsJones* recruited a combination of journalists and scholars to comment on sport's relationship to politics and culture. The website included book and film reviews, a sport history column, commentaries on women's sports—a topic *ESPN.com* practically ignored at the time—and discussions of sporting factoids similar to *ESPN the Magazine*'s "Answer Guy" segment. Its stated mission was to "take sports back from the loudmouthed, cynical, corporate sports media." "We think that the sports world is a mess now," wrote the *SportsJones* editors. "We need to get back to the good ol' days."⁵¹ The website suggested that the Internet—despite media ideologies that disregard its potential for seriousness—can foster greater journalistic integrity than the corporate sports media establishment. In 2000 the *Columbia Journalism Review* published an impassioned letter by *SportsJones* executive editor Jeff Merron that championed online sportswriting and castigated the influential journal for ignoring the medium in a special issue on sports journalism it released earlier that year. Also in 2000, *SportsJones* became the first online publication to have an article chosen for inclusion in the annual *Best American Sports Writing* anthology, Pat Toomay's "Clotheslined." *Sports Illustrated* called *SportsJones* a "sports salon," and ESPN dubbed it "the thinking fan's sports site." "The editorial content at *SportsJones*," raved the *Fort Worth Star-Telegram*'s Tommy Cummings, "is the kind of thought-provoking effort one would expect if *Mother Jones* or *Atlantic Monthly* had sports sections."⁵² The website anticipated *Page 2*'s deep-thinking style.

ESPN acquired *SportsJones*—which had struggled to stay afloat since its launch—shortly after it brought Simmons in-house. It permanently hired Webb, Merron, and managing editor Eric Neel, and *Page 2* immediately started using them to produce content similar to their work at *SportsJones*. Merron, for example, began the series "Reel Life," which compared historical sports movies to the actual events upon which they were based, and Neel wrote the sports and culture column "Critical Mass." *Page 2* also started posting book reviews and featuring writers whose work skewed toward the academic, such as Todd

Boyd and David Shields. Critics such as journalist Steve Klein, however, worried that ESPN's corporate interests would dull the edge that made *SportsJones*, along with its indie counterparts, unique.[53] To be sure, while ESPN purchased *SportsJones* for its daring, it certainly did not encourage the defunct website's former staffers to say anything too critical of their new employer—a constraint they obviously did not face before the site's acquisition.

Though *SportsJones* helped to establish *Page 2*'s alternative take on popular culture, Simmons's ascendancy eventually overshadowed its creative and editorial footprint. Merron's film commentaries, Neel's cultural critiques, and other *SportsJones* holdovers—such as the book reviews and commentaries on women's sports—faded as *Page 2* increasingly organized itself around Simmons's style. ESPN's acquisition of *SportsJones'* brand and personnel enabled *Page 2* to bill itself as an innovator in online alternative sports commentary while eliminating a competitor whose existence was founded in part on critiquing corporate entities like ESPN.

Page 2 emphasized its apparent originality in a commemoration Kevin Jackson wrote on the site's tenth anniversary. The piece fashions a satiric interoffice memo from *Sports Illustrated* to Ralph Wiley written before he left the magazine to join *Page 2*. "Look, Ralph," Jackson's imagined memorandum states, "we very much value your riffs on jazz, politics, history, race, etc., but we're a sports magazine and there are only so many pages available each week. So you'll just have to put up with word limits like everyone else until there's an invention that will somehow miraculously allow infinite space for your copy." The memo suggests that *Sports Illustrated*, and print publishing more generally, could not do Wiley's unique talent justice. *Page 2*, in contrast, had the vision to use the Internet to realize his writing's potential. The article suggests—in no uncertain terms—that *Page 2* was technologically and culturally groundbreaking despite the fact that independent sites like *SportsJones* were fostering similar online content well before its launch.

In keeping with his populist image, Simmons often dismissed the progressive and culturally aware complexity that *SportsJones* and similar outlets exuded. For instance, he charges that the *Best American Sports Writing* series habitually passes over works on mainstream topics in favor of those that focus on traditionally underrepresented groups and themes: "Many of the stories [selected for inclusion in the anthology] don't even have anything to do with major sports anymore; for instance, if you're a blind, club-footed, diabetic, hemophiliac long-distance runner in Cambodia, and someone did a piece on you in a major magazine, and you did not end up in this book, you really need to reevaluate things."[54] He laments that the *Best American Sports Writing* editors allow their political correctness to overtake their responsibility to praise the year's finest work. In doing so, Simmons indicates that the collection does a disservice to the regular fans with whom he aligns, who presumably prefer to read about conventional subject matter.

Despite his antielitist grievances, when Simmons compiled a list of the "best sports pieces ever written" in a 2008 edition of his mailbag, nearly every selection had been included either in a yearly edition of *The Best American Sports Writing* or in Halberstam's *The Best American Sports Writing of the Century*.[55] In the same piece, the Sports Guy makes the case that David Foster Wallace's 1996 *Esquire* article "String Theory," a philosophical commentary on journeyman tennis pro Michael Joyce, is superior to the writer's more popular, but similarly heady, *New York Times Magazine* rumination on tennis superstar Roger Federer, "Federer as Religious Experience." Though deployed from the populist and interactive space of his mailbag, Simmons's canonizing participates in the very snobbery he condemns.

Simmons continually claims his writing style grows directly out of the print canon. He asserts that *The Book of Basketball* is inspired by William Goldman and Mike Lupica's *Wait Till Next Year* (1988), a work he includes in a column devoted to the best sports books ever written; notes that David Foster Wallace's inventive prose partly motivated his signature use of footnotes; and locates Halberstam's *The Breaks of the Game* (1981)—despite his and the Pulitzer Prize winner's seemingly vast stylistic differences—as his single greatest creative influence.

> Through college and grad school, as I was slowly deciding on a career, I read [*The Breaks of the Game*] every year to remind myself of how to write—how to save words, how to construct a sentence, how to tell someone's life story without relying on quotes, how to make anecdotes come alive. It was my own personal writing seminar. . . . Every two years, I read that book again to make sure that my writing hasn't slipped too much. Like a golfer visiting his old instructor to check on his swing.[56]

Although his writing is designed for the Internet, Simmons situates his craft firmly within the esteemed tradition of print reportage that Halberstam represents. He does, however, suggest his predecessor's more conventional writing style—despite its presence on *Page 2*—was out of place online. "Halberstam is one of my heroes and one of the greatest writers ever, but he had no idea how to write on the Internet."[57] Simmons thus situates his work as a simultaneous rebellion against and product of the print canon Halberstam signals.

Bourdieu claims that "an art which ever increasingly contains reference to its own history demands to be perceived historically; it asks to be referred not to an external referent . . . but to the universe of past and present works of art." Simmons suggests his work constitutes an uncommonly sophisticated brand of Internet journalism that is entrenched in and enhances print traditions. As he noted regarding his 2009 decision to end his regular *ESPN the Magazine* column: "I got bored with the space of having to write 1,200 words, and with the deadline six days in advance. It is impossible to write a great sports column six days in advance."[58] His online writing—and, by extension, *Page 2*—grows out of print sportswriting's most respected traditions but is unfettered by its industrial, technological, and professional constraints. Simmons uses the Internet's immediacy and his relationship to the print canon to brand his work as an exceptional variety of online writing that, to borrow Thompson's phrase, sings like a beast in heat.

"Bill Simmons, Establishment"

Regardless of Simmons's calculated dissidence, critics have maintained the writer came to stand firmly as a personification of the corporation. Leitch best expressed this sentiment in a 2009 *Deadspin* article titled "Bill Simmons, Establishment."[59] By 2009 Simmons not only was *Page 2*'s featured columnist, but also enjoyed top billing on *ESPN.com* over Rick Reilly. Reflecting his increasingly crossover appeal, the Sports Guy's work gradually affected a more conventionalist tenor that combined his sarcasm with Reilly's tendency toward vanilla themes and middle-aged sentimentality. His 2012 article "The Consequences of Caring," for instance, tenderly outlines his three-year-old daughter's tearful reaction to her favorite team losing and explains the joy he feels at observing his child's development into a passionate sports fan. The fatherly piece—which marks a transition in his work from ogling women to doting on his daughter—won an Online Journalism Award and was even linked to by *Oprah.com*.

Another clear marker of Simmons's establishment appeal is his position as author of two *New York Times* best-selling books—the first ESPN Books titles since the *SportsCentury* coffee-table book to earn the distinction. ESPN's marketing placed more emphasis on Simmons's status as a best-selling author than his original role as a "normal" sports fan. Simmons, however, performs a careful distance from his mainstream success. For instance, when he appeared on the program *SportsNation*—an interactive and social media–driven TV show that grew out of the fan-driven sensibility he helped build—to promote *The Book of Basketball*, he indulged a comic sketch that endeavored to discover whether the seven-hundred-page book could stop a bullet (it stopped a 9mm, but a .45 punched through). Aside from making light of his heavy volumes, Simmons insists the books are not simply attempts to wring additional revenue out of his columns. He likens *Now I Can Die in Peace*—which essentially repackages his many Red Sox articles—to "a director's cut of a DVD, with the footnotes serving as commentary," and promises that he would not have authorized *The Book of Basketball*'s paperback release if he did not believe it was better than the hardcover version.[60]

At the same time, Simmons treats the book medium with a special reverence. The reformed blogger claims his two books "feel more substantial" than the online work out of which they grew. "I've written a kajillion columns," he writes, "but who knows? The Internet could be wiped out someday. You always have a book." Simmons reinforces the notion that books are, as sociologist Laura U. Miller's puts it, a "sacred product" with the "purported ability to transcend vulgar economic considerations for the sake of . . . loftier goals"—an attitude that Ted Striphas describes as "one of the most entrenched myths of book culture." Accordingly, Simmons claims his books are not simply products of his labor, but also "hardcore evidence that I existed."[61] He uses his online content to fuel his books while employing the book's symbolic value to inflect his Web-based work with prestige.

Furthermore, Simmons leverages the credibility he has acquired to distance himself from the sports blogosphere he helped to spawn. He dismisses most blogs as unprofessional and even unlawful—a reinforcement of the attitudes against which he struggled to legitimize his early work. "How can we have so many libel/slander laws in place for newspapers," Simmons asks, "and yet the Internet is like the Wild West? People can steal material, slander people, rip them to shreds, make up news . . . [Y]ou can get away with anything now." In a similar article—and despite his near-obsessive use of the service—Simmons bemoaned Twitter's impact on professional journalism.[62] He opens the piece by praising John Powers's *The Short Season* (1979) and Halberstam's *The Breaks of the Game*—two books he claims are great in large part because of the tremendous access these writers received. He then suggests Twitter, and other social media like it, threatens this type of journalism by enabling athletes to communicate directly with fans. Simmons's criticism of social media reinforces the professional boundaries he cultivated his renown by defying. This selective gatekeeping allies him with celebrated journalists like Halberstam while suggesting his work does not succumb to Web-based writing's disorderly trappings. By extension, Simmons suggests he has the unique authority to decide what counts as legitimate online sportswriting. His responses to blogging and Twitter position him as a vigilant guardian of traditional sports journalism who exempts his and ESPN's online writings from the surprisingly conservative media ideology he advances. These comments suggest the Sports Guy is as much an entrepreneurial opportunist as a dissident nonconformist. Simmons's professional trajectory mirrors ESPN's broader production and incorporation of alternative voices to build antiestablishment credibility that will expand its reach across platforms and audiences.

Jumping Media Platforms and Juggling Media Ideologies

With *ESPN the Magazine*, ESPN constructed a youthful and TV-inspired contrast to *Sports Illustrated* that provided it with a presence in print culture while defending its market share of cable sports television. With *Page 2*—and Bill Simmons in particular—ESPN established a foothold in online culture while using print's comparative respectability to distinguish itself from Internet writing's sloppy image. Broadly, then, ESPN's forays into print—literal and symbolic— illustrate how media convergence finds old and new media "interact[ing] in ever more complex ways."[63] Print products emerge out of TV, Web outlets are rooted in print, and books sprout from online columns. In the process, they indicate that ESPN regulates these boundaries and brokers their expansion.

4

ESPN Original Entertainment

Branding Authority across Genres

> EOE is our foray into putting the "E" for Entertainment
> back into ESPN.
>
> —Len Deluca, ESPN senior vice president of program-
> ming[1]

> ESPN Original Entertainment is non-traditional, non-
> seasonal, long-form programming that doesn't neces-
> sarily have to have the X-and-O hardcore fan. It needs
> the casual sports fan and needs to appeal to women
> and to younger sports viewers, and ultimately that is
> going to bring more people to the set to sample ESPN.
>
> —Mark Shapiro, senior vice president, ESPN Original
> Entertainment[2]

Newsweek interviewed ESPN president Chet Simmons two months after the network's 1979 launch. Most of the press ESPN had received up to that point was limited to sports and trade publications. *Newsweek*—the United States' second-highest-circulating general interest magazine after *Time*—provided a chance for ESPN to reach beyond its core, and still very small, audience of male "sports junkies." Recognizing this opportunity, Simmons promised that the new network was developing plans to expand its programming outside of live events and news. He claimed ESPN was considering "a sports game show, a sports kiddie program, and even a sports soap opera."[3] Despite Simmons's bold statement, ESPN's experiments in different genres—such as the stage dramas *The Babe* and *Lombardi: I Am Not a Legend,* the financial news programs *Business Times* and *Nation's Business,* and the trivia game show *Sports on Tap* (1994–95)—were few, short-lived, and made by external production companies until *SportsCentury.*

Based in part on *SportsCentury's* success—and building on ESPN's transmedia expansion with *ESPN.com* and *ESPN the Magazine*—ESPN formed the subsidiary production company ESPN Original Entertainment in 2001. ESPN used EOE to capitalize on popular media genres' potential to attract "casual fans," or those who enjoy sports but are not voracious devotees.[4] For instance, EOE's first production, *2-Minute Drill* (2001), was a game show based on the popular British program *Mastermind* and created by *Who Wants to Be a Millionaire* producer Michael Davies. *Pardon the Interruption* (2001–present)— EOE's longest-running and most successful production—expanded on the syndicated film-review program *Siskel & Ebert's* antagonistic banter by having Tony Kornheiser and his *Washington Post* colleague Michael Wilbon, both of whom frequently appeared on *The Sports Reporters,* debate the day's sports news. *Pardon the Interruption* even evokes *Siskel & Ebert's* signature image of one host offering an enthusiastic thumb's up and the other presenting a disapproving thumb's down by adopting a logo with two hands pointing combatively at each other.

Shortly after its launch, EOE ventured into reality and documentary programming, made-for-TV docudramas, and scripted series. The subsidiary exploited these genres' demographic range and packaged them across platforms to intensify ESPN's efforts to reach new audiences, deepen established customers' relationship to its brand, and promote its other material. Moreover, ESPN used these EOE productions to assert its importance to American sport and media culture. EOE's docudramas and fictional series, for instance, routinely integrated ESPN personalities, footage, and logos. They emphasize ESPN's centrality to the historical settings EOE productions reconstruct and the fictional worlds they build while adopting formats that place its brand in new environs.

Expanding the Tent

Based on Mark Shapiro's success running *SportsCentury* and ESPN Classic, ESPN put him in charge of EOE in early 2002, a post he held until leaving ESPN in 2005. ESPN's upper management was particularly impressed by his development of the Sunday-evening ESPN Classic sports movie series *Reel Classics* (2000–2006), which programmed famous sports films ranging from *The Love Bug* (1968) to *Caddyshack* (1980). Like Classic's repackaged event

The title card from ESPN Classic's *Reel Classics*, which exhibited and contextualized "classic" sports films.

footage, the program provided intermittent commentary that contextualized the featured film and humorously explained its relationship to sport culture. *Washington Post* columnist Norman Chad and comedian Jeff Cesario initially hosted the program. Shapiro, however, replaced them with the higher-profile Burt Reynolds—star of the well-known sports films *The Longest Yard* (1974) and *Semi-Tough* (1976)—in 2003. Shapiro's work at EOE extended *Reel Classics'* mainstream aspirations. "Our mission," he claimed shortly after assuming control of the new subsidiary, "is to develop and provide nontraditional forms of entertainment programming to bring more people under the ESPN tent."[5]

To attract more and different viewers, Shapiro started "tapping into what was hot, what was trendy, and what was catching fire at the time." Pushing further ESPN2's efforts to compete with MTV for younger audiences, EOE would produce content to lure consumers away from the networks as well as niche cable outlets like E!, BET, and the History Channel. For instance, from 2001 to 2004, it produced the *Friday Night Block Party*, a four-hour block of summer programming on ESPN2 designed to attract young urban African American and Latino viewers by adopting a hip-hop-infused aesthetic and featuring the rapper Mos Def as host. "We are starting to talk to people in the music business, people in the fashion business, people in the entertainment business who are all very interested in the connection of fashion, music, entertainment, and, of course, sports," said ESPN/ABC Sports president of customer marketing and sales Ed Erhardt.[6] EOE even more aggressively engaged entertainment and story-driven genres it presumed would attract women without alienating its chief viewership. In fact, it began to advertise its programs on Lifetime.

Some critics worried that EOE's adventurous programming would dilute ESPN's brand. "ESPN should stick to sports," complained *Sports Illustrated*'s Chris Ballard, "for the same reason that CNBC shouldn't make an Alan Greenspan biopic and the *Wall Street Journal* shouldn't publish salacious bond-broker-meets-heartbreaker fiction." Shapiro maintained, however, that live sporting events and news would remain ESPN's primary content and that EOE material would constitute no more than 7 percent of the network's overall material. Moreover, he suggested this relatively small fraction of nontraditional content would have greater potential to attract new viewers than additional sports programming. "There's always going to be a small percentage where you're going to put programming on that doesn't revolve around major sports. So you can do darts and billiards, or you can do made-for-TV movies, scripted drama, reality TV, and game shows. And I felt that [nontraditional programming] was far more entertaining than third-tier sports."[7] This content was also less expensive to produce than live programming and could be strategically repackaged throughout the year. Though EOE programs did not rival the ratings marquee sporting events garnered, their potential to recruit different audiences, ability to be reused, and relatively low production costs made them an economical supplement to ESPN's bread and butter. "Producing an hour of drama on ESPN is costly," Shapiro claimed. "But when compared to securing sports rights, it's like shopping at Wal-Mart versus going to Giorgio Armani."[8]

Beyond *Pardon the Interruption*, EOE experimented with a variety of news and talk shows that adopted market-tested templates. *Quite Frankly with Stephen A. Smith* (2005–7) and *Rome Is Burning* (2003–12)—Jim Rome's second stint at ESPN after *Talk2*—were personality-based programs rooted in sports talk radio. *Cold Pizza* (2003–7), which was rebooted as *First Take* in 2007, was a morning news program inspired by NBC's *Today* and ABC's *Good Morning America* that combined sports updates with reports on music, fashion, and culture. *ESPN Hollywood* (2005) commissioned *Entertainment Tonight* producer Andy Meyer to build a show that covered sports tabloid news and gossip—athletes' fashion choices, dating rumors, and so forth. The similarly fleeting and unsuccessful late-night talk show *Mohr Sports* (2002) featured comedian Jay Mohr and included zany sketches and edgy musical guests like Slayer and the Vandals. *Around the Horn* (2002–present), EOE's longest-running talk show after *Pardon the Interruption*, combines the style of a debate program with a game show by having a host award commentators points for their quips. Other game shows developed more familiar formats, such as *2-Minute Drill* (2001); *Stump the Schwab* (2004–6), a sports trivia show that aped Comedy Central's *Win Ben Stein's Money* (1997–2003); and *Teammates* (2005), an adaptation of *The Newlywed Game* that asked pairs of teammates personal questions about their counterparts.

While studio talk and game shows composed a smooth transition from ESPN's typical fare, Shapiro sought to craft a foothold in reality TV, which had become one of the United States' most popular and profitable genres by the century's end—especially among women and younger viewers. Moreover, ESPN's established focus on sports coverage lent itself to the subgenre of competition-based reality TV. In 2002 EOE launched *Beg, Borrow, and Deal*, a program inspired by CBS's *The Amazing Race* (2001–present) wherein a group of young people travels around the country fulfilling sports-related tasks. Shapiro described the program, which was canceled after two underwhelming seasons, as "a gripping story, very gritty, very urban, very young. It has some sex appeal to it and some infighting. It makes for good television." *I'll Do Anything* (2004) borrowed from the syndicated gross-out program *Fear Factor* (2001–6, 2011–12) by making contestants do outlandish things in order to help someone else realize their sports fantasy. *The Contender* (2006–7), which originally aired on NBC and was created by *Survivor* producer Mark Burnett, brought together aspiring boxers to compete in a weekly tournament wherein the losers were forced to leave the show.[9] Similarly, *Knight School* expanded on NBC's *The Apprentice*—another Burnett brainchild—by giving walk-on basketball players a chance to compete for a spot on the legendarily temperamental coach Bob Knight's Texas Tech University roster. Like Donald Trump on *The Apprentice*—though without the marketable catchphrase or hairdo—Knight would select the player to be cut and sent home each week while peppering episodes with his signature rants.

Other EOE reality programs combined popular formats with an effort to promote ESPN and its partners. *Dream Job* (2003–4), an *American Idol* imitator, allowed aspiring anchors to compete for a position at ESPN and to be evaluated by an expert panel. (ESPN Deportes' *Dream Job El Reportero* [2013–14] later did the same for Spanish-speaking anchors). *Madden Nation* (2005–8) is a traveling tournament organized around EA Sports' popular *Madden NFL* video game. Not coincidentally, ESPN and EA Sports inked a fifteen-year contract to integrate their brands merely months before *Madden Nation* premiered. Accordingly, the reality program situates *Madden NFL* as the premiere sports video game. Along these lines, *Dream Job* suggests ESPN stands as the pinnacle of the sports media profession. Like *ESPN the Magazine*'s and *ESPN.com*'s frequent inclusion of ESPN personalities as commentators, *SportsCenter* anchors hosted many of these EOE reality and game shows. While the nontraditional formats sought out new viewers, ESPN used its recognizable anchors to compel audiences that already followed their work on *SportsCenter* to try these new programs.

ESPN's noncompetitive reality programming also adopted popular formats. *The Life* (2001–5) blossomed from a recurring segment in *ESPN the Magazine* that profiles athletes' lives away from sports in a youthful and urban style. The production—which paid special attention to athletes' conspicuous consumption and relationship to popular trends—was often scheduled as part of ESPN2's *Block Party*. Similarly, *It's the Shoes* (2006), hosted by hip-hop personality Bobbito Garcia, used the template of *MTV Cribs* to explore athletes' and celebrities' extravagant sneaker collections. EOE's more straightforward reality programs—such as *D-League* (2001), *The Season* (2001–5), *Timeless* (2005), *Bound for Glory* (2005), *Free Agent* (2006), and *Primal Quest* (2006)— simply offered longer-form versions of the human-interest features ESPN often included on *SportsCenter*'s Sunday edition and *Outside the Lines*.[10]

Like the separation ESPN asserts between its event coverage and reportage, EOE suggested its productions were distinct from and did not conflict with ESPN's news gathering. ESPN steadfastly promised that the athletes who agreed to appear on *Teammates* or *It's the Shoes*, for example, would not receive preferential treatment in its news coverage and that the network's inclusion of them in EOE programs would not give it greater access than its competitors. Moreover, these programs evaded criticism by presenting largely uncontroversial content with little that was newsworthy aside from the presence of celebrities.

This was not the case, however, with the 2006 reality program *Bonds on Bonds*, which featured the embattled baseball player Barry Bonds as he pursued Major League Baseball's all-time home run record and faced widespread speculation that his effort was aided by performance-enhancing drugs. Unlike most EOE productions, a third party created *Bonds on Bonds*. Bonds's staff approached Tollin/Robbins Productions, which made the celebratory and Academy Award–nominated documentary *Hank Aaron: Chasing the Dream* (1995), about fashioning a comparable program that would provide a sympathetic take on the notoriously prickly Bonds as he challenged Aaron's record. Its episodes opened with Bonds's confessional voice-over atop footage of him on and off the field: "This is *Bonds on Bonds*. There's no better person to get it from than me. Period. . . . I'll tell you the truth, I'll tell you who I am, I'll tell you what I go through, and I'll let you in my life. Unscripted. For real. Don't judge me. Get to know me. Then you can judge me." At one point in the first episode, the ballplayer wept while discussing the many pressures he endures that his critics apparently fail to appreciate. While *Bonds on Bonds* claimed to offer a uniquely candid peek at its subject, the ballplayer maintained final approval of its content. Unsurprisingly, the reality show spent little time discussing the drug allegations he was facing—charges that have effectively blackballed him from Major League Baseball.

ESPN staunchly maintained that *Bonds on Bonds* was strictly an entertainment program, and it even prefaced segments with a disclaimer that made clear Tollin/Robbins—not ESPN—was responsible for the show's "content and vision." Nevertheless, *60 Minutes'* Mike Wallace spurned it as "checkbook journalism," and the *New York Times'* Selena Roberts said it demonstrated "ESPN's deficit of integrity." Tollin/Robbins's Mike Tollin defended *Bonds on Bonds* by insisting that the reality show "was not a journalistic enterprise," and John Walsh likened it to an "authorized biography." Moreover, ESPN senior vice president and director of news Vince Doria promised the network would not report on any news gathered during *Bonds on Bonds'* production and that its news programs would not promote the show.[11] ESPN eventually canceled the controversial and low-rated series before its planned ten-episode run elapsed. Though a critical failure, commercial disappointment, and blemish on ESPN's reputation, *Bonds on Bonds* neatly encapsulates EOE's purpose: to filter provocative and broadly appealing subject matter through marketable genres.

True Events, Fictionalized

Complementing its reality television programming, EOE produced a handful of made-for-TV movies—many of which were made by Orly Adelson Productions, which had a "first look" deal with the subsidiary—based on noteworthy sports figures and events. Like most "based on a true story" productions, these films anchor their stories in the actual world and capitalize on viewers' familiarity with the people and circumstances they depict. They are also subject to the complaints routinely lodged against historical films. As film critic Frank Sanello claims, "Commercial imperatives most often fuel cinematic rewrites of history. Complex economic and social issues are pureed into easily digestible bits of information intended for consumption by Hollywood's most soughtafter demographic: the lowest common denominator." Even more damning, film scholar Pierre Sorlin claims that "historical truth is generally ignored by the producer of historical movies." In contrast to these critiques, film historian Robert A. Rosenstone defends historical films by claiming they can furnish productive reconsiderations of the past. They compose, he claims, "a new form of history, what we might call history as vision."[12] Moreover, because these productions are not beholden to the constraints that available archival data present, they have the aesthetic flexibility to inflect their "visions" with entertainment.

Most of EOE's historical films fall within the docudrama subgenre. In contrast to other historical films, docudramas, according to Derek Paget, maintain a closer relationship to indexical images. They often evoke and strategically incorporate indexical footage to create verisimilitude and to broadcast their relationship to the historical settings they engage. Moreover, Paget locates docudrama as "first and foremost a televisual form" that uses the historical film's relative flexibility to filter content through dramatic—and often melo-dramatic—forms that attract larger audiences than documentaries. Steven Lipkin characterizes made-for-TV docudramas as "rootable, relatable, and salable"; they use their derivation from actual and familiar events to draw a diverse swath of viewers.[13]

Sporting content lies at the foundation of the made-for-TV docudrama. ABC's 1971 "Movie of the Week" *Brian's Song*—based on a chapter in Chicago Bears running back Gale Sayers's autobiography, *I Am Third* (1971)—provides a tear-jerking examination of Sayers's friendship with his cancer-stricken teammate Brian Piccolo. Initially competing for the same job, the reserved African American Sayers (played by Billy Dee Williams) and the outgoing Italian American Piccolo (played by James Caan) composed an unlikely, but oddly complementary, pair and were the Bears' first set of interracial roommates in training camp and on the road during the season. Piccolo helped Sayers to come out of his introverted shell, and Sayers motivated the less talented Piccolo to improve his game. Piccolo, however, was suddenly diagnosed with cancer and passed away. *Brian's Song* celebrates the pair's unique friendship and mourns Piccolo's untimely death. As the film's last lines, presented in a solemn voice-over by the actor playing Chicago Bears owner George Halas, sadly proclaim, "Brian Piccolo died of cancer at the age of twenty-six. He left a wife and three daughters. He also left a great many loving friends who miss and think of him often. But when they think of him, it's not how he died that they remember, but how he lived. How he did live." Like the studio-era Hollywood "male weepies" *Knute Rockne: All American* (1940) and *Pride of the Yankees* (1943), *Brian's Song* combines sport and melodrama—

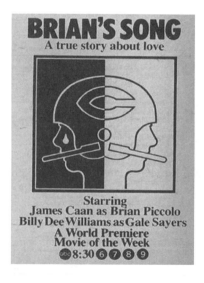

ABC's *Brian's Song* combined sport and melodrama to attract a crossover audience.

while exploiting its interracial subject matter's social currency at the time of its release—to attract a crossover audience. One of ABC's original advertisements for it emphasized these marketable qualities by billing the film as "a true story about love" and including profiles of a black face and a white face encased in Chicago Bears helmets. The black face—Sayers's face—has a single tear streaming down its cheek.

Brian's Song premiered the year after ABC launched *Monday Night Football*. Because it was a prime-time program, *Monday Night Football*'s success was contingent upon attracting a far broader audience than typical weekend game telecasts, a feat it accomplished by infusing the program with a bevy of dramatic and technological accouterments. *Brian's Song*, which initially aired on Tuesday, November 30, exploited this expanded audience and benefited from publicity that the previous evening's *Monday Night Football* telecast—which featured a Bears game—provided. *Brian's Song* also incorporated actual game footage and gave cameo roles to real players and coaches—a common trope in historical sports films that both *Knute Rockne* and *Pride of the Yankees* used to enhance their realism and salability. These strategies paid off considerably. *Brian's Song* became the fourth most watched film ever to air on television—after *Ben-Hur* (1959), *The Birds* (1963), and *Bridge on the River Kwai* (1957)—and it propelled both Caan and Williams to stardom. Based on this success, the film even had a brief theatrical run.[14] It earned multiple awards, including the Emmy for Outstanding Single Program and a Peabody. It also garnered commendations from the American Cancer Society and the National Association for the Advancement of Colored People for its contribution to cancer awareness and its celebration of interracial harmony.

Douglas Gomery claims *Brian's Song* "made the [made-for-TV movie] genre respectable" and "created a form Hollywood still uses to tackle social issues in a controversial yet noncontroversial way." In fact, the ABC movie's success precipitated the 1973 Hollywood feature *Bang the Drum Slowly*—an adaptation of Mark Harris's 1956 novel that starred Robert De Niro as a baseball player who perishes from Hodgkin's disease—which mimicked its dramatic recipe.[15] While *Brian's Song* enjoyed unprecedented popular and critical acclaim among made-for-TV movies, television scholar Jennifer Fuller observes that the genre withered into a tradition now often mocked as the tacky "Disease of the Week" film. TV docudrama's more respectable iterations, Fuller asserts, became "the domain of premium cable channels, which use the genre to bolster the marketing claim that they privilege 'quality' over ratings."[16]

In fact, HBO subsidiary HBO Original Films' first production, *The Terry Fox Story* (1983), used *Brian's Song* as its template. The film examines how Terry Fox, a young cancer-stricken Canadian athlete who lost a leg to his ailment, jogs across Canada to raise money for research. Though Fox dies before fulfilling his goal, his courage transforms him into a national hero. HBO has since produced several other sports-themed docudramas that engage provocative stories and remember significant historical events, ranging from a Mike Tyson biopic to a dramatization of New York Yankees outfielder Roger Maris's effort to overtake Babe Ruth's single-season home run record. While other cable TV outlets made sports docudramas, HBO's consistent production of them—in combination with the channel's tradition of acclaimed original movies—established the premium cable outlet as the subgenre's most respectable voice by the twentieth century's end.

EOE's docudramas followed HBO's lead of selecting recognizable and polarizing subject matter, beginning with *A Season on the Brink* (2001), an adaptation of sportswriter John Feinstein's 1986 chronicle of a season shadowing Bob Knight and the Indiana University men's basketball team that premiered almost exactly one year after the coach's controversial termination. Like EOE's forays into game shows and reality TV, docudramas expand the network's audience. What's more, these feature-length productions—on average—keep viewers tuned in longer. "Relative to other programming," says ESPN senior vice president of research and sales development Artie Bulgrin, "movies are the stickiest. People spend more time watching movies per episode than they do watching sports [events]. . . . Time is ratings; it's the most important component of ratings."[17]

As with *A Season on the Brink*—and like the EOE reality and game shows' adoption of market-tested formats—most of the subsidiary's docudramas adapted notable works of sports writing. *The Junction Boys* (2002) is based on Jim Dent's best-selling book of the same title about Bear Bryant's disciplinarian coaching tactics, *Codebreakers* (2005) expands on a chapter in Bill McWilliams's *A Return to Glory* (2000) that outlines a 1951 cheating scandal that dismantled the United States Military Academy football team, *Four Minutes* (2005) adapts a 1999 Frank Deford *Sports Illustrated* feature that celebrates Roger Bannister's 1954 four-minute-mile run, and the miniseries *The Bronx Is Burning* (2007) takes as its model Jonathan Mahler's historical novel about the 1977 New York Yankees' championship run against the backdrop of New York City's racial and class tensions, a divisive mayoral election, and the "Son of Sam" murders. Along slightly different lines—but still operating within the category of adaptation—*Hu$tle* (2004) dramatizes Pete Rose's banishment from baseball for gambling by building on "The Dowd Report," an investigation that detailed the ballplayer's transgressions and led to his expulsion. The productions use their founding documents both as familiar selling points and to suggest they are rooted in credible source material.

Lipkin claims docudrama provides a handy tool "when actual documentary materials either do not exist or by themselves are incomplete or insufficient to treat the subject adequately." To this end, EOE uses the genre to engage subject matter in ways that neither ESPN's vast archives nor the texts on which these productions are based readily allow. Nevertheless, EOE often steadfastly asserts its films' fidelity to their founding documents. ESPN public relations representative Paul Melvin, for instance, claimed *A Season on the Brink* strove to "stick as true to the book as possible." Despite the film's ostensible intentions, John Feinstein dismissed it as "cartoonish trash."[18] EOE, however, excuses its productions' dramatic deviations by claiming they operate in the service of building compelling stories that work within television's medium-specific constraints. For example, and like many docudramas, *Hu$tle* opens with a disclaimer that affirms its reliability and pardons its embellishments: "This picture is based on facts set forth in the 1989 Dowd Report to the Commissioner of Major League Baseball regarding Pete Rose. While this film is a dramatization of actual events, certain images, names, incidents, orders of events, and dialogue have been fictionalized."

Similarly, although Roger Bannister's four-minute mile is an unquestionably historic sporting achievement, the runner led a spartan—and rather dull—life devoted to his athletic and academic training. *Four Minutes*, which producer Gerald W. Abrams concedes is a deliberately biased "love letter to Bannister," takes several measures to make the runner's biography more engaging.[19] It invents the craggy but inspirational coach Archie Mason (played by Christopher Plummer)—a generic standby in the sports film—and includes Bannister's future wife as his love interest, even though the couple did not meet until after he ran his famous race. It also exercises the aesthetic freedom to build recognizable intertextual resonances. The film opens with a scene of Bannister running in slow motion barefoot along England's coastline in his white training outfit—a direct evocation of the 1981 Academy Award–winning film *Chariots of Fire*'s first moments that signals *Four Minutes*' engagement with similar themes and gestures toward its filmic quality.

Though *Four Minutes* spices up Bannister's relatively staid life, screenwriter Frank Deford insists the adaptation was "totally literal" when it came to the runner's athletic career. Deford suggests the film's aesthetic liberties were harmless as long as they did not "mess with" the historical event around which the production was organized and that it commemorates. Indeed, he implies that these dramatic flourishes emphasize the feat's significance more forcefully than would Bannister's actual story. Film historian Robert Toplin agrees with the premise upon which Deford's explanation rests and suggests critics should forgive filmic representations that are not "literally true" if they operate in the service of more important "symbolic truths."[20]

EOE docudramas combine their creative flexibility with formal practices that cultivate realism and authenticity. Lipkin mentions three primary practices docudramas employ to build varying degrees of verisimilitude: modeling, sequencing, and interaction. Models reconstruct references iconically, sequences arrange indexical and iconic footage in succession, and interactions combine indexical and iconic elements simultaneously.[21]

EOE docudramas adopt all three of these practices to varying degrees. In *A Season on the Brink*, Brian Dennehy, who stars as Bob Knight, reproduces several of the coach's famous tirades, and *The Bronx Is Burning* re-creates a Miller Lite commercial wherein New York Yankees manager Billy Martin (played by John Turturro) and owner George Steinbrenner (played by Oliver Platt) lampooned their contentious relationship. These productions also model the historical world by making iconic footage appear indexical. *A Season on the Brink* features various "interviews" with actors playing local citizens, Indiana University administrators, and players' parents who share their perspectives on Knight's coaching style. Along these lines, *Codebreakers* and *Four Minutes* include content fashioned to resemble old newsreel footage, and *A Season on the Brink* and *Hu$tle* use video sequences made to appear like archived game telecasts and TV press conferences. The films use the fake indexical content to point out their engagement with the historical world—and visual records from it—without having to traverse the constraints that available archive content imposes. The docudramas further cultivate realism without relying on indexical footage by concluding with captions that explain what became of their main characters after the events covered in the films transpired, a standard convention in docudrama and documentary. The captions build on the adapted events and phony documentary footage to suggest the iconic material these docudramas present is rooted in the actual world and reliably contextualizes the featured events.

Nearly all of the EOE docudramas also sequence indexical and iconic footage. *A Season on the Brink*, for example, includes actual footage of Indiana University basketball games from the season on which it reflects. It transitions from long, panoramic video shots cribbed from game telecasts to film footage that re-creates the featured events. Beyond anchoring its iconic representations in the real world, the indexical video content allows the film to reproduce a game atmosphere without having to devote the resources needed to reconstruct a game realistically. The iconic game footage is composed exclusively of medium and close-up shots that do not include the thousands of spectators present at the actual game. *Codebreakers* opens with actual newsreel footage that com-

A Season on the Brink integrated actual archived game telecasts with filmed footage to reproduce inexpensively a game atmosphere at Indiana University's Assembly Hall.

ments on the 1951 Army football team's high hopes leading into the season. It cuts directly from this archived material to iconic footage that mirrors its sepia tone in order to demonstrate the film's derivation from—and artful resemblance to—the source material it displays and the historical world it indexes.

Several of the films also include indexical footage with their closing credits, another common docudramatic convention. *A Season on the Brink* displays TV footage of Indiana University president Myles Brand's March 2000 announcement that he was dismissing Knight along with various snippets of press conferences and interviews wherein the churlish coach lashed out at reporters. The archived moments suggest that the surliness Knight demonstrated during the historical moment *A Season on the Brink* examines escalated and eventually crossed the line. *Hu$tle*'s credit sequence includes footage from a 2004 interview wherein Pete Rose admitted to ABC News' Charles Gibson that he gambled on baseball—a point he had never before divulged. The footage situates the closing captions' explanation of the characters' fates in the actual world while inviting comparisons between the docudramas' representations and the real people they depict.

Of EOE's docudramas, *The Bronx Is Burning* most seamlessly integrates indexical and iconic footage. At several points in the film, it showcases characters watching actual ABC telecasts of the 1977 World Series cribbed from ESPN's archives. It also includes scenes in which interview footage with the miniseries' characters is inserted into actual game coverage that features their likenesses up to bat. The scenes imitate ABC's innovative incorporation of pretaped interviews into its baseball telecasts—a practice borrowed from *Monday Night Football* to inflect games with greater human interest. Similar to Woody Allen's *Zelig* (1983) and Robert Zemeckis's *Forrest Gump* (1994), other moments of *The Bronx Is Burning* splice Oliver Platt as George Steinbrenner into ABC footage of Cosell interviewing the actual Steinbrenner. Lipkin claims docudramas that integrate indexical and iconic footage have the greatest "potential persuasive

The Bronx Is Burning integrated footage of the actor playing Reggie Jackson (Daniel Sujatha) into archived footage of ABC's Monday Night Baseball that depicts the actual Jackson up to bat.

The Bronx Is Burning reproduced interviews that ABC's Howard Cosell conducted with New York Yankees owner George Steinbrenner by splicing actor Oliver Platt as Steinbrenner into the archived footage.

power" because of their relative proximity to real events.[22] *The Bronx Is Burning's* combination of archived footage and iconic material highlights this proximity to suggest that its depiction of the 1977 season is based in—and faithful to— the actual events upon which it reflects while providing perspective on those events that extant indexical footage cannot.

Scholarly discussions of docudrama focus primarily on assessing the genre's claims to illuminate the historical world in realistic and persuasive ways. But beyond simply mediating the past, these productions selectively reinforce the reliability of the archived content they put to use and the authority of the sites that manufacture it. For instance, *A Season on the Brink's* credit sequence prominently includes among its footage of Knight's many outbursts a snippet of the coach castigating ESPN's Jeremy Schaap that was taped for use in a 2000 segment of *Outside the Lines*. The Pete Rose confession woven into *Hu$tle's* closing credits and the TV footage *The Bronx Is Burning* integrates were ABC productions. To be sure, EOE could easily and inexpensively use this Disney-owned content to season its representations with authenticity. However, these aesthetic choices also betray an effort to build historical worlds that place ABC and ESPN at the center of the important events they showcase. *A Season on the Brink's* inclusion of Schaap's *Outside the Lines* interview suggests ESPN was a key journalistic voice probing the story behind Knight's dismissal. *The Bronx Is*

Burning and *Hu$tle* emphasize ABC's importance to documenting the historic 1977 World Series and to uncovering Pete Rose's gambling. If the historical worlds docudramas construct, as Lipkin argues, "contribute to a culture's vision of itself," then ESPN Original Entertainment's docudramas indicate these productions also build pasts that aid distinct interests.[23] EOE uses docudrama's historical flexibility to stress ABC and ESPN's indispensability to the circumstances its productions reconstruct.

While some docudramas explain their approach by suggesting there "is no other way to tell" their stories—or that sufficient indexical data are unavailable—this justification does not completely hold when it comes to EOE's many engagements with the genre. In fact, ESPN has made documentaries—driven by a combination of interviews and archived footage—on topics far more obscure than those its docudramas consider. Like *SportsCentury*'s profiles, however, the EOE docudramas are not principally designed to illuminate sport's history. Rather, they suggest ESPN can reliably and dramatically mediate sport's past, emphasize ESPN's and ABC's presence at and importance to significant sporting moments, and, perhaps most crucially, put to use familiar dramatic formats to satisfy ESPN's typical male audience and draw in casual fans who otherwise might not sample it.

The Complete Angler (2002), a documentary film essay branded as a "video tone poem," marks a thematic and formal departure from EOE's typical fare that seems more fitting for PBS than ESPN. The slow-paced, first-person production adapts writer and painter James Prosek's *The Complete Angler: A Connecticut Yankee Follows in the Footsteps of Walton* (1999), a meditative homage to Izaak Walton's *The Compleat Angler* (1653). Part existential quest and part celebratory exegesis, the production outlines the romantic young artist's efforts to achieve aesthetic enlightenment through fishing the same English waters Walton described centuries earlier. Prosek's exodus began, in fact, as a Yale University project overseen by prominent literary critic Harold Bloom. Fittingly, the documentary brims with literary allusion. Bloom makes a cameo to read William Butler Yeats's "The Song of Wandering Aengus" (1899)—a poem about a trout transforming into a beautiful woman that he dedicates to Prosek's odyssey—and Prosek evokes Mark Twain's *A Connecticut Yankee in King Arthur's Court* (1889) and Alfred Tennyson's "The Brook" (1887) to explain his journey. The documentary concludes with Prosek's literary epiphany: "Don't you see, the book's not about fishing; it's about life. Or, rather, the book is about fishing, and fishing is life." Though anomalous within the EOE oeuvre, the video documentary earned ESPN its second Peabody and, as a result, was perhaps even more successful than EOE's docudramas in fulfilling the subsidiary's mission to venture beyond ESPN's stereotypical audience.

In addition to capitalizing on the EOE feature films' relative "stickiness" and demographic reach, ESPN used these productions to fortify and publicize its other material. For instance, in 2001 ESPN purchased the Bass Angler Sportsman Society, a fishing organization that publishes a magazine and runs the annual Bassmaster Classic tournament. ESPN was initially planning to use BASS as the foundation for an offshoot channel devoted to outdoor sports that would complement the Great Outdoor Games, a less successful variation of the X Games that ESPN ran from 2000 to 2006.[24] Fishing, and outdoor sports more generally, is stereotypically considered a rural and lowbrow activity. Part of ESPN's goal in developing the Great Outdoor Games and acquiring BASS was to market these niche sports to fans that might otherwise dismiss them. *The Complete Angler*, a production explicitly immersed in highbrow cultural traditions, complements this effort by broadcasting fishing's relationship to art and literature.

Other EOE productions were simply scheduled to enhance complementary ESPN programming. "Ratings are a function of compatibility and flow," Shapiro frankly states. "When we make a made-for-TV movie, we will surround it with relevant programming." *A Season on the Brink*—which Richard Sandomir complained was "promoted to the point of seasickness"—premiered on the evening of "Selection Sunday," the day when the NCAA basketball tournament brackets are released.[25] Aside from capitalizing on the excitement surrounding Selection Sunday, ESPN maximized the production's audience by simultaneously airing a version with curse words (a vital part of Knight's vocabulary) on its flagship channel and a "clean" version on ESPN2. The unedited version, which, according to *Variety*, contained more uses of the word *fuck* than any program in cable TV history, drew six times more viewers than its pasteurized counterpart.[26] It also scheduled a special *Outside the Lines* discussion of the film after the premiere. Adopting the same strategy, *The Junction Boys* and *Codebreakers* debuted directly after ESPN's presentation of the Heisman Trophy award ceremony. ESPN banked that the made-for-TV movies' relative stickiness would retain those viewers who watched the ceremony while attracting others who might not care so much about who wins the Heisman but do have an interest in dramatically overwrought stories about men facing difficult obstacles.

Transmedia Tales

ESPN also marketed EOE content across its platforms. *Page 2* featured interviews with *A Season on the Brink*'s Brian Dennehy, *The Junction Boys*' Tom Berenger (who starred as Bear Bryant), and *Four Minutes* screenwriter Frank Deford discussing their experiences working on the films. Jeff Merron's *Page 2* series "Reel Life" also included a segment on *The Junction Boys*. Though Merron points out several of *The Junction Boys*' creative exaggerations, he ultimately endorses the film as a faithful representation. He even includes an interview with one of Bryant's former assistants, who claims that Berenger's performance so uncannily resembled the legendary coach that it gave him "chills."[27]

While all EOE productions had at least some cross-platform promotional presence—whether via a related *SportsCenter* segment or advertisements in *ESPN the Magazine*—others were designed to operate as transmedia packages that straddle platforms. Jenkins defines a transmedia story as one that "unfold[s] across media platforms, with each new text making a distinctive and valuable contribution to the whole. In the ideal form of transmedia storytelling, each medium does what it does best. . . . [A]ny given product is a point of entry into the franchise as a whole."[28] Expanding on *A Season on the Brink*'s and *The Junction Boys*' adaptations of popular works of sportswriting, several EOE productions teamed with ESPN Books to release projects composed of complementary books and films. These transmedia tales have the potential to be even stickier than EOE's feature-length films; the books and films promote each other while offering content divergent enough to recruit slightly different demographics.

EOE's *3* (2004) is a docudrama and book on the life and tragic death of NASCAR driver Dale Earnhardt. The book—a glossy and oversize volume released just prior to the film's premiere—was marked as "Inspired by the ESPN Original Entertainment Movie," included a promotional sticker on its cover that reminded consumers when the film would premiere, contained several images from the movie's production with captions that called attention to its historical accuracy, and ended with a full-page advertisement for the film. Though sold as a stand-alone product, the book essentially functions as a press kit for the movie.

Both the book and the film filter Earnhardt's story through a melodramatic format that emphasizes the racer's relationship with his father, Ralph—also a driver—and his son Dale Jr., who followed in his forebears' footsteps and actually took second place in the 2001 Daytona 500 race wherein Dale Sr. was killed. The film outlines how racing helped the Earnhardts to escape poverty and provided a site of male familial bonding. It ends by cutting from Earnhardt's death on the track to him and his father reuniting in the afterlife. The production's final moment—in true melodramatic fashion—indicates that Dale's and Ralph Earnhardt's spirits live on as Dale Jr. continues their legacy on Earth. Importantly, NASCAR attracts ESPN's second-largest female audience after the National Football League. Similar to *Brian's Song*'s capitalization on *Monday Night Football*'s widespread popularity, *3* uses melodrama to build on the crossover audience NASCAR yields—a potential demographic the project stretches even further by straddling print and TV.

In 2006 ESPN celebrated Muhammad Ali's sixty-fifth birthday with fifty-two hours of commemorative programming and a slew of related content. *Ali Rap*, a project composed of a book and documentary, was the event's main attraction. *Ali Rap* used Ali's iconic rhyming quips to suggest that the boxer anticipated rap's emergence. Though they advance the same basic argument, the *Ali Rap* book and documentary otherwise share few similarities. The book is a glossy pastiche of Ali quotes and complementary images edited and designed by George Lois, an *Esquire* magazine photographer who did several shoots with the boxer during the height of his fame, most famously a 1968 spread that depicted Ali as a political and religious martyr by riddling his body with arrows to mimic Francesco Botticini's fifteenth-century painting of Saint Sebastian. ESPN also elected to publish Lois's book in cooperation with Taschen, a German publisher that specializes in art books. Though certainly ornate in its construction, *Ali Rap* is no more extravagant than the *SportsCentury* coffee-table book or even *3*'s movie tie-in. ESPN Books could have produced an identical volume and claimed a larger percentage of its profits. It teamed with Taschen, however, to take advantage of the publisher's association with the art world. In fact, in 2003 Taschen released *GOAT [Greatest of All Time]: A Tribute to Muhammad Ali*. The project's "Champ's Edition," of which Taschen produced just one thousand copies, was a seventy-five-pound book signed by Ali that included several museum-grade prints and an original inflatable sculpture by the artist Jeff Koons (who also signed the book). The lavish item sold for fifteen thousand dollars. Taschen owner and founder Benedikt Taschen claimed he wanted *GOAT* to be "the most comprehensive piece of work ever done on anybody in the history of the world," and the German magazine *Der Spiegel* named it "the most megalomaniacal book in the history of civilization." Conscripting Taschen to help produce *Ali Rap* situates the book as an outgrowth of *GOAT*, even though the products are unrelated.

Hosted by hip-hop icon Chuck D, the *Ali Rap* documentary claims, "Ali used the language of the street to get his point across." It collects a diverse group of rappers and celebrities to recite some of Ali's best-known quotes and, in doing so, installs the boxer as rap's founding father. As the *Ali Rap* book places the project within contemporary art culture, the documentary tailors itself to the young, urban audience that EOE productions like *The Life* and *It's the Shoes* strove to capture. Though adopting different styles, the *Ali Rap* project's parts—along with the myriad other content ESPN produced and scheduled to celebrate Ali's sixty-fifth birthday—combine to position ESPN as the steward of Ali's visual history. Moreover, *Ali Rap* suggests ESPN uncovers an important new dimension of the boxer's famous life story and cultural import that it packages for separate—though not mutually exclusive—audiences.

ESPN adopted a similar approach with *Ruffian* (2007), which comprised a memoir by sportswriter William Nack and a docudrama about the champion filly racehorse that broke her leg during a nationally broadcast 1975 match race and was euthanized as a result. ESPN released the project one year after the champion racehorse Barbaro met a similar end at the 2006 Preakness Stakes. Like *3*, the docudrama celebrates Ruffian's rise to stardom and laments her unfair death. Because of the dramatic limitations a horse protagonist poses, *Ruffian* tells the filly's story through focusing primarily on her introverted trainer Frank Whitely (played by Sam Shepard) and the eager young sportswriter William Nack (played by Frank Whaley)—both of whom become enamored by the uniquely talented horse and are devastated by her passing.

Published by ESPN Books, Nack's *Ruffian: A Racetrack Romance* offers a nostalgic reflection on his relationship to the horse. Like *The Complete Angler*, it adopts a poetic tone steeped in literary reference. The book begins, in fact, with a somber epigraph from T. S. Eliot's "Choruses from 'The Rock'" (1934). As ESPN used the anniversary of Barbaro's 2006 death to schedule the film's release, Nack opens the memoir with his recollections of watching Barbaro's fateful final race. The horse's death transports him—in a surge of "involuntary memory" that recalls the opening moments of Marcel Proust's *In Search of Lost Time* (1913–27)—to the scene of Ruffian's 1975 demise:

> Seeing this, I felt as though I'd been transported back in time again, doing it all over once again, running madly through the clubhouse and down the stairs two at a time, gulping sunlight as I stepped onto the Pimlico racetrack. Piddling along with my head down, I walked toward the stricken horse as if in sleep, fumbling and feeling my way along the damp walls of the same recurring nightmare that long ago I'd come to know so well, the one where Ruffian had come and gone in a thrash of dying light.[29]

From that intense moment of reminiscence, Nack recounts his experience covering—and growing to love—Ruffian. Beyond its Proustian introduction, Nack's poetic account evokes W. C. Heinz's "Death of a Racehorse" (1949), one of sportswriting's most celebrated works, to explain Ruffian's passing and borrows from *Brian's Song*'s dramatic format to describe his "romance's" development and sad end. Akin to EOE's other docudramas, *Ruffian* uses melodrama to attract a broad audience—a quality the Walt Disney Company exploited by premiering the film on ABC in conjunction with the network's Saturday-afternoon coverage of the

2007 Belmont Stakes. Simultaneously, and like *Ali Rap*'s Taschen-published art book, Nack's lyrical tome supplements the mainstream film while courting a readership with more recognizably literary tastes.

A Real Company in Fictional Worlds

Not long after he joined EOE, Shapiro cited fictional series as a crucial way the subsidiary would deliver ESPN a new and devoted fan base: "This is the next step in an effort to expand and stretch our brand to reach that moderate casual sports fan that likes to get hooked and invested in real drama but is not interested necessarily in X's and O's." EOE's first series, *Playmakers*, took advantage of the National Football League's mainstream appeal by examining a fictional pro football league's scandalous underbelly through a particularly troubled franchise—the Cougars—from an undisclosed American city. The melodramatic series, which *Salon*'s King Kaufman aptly labeled "a soap opera with pads," took inspiration from Oliver Stone's *Any Given Sunday* (1999) to explore professional football's seamy contours.[30] Linebacker Eric Olczyk suffers from posttraumatic stress after paralyzing an opponent, veteran running back Leon Taylor begins taking performance-enhancing drugs to keep up with his younger competition and is embroiled in a domestic abuse controversy, hot-shot running back Demetrius "D. H." Harris is addicted to crack, matinee idol quarterback Derek McConnell is addicted to painkillers and sex, wide receiver Thad Guerwitcz is a closeted homosexual, and Coach George is suffering from cancer. All the while, the Cougars' Machiavellian owner, Gene Wilbanks, does whatever necessary to protect his business interests—no matter the cost to his employees' physical, emotional, or financial health. "The show is not really about football," admits *Playmakers* creator John Eisendrath. "It's about guys—the relationships men have with each other, with their colleagues, their bosses, their wives."[31] The program also contrasts the stereotype of football players as macho simpletons by including confessional voice-overs wherein featured characters articulate their deepest feelings and anxieties.

Playmakers' second episode, titled "The Pissman," showcases its melodramatic sensationalism. The episode begins with D. H. preparing to provide a urine sample to a menacing doctor—the Pissman. "Union says you have to take this shit," D. H. brashly says as the Pissman and his entirely white staff scrutinize the black running back's bare, sculpted body. "Stripping down for the Pissman and getting eyeballed by a guy you know wants to toss your salad. You do blow, you're pissing it for seventy-two hours. I did some the day before yesterday. You do the math." The episode centers on how D. H. beats the test and examines how several of his teammates are dealing with different types of drug issues. The introductory scene cuts from D. H. to Derek McConnell taking an ice bath after a punishing game while ingesting painkillers by the handful. As the quarterback says in a world-weary voice-over: "Life expectancy of an average American is seventy-six. Life expectancy of a pro football player is fifty-eight. No shit. It's not easy cutting 20 percent off your life. You need help," he confesses as the camera focuses in on the various pill bottles next to him. Seconds later, the team doctor confronts Mc-Connell about kidney damage he is suffering because of anti-inflammatories and warns him to scale back. "If I don't use, I don't walk, let alone play," McConnell curtly replies. Coach George similarly disregards the doctor's warnings and, along with Wilbanks, pressures the physician to let McConnell continue medicating despite the health risk. Meanwhile, Taylor starts taking steroids to jump-start his lagging play, and Olczyk receives a prescription for antidepressants to deal with his football-related travails.

"The Pissman" makes clear the irony of certain players taking illegal drugs on the sly, while others are encouraged to take prescription drugs. What's more, it suggests that the Cougars' owner—and, by extension, the league he represents—cares about players' well-being only insofar as they are able to compete on the field. In fact, Wilbanks tips off D. H. about the league's "random" drug test and advises the running back to do whatever necessary to pass it. Taking the hint, D. H. persuades an impressionable teammate to provide him clean urine and pays an unscrupulous physician to inject the sample into his bladder. He passes the test. The episode ends by cutting from the back-alley doctor injecting clean urine into D. H. so he can play to the team doctor injecting McConnell with team-sanctioned drugs also so he can play. "We gotta keep the horses on the track," the compromised team physician resignedly states after administering the quarterback's treatment. "If you think about it," responds McConnell in a sullen voice-over that returns to his earlier ruminations about football players' alarmingly brief life expectancies, "that's what it's all about: keeping the players on the field no matter what. So you don't think about it—any of it. The needles, the pills, the fact that six days a week you can't stand up straight. You deny it all. You have to. Because if you ever really think about what's happening—playing this game is costing you eighteen years of your life—you'd never play another down." "The Pissman," along with *Playmakers'* other episodes, offers a damning interrogation of professional football's treatment of players as disposable parts who sacrifice their bodies and minds for the benefit of avaricious owners indifferent to their employees' plight beyond its impact on their revenues.

Playmakers aired on Tuesday evenings during the football season and benefited from publicity on ESPN's *Sunday Night Football* as well as its institutional affiliation with ABC's *Monday Night Football*. Before the series premiered, Shapiro claimed he hoped it would double ESPN's Tuesday-evening ratings from the previous year.[32] Ratings actually increased fivefold, and *Playmakers* was cable TV's highest-rated show among women in that time slot.[33]

Despite *Playmakers'* successful ratings and positive critical reviews by non-sports-specific publications such as *Entertainment Weekly* and *Variety*, many took exception to its crudeness. Sandomir described it as "a new low" for ESPN that makes "pro football look like a dreadful underworld of pain, needles, drugs, and venal owners." The National Football League most vocally expressed its disapproval. Commissioner Paul Tagliabue called it a "gross mischaracterization of our sport" that "traded in racial stereotypes."[34] NFL Players Association executive director Gene Upshaw reiterated the commissioner's plaint. He dismissed the program as "racist" and suggested that ESPN should avoid such incendiary representations—fictional or otherwise—given its business partnership with the league.[35]

Though he did not deny *Playmakers'* edginess, Shapiro claimed its representations were based—albeit loosely—on fact. "LexisNexis is our best friend," he boasted. "We're pulling from the headlines." The series frequently used actual sports controversies to explain the incidents its characters endure. Olczyk gives Taylor advice about the domestic abuse charges he faces by appealing to NBA player Jason Kidd's ability to salvage his image after dealing with a similar situation in 2001. In response to rumors that McConnell is gay, Wilbanks orders the quarterback to hold a press conference to assert his heterosexuality. The devious owner rationalizes his recommendation by telling McConnell that the strategy worked for New York Mets catcher Mike Piazza, who faced similar rumors in 2002 and held a press conference to set the record *straight*. Toward the end of the series, McConnell gives Olczyk tips on how to regain his girlfriend's trust after she discovered he had impregnated another woman. "You're going to buy her some nice jewelry," McConnell slyly advises. "I'm talking Kobe nice." Here, McConnell references the opulent ring Kobe Bryant purchased his wife after admitting to adultery and being charged with sexual assault in 2003—an incident that occurred merely months before *Playmakers'* premiere. The stories *Playmakers'* plotlines reference—which ESPN's news programs covered incessantly—place the fictional program in dialogue with the actual sporting world. Though it situates its fictional stories in conversation with the real sports world, *Playmakers* never explicitly mentions any NFL-related controversies. The series, Semiao avers, "is no more about life in the NFL than *Gomer Pyle* [*USMC*] is about the Marine Corps."[36] The NFL, however, did not see it this way—and *Gomer Pyle* did not have a business agreement with the Marine Corps.

The dispute *Playmakers* elicited between ESPN and the NFL—an organization often sarcastically called the "No Fun League" because of its obsessive image consciousness—made the program even more popular. "There's an old Hollywood saying," Semiao cynically commented, "that it doesn't matter what they say, as long as you spell the name right." Despite the EOE program's success, ESPN elected not to renew it. As Shapiro said, "We're not in the business of antagonizing our partners. . . . To bring [*Playmakers*] back would be rubbing it in our partner's face."[37] While Shapiro expressed disappointment over what he considered the league's oversensitive objections, he proudly cited *Playmakers* as proof that ESPN could produce a fictional drama with mainstream appeal.

Similar anxieties about ESPN's business relationships constrained EOE's development of a follow-up to *Playmakers*. It abandoned a series called *The Fix*—which centered on a college football conference that conspires to fix a game—to ensure it would not offend the NCAA. Shapiro then commissioned Bill Simmons to script a docudrama on baseball player Alex Rodriguez's 2003 trade from the Texas Rangers to the New York Yankees—a transaction wherein the Yankees swiped the star away from their rival Boston Red Sox after the MLB Players Association vetoed his deal with the team. Again, ESPN canceled the production, which used the working title *Chasing A-Rod*, for fear of irritating the MLB—a decision Shapiro calls "his biggest disappointment at ESPN." "When that happened," Shapiro claims, "I said, 'I'm tired of doing things that get turned down because of our relationships. Let's do poker.'"[38] *Tilt* (2005), EOE's second fictional series, which explored high-stakes poker in Las Vegas, grew out of the industrial constraints that *Playmakers'* brief and controversial run brought into focus.

Created by the producers of the Hollywood film *Rounders* (1998), *Tilt* centers on a group of young gamblers who band together to expose the diabolical poker legend Don "the Matador" Everest (played by Hollywood tough guy Michael Madsen) as a murderous con man. The series was at least as racy as *Playmakers*. One episode, for instance, showcases the Matador orchestrating a Mob-style execution. ESPN even highlighted the series' mature themes by preceding episodes with a disclaimer, which functioned as much as a promise as a warning. Additionally, *Tilt* is even more firmly anchored in the actual world than its predecessor. Its entire plot revolves around a poker tournament that features real professional gamblers playing themselves and that is being telecast by ESPN in a manner that mimics the network's World Series of Poker coverage. Though it was more directly situated in the actual world, *Tilt* did not threaten a valuable partnership. To be sure, professional poker is not concerned with the family friendliness that the NFL tries so hard—and so curiously—to maintain. The program's cancellation after one season was a result of poor ratings. EOE's experimentations in scripted drama suggest the company's business relationships place horizons on precisely how realistic its fictional content can be.

Like EOE's docudramas, *Playmakers* and *Tilt* built verisimilitude by incorporating products and brands from the actual world. Beyond manufacturing realism and offsetting production costs, these product and brand placements serve strategic promotional ends. *Playmakers'* Cougars, for instance, are outfitted in Under Armour gear, and *Tilt's* characters conspicuously prefer to drink Bud Light. Over the course of its history, ESPN has permitted its logos and personalities to be used in a variety of films that range from the comedy *Dodgeball* (2004) to Stephen Spielberg's action-thriller *War of the Worlds* (2005). Chris Berman alone has had cameos in *Necessary Roughness* (1991), *Little Big League* (1994), *Eddie* (1996), *Kingpin* (1996), *The Waterboy* (1998), *The Longest Yard* (2005), *Draft Day* (2014), and the HBO comedy series *Arli$$* (1996–2002). The comedies *Mr. 3000* (2004) and *Herbie: Fully Loaded* (2005)—both Disney productions—feature main characters who are ESPN employees. While Walt Disney Company productions have an obvious incentive to feature ESPN logos and talent, Semiao claims that ESPN encourages all films and TV programs to incorporate its brand as long as they do not compromise it: "If somebody wants to have a sports broadcaster in their film, it should be ESPN."[39]

Playmakers and *Tilt* adopt similar practices. *Playmakers'* Coach George, for instance, intently watches a segment of *Around the Horn* wherein its commentators discuss Taylor's declining skills. Another episode ends with Jim Rome's commentary that uses Taylor's domestic abuse situation to critique violent athletes in general. "Kick these guys off the team," Rome fumes. "Suspend them

Angela Basset plays an ESPN reporter in the film *Mr. 3000* (2004). ESPN nurtures product placements as long as they do not compromise its brand.

indefinitely; make an example of them. Al Unser Jr., Glenn Robinson, Pedro Astacio, Jose Canseco, Will Cordero, Mike Tyson, Mike Fitzpatrick, Leon Taylor. A good guy who did a very bad thing." Along these lines, *Tilt* uses the style of ESPN's poker coverage in scenes that depict telecasts of its characters competing. It mimics ESPN's graphics packages, adopts point-of-view shots like ESPN's that show viewers which cards players possess, and includes postgame interviews conducted by ESPN poker analysts Norman Chad and Lon McEachern. Early in the series—in a solemn voice-over similar to those *Playmakers* employs—one of *Tilt's* main characters laments that ESPN's popular poker coverage has caused fans to underestimate the game's difficulty. "It's obvious when ESPN is showing you the cards they're holding," he remarks.

Shapiro admits that *Playmakers'* and *Tilt's* inclusion of ESPN logos and personalities was "very orchestrated." "We felt we were the everyday fan's news resource for sports and so if you're going to have this fictional world, there's no way they would be going about their day-to-day without some element of ESPN being part of their life."[40] Beyond endorsing ESPN's importance, these brand placements exclude competing organizations. They create settings where ESPN is not simply the most powerful sports media outlet but the only one

Playmakers incorporated portions of ESPN's *Around the Horn* wherein the talk show's featured guests comment on the fictional series' characters.

ESPN's Norman Chad appeared as himself in ESPN's scripted series *Tilt*.

worth mentioning. In doing so, they suggest that ESPN's broader effort to assert and maintain its authority extends into fictional worlds.

"All Things to All People"

"Our mission," Shapiro claimed shortly after joining EOE, "is to forge new highways of sports entertainment. I believe we can be all things to all people." The subsidiary's sometimes-bold experimentations were possible in part, EOE producer and top Shapiro lieutenant Michael Antinoro claims, because of ESPN's recognizable brand and devoted core audience. The subsidiary, he asserts, "was kind of like an incubator. We could try whatever we wanted to try, and [fans] would sample it because it was ESPN." Indeed, EOE was on the front wave of the cable TV trend of channels relying on original programming to build their brand identities. Critics, however, disparaged many of EOE's creations. Will Leitch even claims his 2005 development of *Deadspin* was prompted in part by his frustration with ESPN's Shapiro-driven ventures into nonsports content, which he thought made "ESPN feel more like a corporation than a thing that was serving fans."[41] The website *Sports Media Watch's* 2009 list of the "Ten Worst Sports Programs of the Decade" included eight EOE productions.[42] Much of the criticism suggested EOE was spreading ESPN too far beyond its wheelhouse.

Though EOE produced few hits and was eventually phased out, its programming was not principally designed to satisfy sports media critics or even to attract large overall audiences. Instead, it urged new viewers to try ESPN and strove to create content sticky enough to get visitors to stay in the media outlet's expanded tent.

ESPN Films

"Unprecedented Documentary Series"
by "Filmmaking Originals"

I think the main legacy of the *30 for 30* project [will be] the affirmation that there is still meaning to be found in sports, beyond the clatter of sports radio and argument-based talk shows. There's an audience grateful for programming representing a deeper level of thinking and feeling about sport.

—Jonathan Hock, contributing filmmaker, ESPN Films[1]

ESPN Films is inherently a part of ESPN, but it's important that our films aren't viewed as just sports—and a lot of people feel that way. So being associated with Tribeca and other film festivals and having someone from ESPN on a panel with people from A&E and Magnolia Pictures makes it seem like ESPN is making films for everybody. And that is very important to us.

—Dan Silver, senior director of development,
ESPN Films[2]

In 2004 ESPN developed *ESPN25*, a multiplatform variation on *SportsCentury* that celebrated the media outlet's twenty-fifth anniversary. Similar to *SportsCentury*, the project launched with "The Moments," a daily series of vignettes that counted down the top one hundred events since ESPN's birth. It also included a slate of countdown-driven series and specials—*The Headlines, Then & Now*, and *Who's #1?*—that offered more detailed organizations of sport's previous quarter century. The programs built on *SportsCentury*'s earnest tone by including ceremonial orchestral music in their introductory sequences—a contrast to ESPN programs' typically peppy soundtracks that stressed their subject matter's historical import. It also extended *SportsCentury*'s multimedia format by publishing a book and facilitating online forums for fans to create their own lists and rankings. "We're going to use it as a chance to really look at what's happened during the past 25 years," claimed ESPN producer John Dahl, "which has essentially been a boom time in sports."[3] *ESPN25* did carefully examine sport's past; however, it presented this past through an insistently self-aggrandizing lens that directly attributes its importance to ESPN.

For example, the *ESPN25* book defines and narrates the era through the emergence of the TV sports highlight and locates ESPN as the organization that codified this revolutionary form.

> Twenty-five years ago, Americans got most of their sports news from the newspaper (remember the "newspaper"?), and from a two-to-three min- ute wrap-up at the very end of the 11 o'clock news. Almost all of that news was local and secondhand. Hard-core sports fans subscribed to *Sports Il- lustrated* and crazed sports junkies subscribed to *The Sporting News*, and it cannot be said that many Americans were unhappy with the state of affairs. There was certainly no Million Sports Fan March to demand better sports reporting. Nonetheless, ESPN provided it. And it did so by adopting, and perfecting, an underutilized, unappreciated method of communication: the sports highlight.[4]

Again much like *SportsCentury*, *ESPN25* ended with a lengthy montage that paired famous sporting moments with pop songs that convey sport's themes and emotional power: David Bowie's "Changes" signals the many shifts that marked the era, Joan Jett's "Bad Reputation" provides the backdrop for a sec- tion on scandal, and R.E.M.'s "Everybody Hurts" punctuates sporting failures. The video ends with a graphic that reads: "*ESPN25*, 1979–2004: An Era That Changed Sports." Like the book, the montage makes clear that any significance that marked sport's previous twenty-five years is wrapped up in ESPN's emer- gence and practices.[5]

"Our challenge," claimed ESPN senior vice president Rosa Gatti of *ESPN25*, "is not to be repetitive and not to be self-serving." It was both. Richard Sandomir panned it as a "four month bacchanalia of self-promotion," and the *Philadelphia Inquirer*'s Don Steinberg decried it as "phantasmagorically extensive."[6] These critiques reflect the complaints lodged against the EOE productions alongside which *ESPN25* aired. They locate the project as overblown, narcissistic, and ir- relevant to the network's established strengths in live sporting event coverage and news.

Shortly after Mark Shapiro left ESPN in 2005, EOE was folded into ESPN Content Development—a "boiler room of ideas" that sought to continue expanding the media outlet's offerings.[7] ESPN Content Development shifted focus from scripted dramas, game shows, and reality programming to documentary, a genre to which ESPN had not devoted considerable resources since *SportsCentury*. ESPN then began to acquire independently produced documentaries, and in 2006 it partnered with New York City's Tribeca Film Festival to create the Tribeca/ESPN Sports Film Festival. These activities culminated with the 2008 development of ESPN Films, a subsidiary that focuses on documentaries.

ESPN Films' highest-profile and most ambitious project is *30 for 30* (2009–10), a series of thirty documentaries made by thirty commissioned filmmakers to commemorate ESPN's thirtieth anniversary. The series offered an artful contrast to *ESPN25*'s hyperbolic self-celebration, expanded on *SportsCentury*'s use of documentary to situate ESPN as an authority on sport history, borrowed from *Page 2*'s recruitment of celebrated authors, and tightened EOE's at times disorderly eclecticism. In ESPN Films vice president Connor Schell's words, *30 for 30* "continues the evolution [of *SportsCentury*] and takes it to another level."[8] ESPN ensures as much by marketing *30 for 30*—which has since expanded into a permanent series and spawned offshoots attached to different ESPN entities—as a collection of innovative and cinematic documentaries that bear the aesthetic imprint of their directors, a star-studded roster that includes Steve James, Barry Levinson, Barbara Kopple, Albert Maysles, and John Singleton. While *SportsCentury* constructed ESPN as a company with the capacity to narrate sport's history through original made-for-TV documentaries, ESPN Films suggests the organization enriches the prestigious genre's artistic potential.

ESPN Films

EOE demonstrated little interest in documentary. Those it did create—such as *Ali Rap* and *The Complete Angler*—received relatively little publicity and premiered on less prominent time slots than its docudramas, miniseries, and scripted dramas. "There was a wondering whether documentary filmmaking was in the future," Dahl explains. "The word *documentary* felt educational as opposed to something vibrant and entertaining."[9] EOE's mostly formulaic engagements with the genre did little to challenge this sentiment.

EOE experimented with independently produced documentaries by acquiring Jonathan Hock's *Through the Fire* in 2005. Hock, a documentarian who began his career at NFL Films and worked on *SportsCentury*, produced *Streetball*, a program on inner-city basketball that composed the centerpiece of EOE's "Block Party." Based on *Streetball*'s success, HBO's *On the Record with Bob Costas* commissioned Hock to produce a short segment on urban basketball. Hock elected to focus on Coney Island high school prodigy Sebastian Telfair. Building on the tradition of *Hoop Dreams* and Darcy Frey's book *The Last Shot* (1994)—which also centered on Coney Island and featured Telfair's cousin Stephon Marbury—Hock's segment explored how Telfair strives to use basketball to improve his and his family's fortunes.

After realizing that there was more to Telfair's story than a short segment could contain, Hock decided to expand the piece into a feature, which he made independently when HBO Sports declined his proposal.[10] The documentary he crafted, *Through the Fire*, premiered at the 2005 Tribeca Film Festival. Based on the film's positive critical reception and potential to complement its basketball programming, ESPN purchased a ten-year license for the documentary's domestic rights. It created additional buzz for the film by facilitating its continued exhibition on the festival circuit. The documentary earned the Audience Award at AFI Fest and collected the Urbanworld Film Festival's Best Documentary prize before premiering on ESPN in March 2006. *Through the Fire*'s DVD packaging includes the logos from the film festivals where it appeared and describes the production as "ESPN's critically acclaimed documentary," even though the media outlet was uninvolved in its production. "It was ironic that ESPN bought it," Hock explains, "because my main incentive in making it independently was that I was tired of everything I was doing being owned by ESPN."[11] ESPN's promotional campaign suggests it did not simply acquire *Through the Fire*, but also attained the film's accolades and independent cachet.

Dahl describes *Through the Fire* as "a foreshadowing of what was to come." "It sent us on a path," Schell explains, "that eventually gets to *30 for 30*." A first stop on this route was ESPN and Tribeca's 2006 creation of the Tribeca/ESPN Sports Film Festival. Film festivals, according to media scholar Marijke De Valck, are "sites of passage that function as gateways to cultural legitimization." They are, in Thomas Elsaesser words, "the Olympics of the show business economy," which provide an opportunity for independent films to gain exposure and distribution while offering corporate media outfits a chance to scout new material and talent.[12] Tribeca and ESPN's partnership, however unlikely, is mutually beneficial. Tribeca cofounder Jane Rosenthal claims that ESPN's brand recognition attracts new visitors to the festival and provides a useful programming function that signals to attendees which selections have sporting themes. Meanwhile, Tribeca brokers ESPN's entrance into a rarefied cultural space. "We want our brand to be in front of people who aren't sports fans," says ESPN Films' Dan Silver.[13] While Tribeca maintains control over the selection

Tribeca/ESPN's Sports Day is an annual family-friendly street fair attached to the Tribeca/ESPN Sports Film Festival.

process, the partnership provides ESPN with a pipeline to procuring productions that appear at the event—such as Diego Luna's *J. C. Chávez* (2007) and Hock's *Lost Son of Havana* (2009)—and a respectable site where it can exhibit its own works. When ESPN has not been able to purchase certain documentaries it covets—Asif Kapadia's *Senna* (2010), for example—it has struck licensing and distribution deals to associate its brand with them. ESPN expanded on its film festival with the Tribeca/ESPN Sports Day, a family-friendly street fair composed of (mostly promotional) sports exhibits and activities. The Sports Day combines with the festival to propel ESPN's extension into new spaces and to broaden Tribeca's audience beyond the stereotypical festival crowd.

Though formed in *Through the Fire*'s and the Tribeca/ESPN festival's documentary-driven wake, ESPN Films initially strove to develop fictional films for theatrical release in partnership with Hollywood studios. These films, according to Semiao—who was named ESPN Films' senior vice president after EOE's dissolution—would enable ESPN to extend its reach without overshadowing its regular television programming.[14] The subsidiary began development on two biopics: one on Vince Lombardi, starring Robert De Niro and written by Academy Award winner Eric Roth, and another on Jackie Robinson, with Robert Redford attached as both an actor and a producer. The projects were shelved, however, after the economic downturn tightened credit lines and made Hollywood studios less willing to invest in sports films, which typically attract smaller international audiences than other genres. Moreover, Semiao claims that Roth's script for the Lombardi film did not sufficiently impress ESPN's potential studio partners: "Eric, God bless him, wrote a shitty script. Just like the best hitter in baseball strikes out now and then, the best player in basketball misses a shot, the best quarterback throws an interception. The best screenwriter wrote a bad script." Given these constraints and the mixed reviews EOE's scripted content received, John Skipper, who took charge of ESPN's content after Shapiro left, believed documentary would compose a more respectable and less expensive focal point for ESPN Films that retained the EOE productions' stickiness. "We are no longer in the movie business for television," Skipper announced. "We can make 10 documentaries for the same $5 million it would cost us to make one movie."[15] ESPN Films has since focused entirely on documentary.

The subsidiary's first original production, Dan Klores's *Black Magic* (2008), is a four-hour exploration of race and basketball in the United States through the lens of historically black colleges and universities. It considers how these HBCUs amplified college basketball's popularity and prompted its integration. It also points out the unexpected challenges these programs have suffered as a consequence of the racial integration they hastened, which allows better-resourced schools to compete for players who otherwise likely would have attended HBCUs. The documentary extends *Through the Fire*'s focus on the intersections between African American culture and basketball while probing the topic's history. Klores and ESPN advertised the documentary's relationship to African American culture by premiering it at Harlem's Apollo Theater. Moreover, Klores claimed *Black Magic* was inspired by Ken Burns's epic treatment of baseball.[16] ESPN emphasized the film's similarity to *Baseball* by initially airing it without commercial interruption in prime time over the course of two evenings and marketing it as a "Dan Klores film" rather than simply an ESPN production. It was the first time ESPN adopted either practice. The careful cultivation of *Black Magic* as an authored TV event helped the film become the highest-rated premiere of any documentary in the network's history and earned ESPN its third Peabody Award.

ESPN Films continued this author-driven format with Spike Lee's *Kobe Doin' Work* (2009), which trains thirty cameras on the Los Angeles Lakers' Kobe Bryant during a single game to provide a novel view of his play. From its opening moments, the production announces its status as a product of Lee's distinctive creative vision. It begins with the solitary filmmaker strutting onto the Lakers' home court to unveil his work: "One game, we had thirty cameras, just on Kobe. Kobe was miked, and with the assistance of coach Phil Jackson, he let us bring a camera into his sacred locker room, and we shot there before the game, at halftime, and postgame. And what you will see is a very intimate portrait of the greatest basketball player on the planet today." Lee insists that his unconventional film, which required tremendous access and an unusually large crew, was possible because of his established status as an auteur and a celebrity basketball fan. "The only reason why Phil Jackson and Kobe and [Lakers owner] Dr. Buss gave me access to all of this," he asserts, "is because they know how much I love the game and I know what I'm talking about. If I was Joe Blow off the corner, and not a well-known filmmaker, that'd be hard. They wouldn't trust someone sticking a mike in their face."[17] ESPN reinforced the production's

Filmmaker Spike Lee introduces *Kobe Doin' Work* (2009) from Los Angeles's Staple Center. The introduction emphasizes the film's position as a "Spike Lee Joint."

position as Lee's handiwork by branding it as a "Spike Lee Joint"—the title all of the filmmaker's productions carry. In doing so, it allied the documentary with celebrated Lee productions like *Do the Right Thing* (1989) and *Malcolm X* (1992).

Similar to Klores's assertion that *Black Magic* grew out of Burns's *Baseball*, Lee claims *Kobe Doin' Work* took inspiration from Douglas Gordon and Philippe Perreno's *Zidane: A 21st Century Portrait* (2006), which provided a similarly multidimensional examination of French soccer star Zinedine Zidane during a match. Lee notes that he attended *Zidane*'s premiere at the Cannes Film Festival and "got thinking . . . this would work even better for basketball."[18] *Kobe Doin' Work* is not as formally daring as *Zidane*, which shows little concern for the game action and includes, for instance, lengthy close-ups of Zidane's cleats rustling through the grass, a slow-paced and haunting score by the Scottish postrock band Mogwai, and brief intertitles that depict Zidane's ruminations on the relationship between soccer and life. *Kobe Doin' Work*, by contrast, adopts the format of a highlight film from Bryant's perspective that features the star explaining his play in a voice-over. Indeed, Lee's film borders on a puff piece that provides no critical commentary on Bryant as an athlete or person. Nevertheless, ESPN and Lee situate *Kobe Doin' Work* as a product of cinema culture designed by a respected artist and inspired by a renowned art film—a status they reinforced by premiering the documentary at Tribeca. Along these lines, Lee insists that even though the production was designed for television, it is a film on par with his other works. "The medium doesn't matter to me," he states. "It's still filmmaking. Anything we do we have the cinema mind-set. Kobe's film, whether it's shown in film festivals or on television, it's a film."[19] Lee's attitude reflects ESPN Films' branding strategy, which allies the subsidiary with film, even though most of its works—including *Kobe Doin' Work*—are shot on video.

Similar to *Black Magic*, and in keeping with ESPN Films' creative aspirations, ESPN initially aired *Kobe Doin' Work* with limited commercial interruption. "We wanted to make it a cinematic experience," Dahl remarks. "If you keep interrupting the flow of the story, it gets really hard to get into it." These presentations allowed ESPN Films to foster a mode of viewership comparable to HBO's and PBS's presentations. Indeed, documentaries' lower production costs compared to scripted content—which was already a cheaper alternative to live event coverage—made it easier to rationalize airing *Black Magic* and *Kobe Doin' Work* with little or no commercial interruption. ESPN complemented the reduced commercials by removing the "bottom line"—a ticker of scores and updates that runs along the base of the screen during programming—for airings of ESPN Films documentaries. While he acknowledges the benefits of including a bottom line in programming, namely, its ability to dissuade viewers from changing the channel, Dahl observes that "if you have a bottom line, you're splitting the audience's attention. For a film, you're trying to get someone engaged in the story; you're asking them to put everything down and get invested."[20] Omitting the bottom line, he suggests, retains audiences by fostering an immersive viewing experience. Dahl claims *The Greatest Game Ever Played* (2008), ESPN Films' documentary on the 1958 NFL Championship, provided a useful test case for this practice. Though the film premiered after the 2008 Heisman Trophy presentation—a time when there was an exceptional amount of sports news circulating—the bottom line's absence did not noticeably drive away viewers. This airing compelled ESPN to continue removing the bottom line for all of ESPN Films' airings, an omission that marks these documentaries as distinctively cinematic and as warranting more careful attention than ESPN's typical content.

Unlike *Black Magic* and *Kobe Doin' Work*, *The Greatest Game Ever Played* aired with regular commercial breaks and was unattached to a distinct directorial voice. However, it complements its predecessors' artistic goals by underscoring ESPN's relationship to film culture. It begins with a spoken introduction by Chris Berman along with shots of 16mm film projectors playing old football footage. "The motion picture," Berman intones. "It is how memories have been captured for more than a hundred years. It is how examples of true excellence are passed down from generation to generation. It records the great moments of our time. To see the heights the NFL has reached, we see its path in the frames of history." *The Greatest Game Ever Played* combines interviews about the 1958 championship with a new colorization of the game's film to suggest ESPN Films enlivens this well-documented sporting event.

Not all ESPN Films productions were so deliberately packaged as cinematic events. Several of the subsidiary's early documentaries—such as *Hellfighters* (2008), *Inning by Inning: A Portrait of a Coach* (2008), *The Streak* (2008), *A Woman among Boys* (2008), and *The Zen of Bobby V* (2008)—received little promotion and premiered sporadically across the network's channels. Though their airings all excluded the bottom line, they were otherwise undistinguished from ESPN's regular programming flows. In fact, Richard Linklater directed *Inning by Inning*, a profile of the University of Texas's unconventional baseball coach Augie Garrido. Despite Linklater's celebrated status as the director of cult classics like *Slacker* (1991) and *Dazed and Confused* (1993), ESPN did not emphasize his involvement in the film as aggressively as it stressed Lee's relationship to *Kobe Doin' Work* or even Klores's attachment to *Black Magic*. "We hadn't figured out how to package and sell these to our audience," Schell says of ESPN Films' initial productions. "There wasn't really a strategy around them."[21] The *30 for 30* series organized ESPN Films' documentaries around a cohesive brand that emphasizes their formal inventiveness, relationship to cinema culture, and derivation from unique directorial perspectives.

30 for 30

The series *30 for 30* is the brainchild of Bill Simmons, who claims he came up with the idea in 2007 while packing away his collection of old sports videotapes. He wondered how ESPN, with its enormous archive, could reasonably claim to be the Worldwide Leader in Sports without consistently producing sports documentaries. Simmons believed a documentary series that featured recognizable filmmakers would both shine a light on ESPN's influence and compose an effective way to commemorate its upcoming thirtieth anniversary. After a series of e-mail exchanges with Schell and other ESPN colleagues, the project was approved, and Simmons was named an executive producer. Simmons and company's initial task was to recruit some big-name participants. "We hoped to land a few respected names early for a 'domino effect' of sorts and only needed two or three names," Simmons explained. "We all started going on meet and greets, and that's when something crazy happened. Something we never anticipated: these people had been waiting for us. They had stories to tell. They just never thought they'd have a chance to tell them." The series would expand on *Through the Fire*, Tribeca, and ESPN Films' initial productions to announce ESPN as a permanent presence in the documentary genre. "We're not just going to say halfheartedly that we're making documentaries," Schell notes of *30 for 30*'s development. "We're going to make them with the best documentary filmmakers in the world. And we're not going to make one of them and see how it goes. We're going to make 30 of them. We're going to make this feel as special as possible. Part of being special is being credible, and the way you become credible is to work with the best people out there." As a celebration of ESPN's thirtieth anniversary, *30 for 30* sought to make up for some of the integrity that *ESPN25*'s many indulgences compromised. John Skipper claims ESPN conceptualized *30 for 30* "with the proposition that we didn't want to do anything too celebratory. There's a sense that we've done enough of that." "I know we love celebrating ourselves," Simmons added, "but there's a better way of doing it. It's with good content that we're not clubbing people over the head with."[22] Moreover, *30 for 30* provided the coherence that ESPN Films' initial documentaries lacked. The brand united the series' selections, however disparate their topics, and encouraged viewers to consume them as a collection. ESPN reinforced *30 for 30*'s seriality by initially programming its films in consistent weekly time slots.

The series built distinction in part by reinforcing documentary's reputation as an exceptionally nuanced TV genre. According to ESPN Films executive producer Keith Clinkscales, "As sports had become more powerful and integral to our social culture, the desire to know more about these figures is just kind of natural. . . . To get to different layers of that is what documentary filmmaking does best. It provides a layer of intimacy that you just can't get from the normal way sports are covered." ESPN emphasizes this attitude by using the phrase "Too Dramatic Not to Be Real" as *30 for 30*'s tagline. Along these lines, ESPN vice president for content development Joan Lynch suggests *30 for 30*'s documentaries can serve the same programming functions as EOE's generically adventurous content. "The stories we're telling are dramatic enough that we don't have to rely on putting scripted programming on our air to be provocative."[23] The series' trailer stresses that *30 for 30* sheds new light on sport's past. It features footage from various films in the series combined with soft piano music and a baritone voice-over that intones, "What if I told you . . .," followed by a statement that contrasts conventional wisdom. For instance, it showcases Muhammad Ali training while the narrator states, "What if I told you, he *wasn't* the greatest." The footage of Ali is taken from Albert Maysles's *Muhammad and Larry*, an examination of Ali's embarrassing 1980 loss to Larry Holmes during the twilight of his career. The trailer suggests Maysles's documentary offers an uncommon take on an icon that is already the subject of many documentaries and biographies.

The series also deliberately contrasts *SportsCentury*'s straightforwardness. "These wouldn't be typical documentaries with highlights and talking heads and a chronological theme," Simmons vowed when introducing the project. "These would be stories with a beginning, middle, and end."[24] *Muhammad and Larry*, for instance, focuses entirely on a bout that *SportsCentury*'s Ali profile mentions only in brief. It does so by combining footage that Maysles and his brother David originally shot for a British television documentary—which was scrapped after Ali's poor showing—with new interviews and content from ESPN's archive. As Shapiro insisted that *SportsCentury* shoot all new interviews to create a distinct look, *30 for 30* stressed its uniqueness by using all original interview content staged by the individual films' directors.

The documentaries emphasize *30 for 30*'s originality by adopting a variety of formal approaches. Steve James's *No Crossover: The Trial of Allen Iverson* is a first-person account wherein James confronts his hometown's racism through exploring its response to basketball player Allen Iverson's involvement in a racially charged brawl while in high school; Adam Kurland and Lucas Jansen's *Silly Little Game*, a lighthearted investigation of fantasy baseball's invention, incorporates animated sequences; and Reggie Rock Bythewood's *One Night in Vegas*, a discussion of rapper Tupac Shakur's friendship with Mike Tyson and murder after a 1996 Tyson bout, integrates comic book–style sequences to accentuate its subjects' outsized statures. Simmons claims that *30 for 30*, unlike *SportsCentury*, privileged imaginative approaches to provocative sport stories over ensuring that it covered the most popular events. "If there was no fresh take on the O. J. trial, the 1980 Olympic hockey team, Magic's HIV-driven retirement or any other 'iconic' story from that time, then screw it. We weren't going to assign those topics just to have them in the series."[25]

For instance, Brett Morgen's *June 17, 1994* inventively examines media coverage of O. J. Simpson's infamous low-speed car chase after being implicated in the murder of Nicole Brown Simpson and Ronald Goldman. Without voice-over narration or talking-head interviews, Morgen presents a pastiche of archived TV footage along with an eerie score to demonstrate how the bizarre occasion transformed into a spectacle that disrupted the media landscape's normal patterns.[26] His documentary presents mainstream and sports news updates on the chase interrupting and combining with coverage of the U.S. Open golf tournament, NBA Finals, World Cup, Major League Baseball, and the New York Rangers' Stanley Cup celebration. It shows, for instance, Chris Berman sprinkling his dispatches from the U.S. Open with new developments on the story and the network's World Cup sportscasters assuring viewers that "coming up at halftime we'll give you . . . the latest on the charges against O. J. Simpson." Morgen also includes B-roll of NBC's NBA Finals broadcast feed that demonstrates Bob Costas, Tom Brokaw, and their producers deciding how they will discuss the breaking story without compromising their event coverage: "Hello, everyone. I'm Bob Costas. It is our professional obligation to cover the ball game tonight. We will do that in what we hope is a professional fashion. We are, of course, mindful of the O. J. Simpson situation, and we will apprise you of any new developments." The NBC footage cuts to Brokaw at the network's headquarters, who describes the Simpson affair as "a modern tragedy of Shakespearean proportion being played out on television." The transition from Costas to Brokaw both showcases how the Simpson chase narrowed the division between sport and mainstream news and comments on popular media's tabloid-driven preoccupations.

June 17, 1994 demonstrates how the same vast media machine that fashioned Simpson into a broadly appealing sport celebrity—indeed, one of the United States' first African American athletes with crossover salability—persecutes him for disrupting that lucrative image. Morgen closes the film by combining the chase's anticlimactic finish and Simpson's apprehension with footage of the media outlets that were obsessing over the story moments earlier returning to their normal patterns with new content. A disembodied newscaster announces "There are other stories in the world of sports today" as the credits roll, accompanied by the Talking Heads song "Heaven," which offers the unsettling juxtaposition of an upbeat tune with lyrics about postmodern ennui. The documentary, which the *Los Angeles Times*' Robert Lloyd calls a "tone poem" and a "meditation, of an elemental sort, not just on sports but on the way of the world," showcases and critiques how popular media generate, cover, sap, and eventually subsume the stories that constitute their commercially driven currents. While *SportsCentury*, by Shapiro's admission, did not attempt to "rewrite" sport history or reimagine the sports documentary's typical conventions, *30 for 30* productions like *June 17, 1994* suggest ESPN Films pushes against the genre's formal customs and, in doing so, interrogates the predictable historical narratives it generates. As Schell asserts, "We wanted to reinvent the genre with every single film."[27]

The emphasis ESPN Films places on *30 for 30*'s formal innovation intensifies *SportsCentury*'s efforts to usurp HBO Sports' position as television's most prominent producer of sports documentaries. This competition for market share, Simmons admits, informed his conceptualization of the project. "I was watching an old HBO Sports documentary," he claims, "and got mad that HBO had this monopoly. . . . I thought, we're a sports network and they're not, but it's always, 'oh, they have a new documentary.'" In a *New York Times* interview, Simmons facetiously claimed to "want nothing more than to destroy [HBO Sports]." Specifically, he observed that although HBO documentaries are "consistently good," they are produced by "a bunch of older sports fans based on what they think people in their age range want to see." In a *30 for 30* podcast Simmons hosted during the series' initial run, he, Schell, and Dahl complain that HBO Sports documentaries' repetitive use of talking-head interviews, archive footage, and voice-over narration by actor Liev Schreiber has rendered the genre trite. On the other hand, *30 for 30*'s comparative adventurousness, Skipper asserted, strove to transform ESPN into "the first stop for documentary makers to tell great stories."[28] Despite ESPN Films' stated ambitions—and daring productions like *June 17, 1994*—most *30 for 30* documentaries actually adopt HBO's basic format. Regardless, ESPN Films' producers maintain that *30 for 30* breathes new life into the "tired" and HBO-dominated genre while attracting viewers who otherwise may have minimal interest in it.

Former HBO Sports president Ross Greenburg claimed that the premium cable outlet's sports documentaries endeavor to "penetrate the American mind" and "sociologically look at our culture through the eyes of sports."[29] The productions, he suggested, grow out of and reinforce the channel's status as exceptional TV. Greenburg shared his thoughts on the competition ESPN Films posed after HBO Sports won the 2010 Emmy for Outstanding Sports Documentary, an accolade it had received several times before. He likened the experience of watching HBO Sports productions to "walking into a gallery and seeing [Michelangelo's] *David*" and, extending his sculptural metaphor, compared ESPN Films' documentaries to "something I chipped out when I was 10."[30] He added that HBO Sports "will always feel" that it "owns" the Outstanding Sports Documentary category.

To enhance its refinement and gain aesthetic ground on its traditionally more respectable competitor, ESPN Films surrounds its works with markers of prestige that HBO Sports' productions do not possess. For example, it positions *30 for 30* as a film series that provides cinematic viewing experiences even though its primary home is TV. "Cinema," film scholar John Ellis explains, "proposes a curious and expectant spectator. . . . The viewer for broadcast TV is rather more a figure who had delegated their look to the TV institution." John Caldwell observes that TV outlets often perpetuate this attitude by evoking film technologies and practices—through both their productions and how they market them—to distinguish content.[31] Prior to each *30 for 30*, the ESPN Films logo appears in front of a white background with the circular light of a film projector shining into it. In doing so, it explicitly links ESPN Films with cinema technologies and exhibition. The *30 for 30* logo—an animated filmstrip with "30 for 30" printed on it and a beam of projected light shining through its center—fashions a similarly cinematic identity for the series. The branded filmstrip moves vertically and is accompanied by a light clicking noise as if it is running through a projector. Aside from the series' trademark, ESPN uses a graphic of old-fashioned red paper movie tickets with "30 for 30" and the tagline "Too Dramatic Not to Be Real" emblazoned on them. Like the ESPN Films documentaries that precede the series, few *30 for 30* productions use any

ESPN Films brands its productions as exceptionally filmic and cinematic by using old-fashioned movie tickets, film stock, and the light from a projector.

actual film stock. Those that do—such as *Muhammad and Larry* and Hock's *The Best That Never Was*—principally employ it only briefly and in an archival and contextual capacity. The overwhelmingly video-based series uses film's relative sophistication to brand itself as cinematic.

Reinforcing *30 for 30*'s cinematic status, ESPN recruited a series of presenting and participating sponsors—a list that includes Cadillac, Honda, Infiniti, and Levi's—to allow the documentaries to debut with limited commercial interruption. Moreover, Dahl claims the commercial breaks that do occur are regulated so they do not take place at times that might disrupt a particularly poignant moment.[32] ESPN also removes the bottom line for all *30 for 30* airings across the network.

Adding to the cinematic image it cultivates for *30 for 30*, ESPN calls attention to the participation of renowned filmmakers and emphasizes the creative flexibility it affords them. Simmons called the series "the greatest collection of filmmakers ever assembled under the same umbrella" when it launched.[33] In many cases, the films resemble the works that made their directors famous. *No Crossover*'s focus on race and basketball resonates with James's *Hoop Dreams*; Barbara Kopple's *The House of Steinbrenner*, which considers George Steinbrenner's reign as the New York Yankees' owner, centers on workers in ways that echo her films *Harlan County, USA* (1976) and *American Dream* (1991); and Barry Levinson's *The Band That Wouldn't Die*, a celebration of the Baltimore Colts marching band's refusal to cease operations after its team's 1984 relocation to Indianapolis, expands on his nostalgic depictions of Baltimore in *Diner* (1982), *Tin Men* (1987), *Avalon* (1990), and *Liberty Heights* (1999).

The *30 for 30* series emphasizes its participating filmmakers' uniqueness by integrating "Filmmaking Originals" sequences into commercial breaks wherein the directors—framed in filmstrip graphics that accentuate their authorial status—explain their aesthetic philosophies and personal relationship to the subject matter they explored. Levinson, for instance, acknowledges that *The Band That Wouldn't Die* spawned from his experience as a Baltimorean and Colts fan who was devastated by the team's sudden departure. He claims that he "felt

The *30 for 30* series emphasizes participating filmmakers' pedigree through intermittent "filmmaking original" segments wherein they explain their artistic philosophies and relationship to their subject matter.

lost" without a pro football team in Baltimore and that the Colts' marching band gave him hope that the city would someday get another team, which it did in 1996. *The Band That Wouldn't Die*, the filmmaker suggests, gave him a chance to explore these memories and emotions. The "Filmmaking Original" segments that aired with *No Crossover* include James explaining how the project enabled him to come to grips with his hometown's racism and his complicity in it.

The *30 for 30* website also stresses the filmmakers' artistry and intimate connection to their subject matter with in-depth biographies and "Personal Statements." Simmons added to these author-driven discourses with his *30 for 30* podcast, which included several of the series' filmmakers discussing their artistic philosophies, creative process, and the production of their film. For example, Brett Morgen claims *June 17, 1994*'s avoidance of voice-over narration and original interviews exemplifies a style of documentary he calls "experiential," wherein the audience is made to feel as if it is witnessing featured events "firsthand." Morgen then dismisses documentaries that rely on talking-head interviews and voice-of-God narration as "the antithesis of cinema" and compares the process of making "experiential" productions like his to "walking a tightrope without a net."[34]

Morgen's ruminations suggest ESPN facilitates idiosyncratic productions and gives commissioned artists the freedom to express themselves however they see fit. Simmons even claims that his greatest contribution to the project was convincing ESPN to let the filmmakers "explore their vision" unhindered, and he asserts that the company's willingness to do so made *30 for 30* "more creative" than the "producer-controlled" documentaries it produced before ESPN Films and that its competition presumably continues to churn out. Schell reiterates Simmons's point and indicates that the directors' talents best serve ESPN when they are left alone.[35]

The commissioned filmmakers repeatedly praise ESPN Films' lack of intervention—comments that ESPN recirculates in its promotional materials. James claims that "the beauty of this whole series is [ESPN] didn't want a series that looked like it was made by the same person. . . . They wanted them to be documentaries with individual visions of their makers." "I've yet to feel that I've had to compromise my vision," adds Hock, who has worked with ESPN Films repeatedly since *Through the Fire*. In fact, Hock's rough cut of *The Best That Never Was* ran far longer than the 50 minutes ESPN initially allotted him. Impressed by the film's potential, ESPN allowed him to expand the documentary to a 102-minute production. Similarly, Alex Gibney's *Catching Hell*, which examines scapegoating in sports, was slated for release as part of *30 for 30*'s initial run but was delayed until 2011. Simmons claims that granting Gibney additional time to complete the project was a no-brainer: "The fact that he's spending MORE time on something that was already great has us really excited."[36] These scenarios and comments indicate that ESPN allows its artists to explore their inspiration in a form, through methods, and at a pace that suits their process.

Gibney locates ESPN Films' willingness to let directors experiment as the main quality that distinguishes *30 for 30* from other TV sports documentaries. "They're saying do it in your style," he claims. "It's exactly the opposite of what you'd expect from a branded cable network, which can be bristling to an independent filmmaker, where you become just a sausage maker."[37] He maintains that ESPN Films established a format for difference within the often uniform sports documentary genre that it cultivates by allying with unique artists whom it urges to explore their creativity. More specifically, Gibney claims *30 for 30*'s formal diversity sets the series apart from HBO Sports' offerings. "HBO has their format," he notes, "but they're rigorously produced with exactly the same style. So you go into a zone—you feel, 'Ok, this is the HBO Sports film zone.' *30 for 30* is doing just the opposite. They're saying, 'each one of these is going to be wildly different.'"[38] As Gibney indicates, and similar to ESPN's dubious assertions that *30 for 30*'s films are distinct from HBO Sports' documentaries, the series' employment of different filmmakers and ESPN Films' willingness to let those artists work autonomously enrich a potentially vibrant TV genre that HBO Sports has made stale. In reality, however, ESPN Films closely monitors both the selection of *30 for 30* topics and the films' creation. It assigns a production team to each film that provides filmmakers with support and offers ESPN periodic progress reports.

The series' focus on its commissioned filmmakers as the documentaries' principal creative forces reflects practices film historian David Bordwell uses to characterize art film, a genre in which "the author becomes a formal component, the overriding intelligence organizing the film for our comprehension." Caldwell notes that TV industries adopt this practice by situating directors as authorial visionaries and deploying these powerful signifiers to position certain content as artful enough to "cut through the televised clutter."[39] The *30 for 30* series' appeals to its directors and their creative freedom borrow from these film and TV industry practices to set ESPN Films apart from HBO Sports, which typically does not market its documentaries through their directors.[40] It also separates the series from *SportsCentury*'s documentaries, which were branded only as ESPN products, and EOE's telefilms, which were primarily publicized through their lead actors. EOE marketed *Hu$tle*, for instance, through stressing the actor Tom Sizemore's involvement as Pete Rose even though Academy Award–nominated filmmaker Peter Bogdanovich directed it. In contrast, *30 for 30*'s focus on directors marks these documentaries as artworks that are more cultured than ESPN's earlier forays into documentary and telefilm.

Several *30 for 30* documentaries actually boast producers who are more famous than their directors. In these cases, ESPN Films includes those producers in its marketing. For instance, actor Morgan Freeman produced *The 16th Man*, an examination of how Nelson Mandela used the South African rugby team to unite his racially divided nation just after Apartheid's end. ESPN Films bills Freeman—who starred as Mandela in *Invictus* (2009), a fictional film on the same topic released one year before *The 16th Man*—as a producer and includes the famous actor alongside director Clifford Bestall in the documentary's publicity. While every *30 for 30* documentary has producers, ESPN Films' marketing calls attention to them only when their names are more noteworthy than the film's director. This practice indicates that ESPN is not simply interested in marking *30 for 30*'s films in relation to the primary creative forces behind their construction, but the most recognizable and influential names associated with them.

While appearing on Simmons's *30 for 30* podcast, Barry Levinson expressed amazement at how willingly ESPN accepted his pitch to make a film on a marching band—a topic he considered far afield from the series' focus. "I'm going to tell you a secret," Simmons responded. "You could have basically told us that you were going to do anything and we would have said yes."[41] Though not without sarcasm, Simmons's comments reflect *Page 2*'s strategic appropriation of Halberstam's, Thompson's, and Wiley's celebrity by implying that *30 for 30* is as invested in associating with the symbolic power authorial names deliver as it is in the content commissioned filmmakers produce.

ESPN further reinforces the *30 for 30* productions' exceptional status by submitting them to and exhibiting them at Tribeca and other festivals. *No Crossover* premiered at South by Southwest, Steve Nash and Ezra Holland's *Into the Wind* debuted at the Toronto International Film Festival, and Jeff Zimbalist and Michael Zimbalist's *The Two Escobars* was unveiled at Cannes. ESPN markets the films' DVDs by including the laurel-wreath trademarks from the festivals to which they were selected—a trope it began with *Through the Fire*. It also uses

ESPN Films' involvement in the festival world to cast itself as a patron of independent film rather than a corporate media outlet looking to exploit the genre's commercial and cultural value. For instance, it organized a panel discussion at the 2010 Tribeca/ESPN festival that featured Morgen, fellow *30 for 30* director Mike Tollin, Schell, and Simmons discussing the sports documentary's future and ESPN's role in it. Similarly, in 2013 ESPN started awarding the Tribeca Film Institute/ESPN Prize—a grant of thirty thousand dollars for a sports film in progress that "capture[s] the human element of the sports world" and "strive[s] to change the way people perceive sports by bringing the dramatic stakes of competitiveness to life." Schell insists that despite the strategic advantages of ESPN's involvement with Tribeca, the partnership is "inherently about trying to support the arts," and Silver calls the cosponsored festival "the most altruistic thing ESPN has done." Schell also maintains that ESPN and Tribeca "have an arm's-length relationship" that requires ESPN to "submit work like everybody else."[42] While Tribeca has no obligation to include ESPN Films productions and ESPN is uninvolved in the selection process, there is an obvious incentive for the festival to indulge its partner—both because of their prized alliance and because of the traffic ESPN's brand brings to the event.

Regardless of the potential conflicts of interest that arise, the *New York Times'* Mike Hale claims that ESPN and Tribeca's union has "raised sports films to new prominence." He also assures readers that "any fears that being in business with the home of *SportsCenter* and *Monday Night Football* might compromise the festival's downtown bona fides would be misplaced." ESPN, Hale affirms, not only belongs in but fortifies the elite artistic world Tribeca represents. "I don't know another company," Schell says of his employer, "that would make a commitment like this to independent cinema."[43] Although many ESPN Films productions are directed by filmmakers who cut their teeth in indie circles, they are far from independent. However, ESPN uses its partnership with Tribeca and presence on the festival circuit to position *30 for 30* as part of the indie film world and to reap this association's benefits. The festival's continued success even compelled South by Southwest to launch its own sports-centered film festival and media exposition, SX Sports, in 2014.

ESPN's efforts to brand *30 for 30* as distinctly artful were, by most accounts, a tremendous success. *New Jersey Star-Ledger* TV critic Allan Sepinwall called it "one of the best ESPN projects in years," and the *Boston Globe's* Chad Finn claimed that it "set a standard for contemporary sports documentaries." Critics specifically located the series' ostensible celebration of ESPN's thirtieth anniversary as a dignified contrast to *ESPN25's* misguided indulgences. Sepinwall applauded it as a "reminder of how great ESPN can be when it acts a little humble and gives you the story without the self-promotion." "This is ESPN using its power for good instead of evil," Sepinwall claimed, "for a celebration of sports rather than a celebration of itself."[44]

However, *30 for 30* is not without self-promotion. Though not as overtly as *ESPN25*, the series persistently positions ESPN as sport's most authoritative voice. Reflecting *SportsCentury*'s profiles and EOE's docudramas, *30 for 30*'s documentaries do this in part by integrating archived ESPN content. Dahl points out that budgetary constraints make it more economical for *30 for 30*'s filmmakers to include ESPN footage, which they can use for free, rather than paying to license similar content that the company does not own. He insists, however, that ESPN does not require filmmakers to use its archived content.[45]

Regardless, ESPN footage's pervasiveness across *30 for 30* suggests the history it chronicles cannot be remembered without ESPN. *Muhammad and Larry*'s use of ESPN coverage, for instance, reminds viewers that, like ABC Sports, ESPN played a role in documenting Ali's important career. Similarly, *June 17, 1994*'s frequent use of ESPN material depicts the media outlet as driving mainstream coverage of one of the 1990s' biggest news items. Along different lines, *Run Ricky Run*, Sean Pamphilion's examination of eccentric pro football player Ricky Williams, uses archived content to subtly critique ESPN. It includes *SportsCenter* footage of Berman complaining that Williams—who briefly retired from the NFL and went on a transcontinental spiritual quest after twice testing positive for drugs—"chose marijuana over football." The documentary implies that ESPN failed to appreciate Williams's intelligence and sensitivity. Its critique simultaneously, however, recognizes ESPN as the media establishment and as sports news' most powerful force.

Other *30 for 30* documentaries engage ESPN's print and online archives to build their arguments and to reinforce the media outlet's expertise. *The Marinovich Project* expands on Stephen Rodrick's 1998 *ESPN the Magazine* article on troubled former University of Southern California and Los Angeles Raiders quarterback Todd Marinovich. *The Ghosts of Ole Miss*, Fritz Mitchell's investigation of the relationship between the University of Mississippi's football

Like *SportsCentury*'s profiles, many ESPN Films productions integrate archived ESPN footage. Brett Morgen's *June 17, 1994* uses *SportsCenter* footage of Keith Olbermann commenting on O. J. Simpson's car chase down Interstate 5.

program and the school's racial integration, adapts Wright Thompson's 2010 *ESPN.com* feature article "Ghosts of Mississippi." Thompson, a Mississippian who often writes about his home state, plays a quasi-authorial role in the film by providing voice-over narration and explaining the research he conducted in the university's archive to uncover the school's divisive and misunderstood past.

Simmons and Schell steadfastly assert that *30 for 30* is a historical and creative endeavor that is unmotivated by ratings or revenues. Skipper even describes it as "a gift to our viewers."[46] Despite these ostensible motives, the documentaries were very deliberately scheduled to capitalize on and enhance ESPN's other programming. Extending the strategy it employed with *The Greatest Game Ever Played*'s premiere—which mimicked *The Junction Boys'* and *Codebreakers'* initial debuts—ESPN first aired the college football–themed documentaries *The U, Pony Exce$$, The Marinovich Project, You Don't Know Bo, The Youngstown Boys,* and *The U Part 2* after the Heisman Trophy presentation to retain the popular event's audience. Similarly, *The Guru of Go, The Fab Five, Survive and Advance,* and *Requiem for the Big East*—just like *A Season on the Brink* and *Black Magic*— premiered after ESPN's Selection Sunday special. ESPN premiered *The Two Escobars,* an exploration of the relationship between soccer and the drug trade in 1990s Colombia, amid its coverage of the 2010 World Cup.

Schell describes the *30 for 30* productions as "evergreen stories that ESPN can broadcast on multiple platforms for years to come." Accordingly, they are programmed across the network's channels to complement their areas of focus: ESPNU commonly airs college-themed selections, Deportes schedules the few that have Latin American themes, and Classic showcases them all because of their common engagement with sport's past. Clinkscales called *30 for 30* "a natural brand extension for Classic." Similar to *SportsCentury*'s migration to the channel after the series' initial run, *30 for 30* reruns have become a staple on Classic that are scheduled both arbitrarily and to commemorate events like Title IX and Black History Month. Classic also developed "ESPN Films on Classic," a series Schell describes as an "on-air film festival" that combines blocks of *30 for 30* productions with other documentaries ESPN acquires.[47] The *30 for 30* productions give these channels more proprietary content while allowing them to create less original material and to purchase fewer third party– produced programs. Combined with documentaries' relatively low production costs compared to live event coverage and scripted content, these practices suggest that while *30 for 30* may not have been designed to generate significant revenues, it was certainly developed in part to save money, appeal to the audiences its different channels attract, and lure new viewers.

Extending and Protecting *30 for 30*

The Peabody Award and International Documentary Association Distinguished Continuing Series prize that *30 for 30* earned after its initial run made it ESPN's most honored project since *SportsCentury*. Based on this success, ESPN opted to continue the series, without its focus on the years between 1979 and 2009. It was initially dubbed *ESPN Films Presents*, but ESPN returned to *30 for 30*—despite the title's inappropriateness—after noticing the brand's resonance. "We did [*ESPN Films Presents*] for a year," Schell explains, "and what we found was that every critic who wrote about it called it *30 for 30* and everybody on social media called it *30 for 30*. At first we tried to combat that, and then it became clear that rather than fight that, we should embrace it. We created a brand that had taken on meaning for people."[48]

Complementing *30 for 30*'s continuation and its documentaries' use across ESPN's channels, ESPN Films developed spin-off series to fuel different properties. For instance, in 2011 it began *SEC Storied*, an outgrowth of ESPN's partnership with the NCAA's Southeastern Conference that aired primarily on ESPNU until the ESPN-operated SEC Network's August 2014 launch. The SEC, in fact, requested that ESPN Films create a documentary series like *30 for 30* to explore its history—an endeavor the series' title reinforces by suggesting the SEC is a "storied" organization. The series, however, does not emphasize participating filmmakers, makes less pronounced appeals to film and cinema culture, and lacks *30 for 30*'s formal diversity. It offers straightforward and mostly celebratory profiles of famous and important SEC figures. *Herschel*, the series' first production, examines how University of Georgia running back Herschel Walker overcame racism and childhood bullying to lead his team to the 1980 national championship, win a Heisman, and enjoy a productive professional career. It ends with Walker praising the University of Georgia as "the start of everything," an endorsement that suggests the SEC facilitated his success in and beyond college. *Lolo* (Louisiana State University runner Lolo Jones), *Abby Head On* (University of Florida soccer player Abby Wambach), and *Croom* (Mississippi State University football coach Sylvester Croom) offer similarly congratulatory biographical portraits. They nurture ESPN's partnership with the SEC by glorifying the conference for a national audience and providing ESPNU and the SEC Network with content that complements their focus and can be flexibly scheduled.

In the summer of 2013, ESPN Films unveiled *Nine for IX* in collaboration with *ESPNW*, a women's sports website launched in 2010. Taking inspiration from Title IX, its nine documentaries focus on women-centered topics and are directed by women, qualities the series broadcasts with the tagline "By Women.

For All of Us." The productions explore—some more pointedly than others—women's struggles for gender equality in sport. For instance, Ava DuVernay's *Venus Vs.* explains Venus Williams's efforts to ensure female tennis players receive as much award money as their male counterparts in Wimbledon, Annie Sundberg and Ricki Stern's *Let Them Wear Towels* outlines women sports reporters' fight to gain access to men's locker rooms for postgame interviews, and Heidi Ewing and Rachel Grady's *Branded* explores the commercially motivated sexualization of female athletes.

Similar to the role Simmons plays in *30 for 30*, former ESPN anchor and *Good Morning America* host Robin Roberts serves as *Nine for IX*'s executive producer and figurehead. Also like *30 for 30*, *Nine for IX* emphasizes its cinematic pedigree by positioning its directors as visionaries with license to explore their inspiration, integrating filmmakers' perspectives on subject matter into the films' presentation and on the *Nine for IX* website, and packaging its documentaries with movie-ticket and filmstrip graphics. Prior to their appearance on ESPN, several *Nine for IX* films' exhibitions reinforced the series' combination of artistic quality with social consciousness. Bess Kargman's *Coach*, a brief profile of Rutgers University women's basketball coach C. Vivian Stringer, premiered at Tribeca and won its Best Documentary Short award. *Venus Vs.* and *Let Them Wear Towels* were unveiled as part of the Center for American Progress's Reel Progress film series. *Nine for IX* composes a variation on *30 for 30* that uses the series' emphasis on director-driven and cinematic documentaries to promote *ESPNW* and to emphasize ESPN's ostensible commitment to women in sport and in sport media.

Even more specific than *SEC Storied* or *Nine for IX*, *Soccer Stories* used a collection of two feature-length and six short documentaries to build anticipation for ESPN's and ABC's 2014 World Cup coverage. Dahl claims the success of *30 for 30*'s *The Two Escobars*—which stands among the series' most acclaimed titles—prompted ESPN Films to produce an entire lineup on soccer.[49] Moreover, and again building on *The Two Escobars*, *Soccer Stories*' documentaries focus entirely on international themes, which are mostly absent from *SportsCentury* and *30 for 30*. Their global emphasis familiarizes ESPN's and ABC's U.S.-based viewership with the World Cup's transnational participants while reaching out to the cosmopolitan audience the event attracts.

ESPN Films director of content development Libby Geist claims the subsidiary strives to ensure that *SEC Storied*, *Nine for IX*, and *Soccer Stories* are not treated or perceived as secondary to *30 for 30*. She asserts that only projects deemed suitable for inclusion in *30 for 30* are green-lighted for production as part of any ESPN Films series. However, ESPN typically reserves documentaries with the broadest potential audience—even if they complement a more specific series—for *30 for 30*. *You Don't Know Bo*, *The Ghosts of Ole Miss*, and *Bernie and Ernie* all concern the SEC and were released after *SEC Storied*'s launch. They were included in *30 for 30*, Dahl claims, because of their "national relevance." Along these lines, Geist claims *The Ghosts of Ole Miss* was originally slated for inclusion in *SEC Storied* but was eventually rebranded as a *30 for 30* production when ESPN Films recognized its potential popularity.[50] *The Book of Manning*—an account of former SEC quarterbacks Archie, Peyton, and Eli Manning's familial bonds—was branded as a *SEC Storied* documentary but programmed like a *30 for 30* to exploit its subject matter's salability. It premiered on ESPN during prime time one week before *30 for 30*'s fall 2013 lineup began and was eventually included in a *30 for 30* DVD box set. *The Ghosts of Ole Miss* and *The Book of Manning* suggest ESPN Films uses *30 for 30*'s brand and the programming practices associated with it to signal and capitalize on its documentaries' relative importance.

Similar practices inform *Nine for IX*'s place in ESPN Films' expanding roster of documentaries. Reflecting the legislation after which it is named, *Nine for IX* composed an unprecedented platform for sports documentaries about women and for women filmmakers in general. ESPN called attention to the series' significance and contribution to Title IX's sociopolitical mission by leading into its first installment, *Venus Vs.*, from a *SportsCenter* hosted by two women, Linda Cohn and Lindsay Czarniak. This uncommon—though not unprecedented—casting decision conspicuously suggests that ESPN participates in and pushes forward the advancements Title IX ushered. Indeed, prior to *Nine for IX*'s launch, only three of the forty-nine total *30 for 30* documentaries concerned women. A different set of three employed at least one female director.[51] The series, then, provides women greater representation but also runs the risk of further marginalizing women's content on ESPN by relegating ESPN Films documentaries about women to the less popular and less aggressively promoted *Nine for IX* series.

ESPN Films is sensitive to these risks and strives to ensure, in Geist's words, that ESPN is not "only telling female stories or working with female directors for *Nine for IX*," a perspective that *ESPNW* vice president Laura Gentile affirms.[52] However, the *30 for 30* lineup in the year following *Nine for IX* included only one woman-themed and -directed production, Nanette Burstein's *The Price of Gold*, which explored the 1994 scandal surrounding U.S. figure skaters Tonya Harding and Nancy Kerrigan. The documentary capitalized on the Harding-Kerrigan incident's status as one of sport's most infamous scandals and premiered directly before the 2014 Winter Olympics. The film's subject matter, coupled with the excitement surrounding the Olympics, gave it exceptionally widespread appeal. Its position as the sole women-centered *30 for 30* film since *Nine for IX* indicates that only those women-oriented documentaries that engage mainstream and immediately marketable topics will be included in the more visible series. Moreover, while *Nine for IX*'s documentaries premiered in prime time on ESPN's flagship channel, they did so across July and August—the sports calendar's slowest season. Although *Nine for IX* certainly provides new, productive, and needed spaces for women's participation on ESPN, the programming practices that separate its documentaries from those in *30 for 30* suggest the media outlet's traditionally limited commitment to women's content remains negligible as part of its most prominent series and during its peak seasons.

Programming "Decisions"

Amid *30 for 30*'s critically acclaimed maiden voyage, ESPN produced and aired *The Decision*, a one-hour July 8, 2010, prime-time special wherein NBA free agent LeBron James announced his plans to leave the Cleveland Cavaliers to join the Miami Heat—to take, as he infamously put it, his "talents to South Beach." James's free agency was among the year's biggest sport stories, and *The Decision* was a coup for ESPN during the relatively slow summer months. But James would give ESPN the rights to transform his decision into *The Decision* only if the network consented to pay all production costs; use Jim Gray, an independent sportscaster, as the interviewer; and donate all proceeds to the Boys & Girls Club of America. ESPN agreed, and *The Decision* became the network's second-highest-rated program of the year (after its live telecast of the NFL Pro Bowl), dwarfing the viewer numbers that even *30 for 30*'s most popular documentaries achieved.

Though a ratings success, *The Decision* was a critical nightmare. Commentators attacked its transformation of a brief announcement into an hour-long program as unnecessarily excessive and charged that the concessions ESPN made to secure James's cooperation—even though the money went to charity—evidence the outlet's disregard for journalistic standards. *Sports Illustrated*'s Richard Deitsch called it "the worst thing ESPN has ever put its name to," and the *National Post*'s Bruce Arthur dubbed it "the most crass, blind, tone-deaf, sycophantic, narcissistic, wretched hour in sports television history." "Does this not-so-subtle form of checkbook journalism," asked the *Washington Post*'s befuddled Leonard Shapiro, "pass the smell test anywhere else but in the Bristol, Conn. offices of the so-called worldwide leader?"[53]

Many of the critiques focused on *The Decision*'s resemblance to a competition-based reality TV show like ABC's *The Bachelor* wherein James dumped the Cavaliers for the Heat—resonances that prompted Buzz Bissinger to rename ESPN, "BSPN; America's bullshit leader."[54] Beyond noting *The Decision*'s formal resemblance to reality TV, these critiques suggest it shared the genre's stereotypical mindlessness. Indeed, the overwhelmingly negative response *The Decision* garnered echoed critical reception of EOE's mostly reviled game shows and reality series.

The series *30 for 30* was designed to be and was received as an antidote to the cultural decay that reality TV represents. As Deitsch observes, "In the same year that ESPN broadcast *The Decision*, the self-aggrandizing shamathon featuring LeBron James, the network also produced some of its finest content since its inception." In Schell's words, "As reality TV was sinking to new lows, we became intellectual and smart."[55] Though *30 for 30*'s ratings did not come close to rivaling those *The Decision* pulled in, its use of the documentary genre and presentation as uniquely artful enables ESPN to counter suggestions that it blindly chases ratings. *The Decision*'s and *30 for 30*'s coexistence suggests ESPN is at once responsible for sports media's proudest and most shameful moments. But this marriage is more complementary than contradictory—a schizophrenia ESPN embraces and transforms into symbiosis to safeguard its continued dominance of a multifaceted industry.

6

Grantland

ESPN's Miramax

What *Grantland* truly represents is an attempt to leverage Simmons's particular sensibility into a freestanding
publication.
—Jonathan Mahler, *New York Times*[1]

Grantland is a prestige product, meant less to run
quality work (though it does do that) than to run work
that's perceived to be quality.
—Tim Marchman, *Deadspin*[2]

In 2009 PEN American Center executive director Steve Isenberg propositioned
ESPN president John Skipper—a former English major with a soft spot for
literature—to cosponsor an annual award. The following year, these seemingly
disparate organizations inaugurated the PEN/ESPN Literary Sports Writing Award, which recognizes an exceptionally literary nonfiction book about
sports. PEN and ESPN added a lifetime achievement award in 2011 to honor
sportswriting's most memorable practitioners. Isenberg claims the partnership
allows PEN to prove it is "not just highbrow."[3] It also enables ESPN to assert
that it is far from lowbrow. The awards expand on *SportsCentury*'s organization
of sport's past, *Page 2*'s recruitment of celebrated journalists, and ESPN Films'
collaborations with Tribeca by suggesting ESPN shares PEN's ability to decide
what counts as "literary."

Complementing the PEN/ESPN Awards' development and riding *The Book
of Basketball*'s and *30 for 30*'s success, Bill Simmons left *Page 2* in 2011 to start

the sports and popular culture website *Grantland.com*—a hip alcove of *ESPN. com* that shares *Page 2*'s interest in popular culture but spans beyond sport. The ESPN-owned project takes its name after Grantland Rice, the "dean of American sportswriters" who is commonly recognized as the sportswriting canon's foundational figure. Despite his site's hallowed namesake, Simmons's work is not typically recognized as literary. "Simmons," Jonathan Mahler flippantly observes, "is not a literary sports writer. You can't capture his resonance with lyrical quotes from his oeuvre, because they don't really exist."[4] Simmons, however, combined Rice's powerful name with adaptations of *30 for 30*'s marketing strategies to brand the website, its content, and its editor as classy. *Grantland* specializes in long-form journalism, employs a combination of recognizable and up-and-coming writers, and situates itself as an outgrowth of and organizing authority over the sportswriting canon. It also teamed with the independent publisher McSweeney's to create *Grantland Quarterly*, a stylish collection of the website's best works packaged as hardcover books. These efforts separate *Grantland* from other sports and pop culture publications and position Simmons as the visionary who curated this exceptionally chic website, which eventually transformed into a multimedia hub that includes blogs, videos, and podcasts.

"To ESPN What Miramax Was to Disney"

Simmons's stock had never been higher in the months leading to *Grantland*'s June 11, 2011, launch. *The Book of Basketball* was a *New York Times* best seller, and *30 for 30* gathered ESPN's fourth Peabody. Furthermore, his contract was set to expire after 2010. The sports media Renaissance man used his rapidly escalating renown to negotiate a freestanding publication organized around his appreciation for the intersections between sports and pop culture. "I was going to do it whether I was at ESPN or not," he claims. "I want to do it with you guys. If you guys don't want to do this, I'm not going to be upset, but I'm going to do it somewhere."[5] ESPN indulged its superstar writer to retain his services and celebrity.

Simmons said his principal goal in developing *Grantland* "was to figure out how to capture the spirit and creativity of *30 for 30* and transfer it to a website." The site, which he claims was modeled after fashionable magazines like *Esquire*, *GQ*, *Inside Sports*, and *Spy*, would specialize in long-form journalism by recognizable writers—an adaptation of *30 for 30*'s engagement with cinema, the documentary genre, and established directors. To do this, he compiled what the *Boston Phoenix*'s Matt Parrish describes as an "A-Team-style masthead of nerdy badasses" from print and the Web. *Grantland*'s original editorial staff included *Awl.com* publisher David Cho, *New York Magazine*'s Lane Brown, *GQ*'s Dan

Fierman, *Harper's* Rafe Bartholomew, and the celebrity consulting editors Dave Eggers, Malcolm Gladwell, Chuck Klosterman, and Jane Leavy. Its staff and freelance writers ranged from *Esquire's* Chris Jones to *Deadspin's* Katie Baker to video game critic Tom Bissell. The website's development resembled *ESPN the Magazine's* recruitment of *Sports Illustrated* employees to fuel its launch. The similarly renowned, but far more diverse, collection of talent Simmons culled for his project, however, demonstrated *Grantland's* comparatively eclectic scope. The website also adopted *30 for 30's* sponsorship model by recruiting Subway—which was already sponsoring Simmons's podcast—Google, Lexis, and Unilever. This allowed *Grantland* to rely less on page clicks and to minimize the presence of ads, much like the ESPN Films documentaries' frequent presentation with limited commercial interruption, while enabling sponsors to identify with an exalted division of *ESPN.com*. "It's the quantity over quality trap," Simmons explained. "Everyone's chasing page views and I'm not sure that's always the way to go. We want to put up longer, more thought out stuff." Because of its personnel and design, Simmons boasted that *Grantland* would be "to ESPN what Miramax was to Disney, a boutique division with more room for creativity."[6]

Simmons's website most directly cultivates a literary image by appropriating Grantland Rice's name. When the site launched, it included the iconic final lines of Rice's "Alumnus Football" on its banner: "For when the One Great Scorer comes to mark against your name, / He writes—not that you won or lost—but how you played the Game." Above the quote, it placed an image of a hand—presumably Rice's hand—holding a fountain pen. Rice, however, famously wrote on a portable typewriter, and many photographs depict him posing next to one. Despite this historical inaccuracy, *Grantland's* design suggests the website continues the lionized sportswriting tradition Rice embodies and—like Rice—approaches the

Grantland's original home page marked the website as literary by including a passage from Grantland Rice's poem "Alumnus Football," an image of a hand (presumably Rice's hand) holding a fountain pen, and a portion of a George Lois photograph used for the *Esquire* magazine cover wherein Gay Talese's "The Silent Season of a Hero" appeared.

craft in an artisanal way. This nostalgic image contrasts blogging's laissez-faire repute and reflects Simmons's effort to brand *Grantland* with a sense of dignity that is not associated with his earlier work for *Page 2*.

Although it adopts Rice's powerful appellation, Grantland was branded as Simmons's aesthetic domain until he left. The link to the website on *ESPN. com* lists it as "Bill Simmons Presents *Grantland*." The site marks a transformation of him from the relatable "Sports Guy" into "Bill Simmons," an editorial visionary who binds the vaunted tradition Rice personifies to the digital age. "What *Grantland* truly represents," Mahler writes, "is an attempt to leverage Simmons's particular sensibility into a freestanding publication" that capitalizes on his salable style and passionate following in a manner similar to how Oprah Winfrey and Martha Stewart evolved into diversified brands that extend beyond their initial TV shows. In fact, *Grantland*'s content all bears Simmons's aesthetic stamp by including footnotes. The boutique website, however, distances itself from *ESPN.com*'s interactivity by excluding comments sections, a decision that gives its contributions an air of polished finality.

ESPN.com situated *Grantland*'s launch as an outstanding media event by embedding a countdown on its main page and slowly rolling out teases to provide readers with a sampling of the kinds of content they could expect. Simmons officially unveiled the outlet with a "Welcome to *Grantland*" editorial note that explained his mission to craft a free website that features uniquely creative voices.[7] During its first several months, for example, the website featured Steven Hyden's commentary on Stanley Kubrick's seldom-discussed first film, *Fear and Desire* (1954); Jay Caspian Kang's discussion of professional baseball player Ichiro Suzuki's complex racial meaning; Tom Bissell's look at how video games use narrative; Anna Clark's analysis of the controversial Detroit Tigers legend Ty Cobb as a metaphor for the city's history; Simmons's thought piece on the differences between movie stars and sports stars; and MacArthur Award winner Colson Whitehead's four-part creative nonfiction essay on the World Series of Poker. Whitehead's contributions, in fact, composed the foundation for a book he published in 2014, *The Noble Hustle: Poker, Beef Jerky, and Death*. While not all of *Grantland*'s articles concern sport, those that do consistently probe its cultural resonances. For instance, Wesley Morris periodically writes the "Sportstorialist" column, a riff on the popular fashion website *The Sartorialist* that comments on the intersections between sport and fashion.

Grantland also situates its content as a daring alternative to mainstream sportswriting. Morris, for example, published a short profile on the New England Patriots' fun-loving tight end Rob Gronkowski less than two weeks after *Sports Illustrated*'s Chris Ballard published his own piece on the budding star.

Ballard's "The Last Happy Man" offers a lively and straightforward account of how Gronkowski has adjusted to his newfound fame and expresses hope that the exuberant young man will retain his accessibility and zeal as he acclimates to the limelight and its attendant pressures. Though demonstrating a similar appreciation for Gronkowski's joie de vivre, Morris's "The Tao of Gronk" places the tight end's marketable persona into a more complex framework by claiming that his mischievousness reeks of straight white male privilege. Gronkowski's racial identity, Morris incisively points out, affords the tight end a degree of goofiness that would be read differently were he not white. The piece functions as a response to Ballard—and to *Sports Illustrated*—that demonstrates *Grantland*'s apparent willingness to wrestle with politically loaded nuances that conventional sports media outlets often elide.[8]

Grantland expands on Simmons's signature use of popular culture to illuminate sport by employing sports vernacular and metrics to explain pop culture. In a column on his beloved *The Breaks of the Game*, Simmons laments art's inability to be organized according to the satisfyingly tidy and mostly quantitative criteria used to make sense of sport. "I believe Michael Jordan is the greatest basketball player ever, and I can prove it. I believe *The Breaks of the Game* is the greatest sports book ever and I can't prove it. Books can't be measured that way—they hit everyone differently, so when we're evaluating them, we can only say, 'You can't mention the greatest books (or albums, paintings, TV shows, movies or whatever) without mentioning that one.'"[9] *Grantland*, however, routinely—and lightheartedly—filters culture through sports-specific analytic frameworks. Chuck Klosterman's "Rock VORP" adopts the arcane baseball statistic Value over Replacement Player, which measures individual players' value by comparing them to a fictional player at the same position with average statistics, to determine which popular rock band has the greatest overall talent. Katie Baker's "Matrimonial Moneyball" creates a comparable statistical model to rank the pedigree of the high-society couples featured in the Sunday *New York Times*' wedding announcements. Along these lines, *Grantland* uses the structure of the NCAA basketball tournament bracket to judge, for instance, the best character on HBO's *The Wire* or the funniest *Chappelle's Show* sketch. These selections make no pretense to accuracy, objectivity, or even usefulness. Rather, they humanize and make fun of sports analysis while packaging popular culture into a defamiliarizing form.

Grantland complements its wide-ranging articles with podcasts, video series, and *The Triangle* and *Hollywood Prospectus* blogs, which, respectively, focus on sports updates and entertainment news. *Hollywood Prospectus* further evidences *Grantland*'s appropriation of sports language to explain culture by evoking the statistics-driven baseball publication *Baseball Prospectus*. Like the main website's use of Rice's hand and pen to signal its distinction, these different sections emphasize their quality through adopting retro technologies as logos. The Grantland Channel uses a film camera as its trademark, and the podcasts employ a vintage radio microphone to suggest their digital content continues these earlier sports media traditions and is produced with similar care.

Grantland also publishes companion articles for ESPN Films' documentaries, and in May 2012 it became the home of *30 for 30 Shorts*, a series of short documentaries that Simmons described as "a logical extension in *30 for 30's* evolution and *Grantland's* evolution too." Connor Schell calls the short films "visual editorials . . . that don't require four-act treatment" and that offer filmmakers greater creative flexibility. "If I can hear [*This American Life* host] Ira Glass introduce it," explained Dan Silver of the series' focus and ambitions, "it would work as a *30 for 30* Short."[10] Aside from fostering convergence between *Grantland* and ESPN Films, the Web-based short films—which gathered a 2014 Creative Arts Emmy Award and inspired ESPNW to create a series of *Nine for IX Shorts*—are more easily circulated than ESPN Films' full-length documentaries. ESPN ensures their shareability beyond its propertied domain by using media players that are compatible with most major social media platforms.

Grantland symbolically distances itself from ESPN's brand—a separation its parent company nurtures—while benefiting from ESPN's resources and cross-promotion. The specialty website contains only a single link to *ESPN.com* and otherwise bears none of the Worldwide Leader's marks. It emphasizes this autonomy by providing its contributors with creative latitude—such as the ability to use profanity—that neither *ESPN the Magazine* nor *ESPN.com* offers. "Grantland's appeal, not least to Simmons," explains *Deadspin* editor Tommy Craggs, "is its seeming independence." *Grantland* was actually set to hire Craggs until he wrote a scathing article about *ESPN.com* blogger Lynn Hoppes. ESPN management balked, Craggs and his *Deadspin* colleagues continued to write about his prospective employer in their characteristically dissident style, and the deal eventually dissolved. Craggs commented on the site's prospects shortly after his aborted hire: "I think [*Grantland*] will be great to the extent that it can keep Bristol at arm's length. I'm pessimistic about that part."[11] Craggs's critique suggests that *Grantland's* independence is a clever facade that obscures its thoroughly corporate innards.

Grantland reinforces its literary image and symbolic distinction from ESPN by capitalizing on long-form journalism's rising prominence online. "Long-form's demographic," observes media scholar Robert S. Boynton, "is the envy of any advertiser: young (fifty percent of the readers are under 34), mobile (thirty percent read primarily on phones or tablets), and well educated (forty-two percent have attended graduate school)." To be sure, this demographic overlaps with the middle-class audience that ESPN and Simmons pursue. Also, like feature-length films, long form is relatively sticky; consumers spend more time with these texts—and the ads they deliver—than other articles.[12]

Mahler complains that the term *long form* is carelessly used to brand longer material as literary. *Grantland*'s David Cho perpetuates what Mahler decries as the gimmicky "cult of long-form" by claiming the site set out "to prove long-form content still had a place online, that everything didn't have to be short bite-size nuggets."[13] Despite Cho's claim, *ESPN.com* featured lengthy articles prior to *Grantland*'s emergence and has continued to include such materials since the website's launch. Many of its narrative and investigative features—such as Wright Thompson's consistently award-winning work—are just as complex, carefully reported, and culturally aware as *Grantland*'s content. Though indisputably long, these *ESPN.com* articles are not explicitly marketed as "long form." Likewise, *Grantland* consistently posts brief reports and analyses that would be at home among *ESPN.com*'s typically more straightforward and news-driven content. Though short, these posts are steeped in *Grantland*'s belabored status as ESPN's home for long form. Like ESPN Films' strategic reliance on documentary, Grantland exploits and reinforces long form's symbolic value to separate further its material—regardless of its word count—from ESPN's typical content and to capture the coveted audience that the trendy generic signifier attracts.

The controversy surrounding Caleb Hannan's 2014 article "Dr. V's Magic Putter" illustrates *Grantland*'s reliance on long form's cachet. Hannan's piece focused on Essay Anne Vanderbilt, the enigmatic inventor of the YAR golf putter. The first-person account revolves around Hannan's quest to learn about this inscrutable figure. In the process, he discovers that Vanderbilt had falsified many of her biographical details—including her claims to possess a doctorate—and is transgender. He also reveals that Vanderbilt, who suffered from clinical depression, had killed herself between his reporting and the story's publication.

Soon after Hannan's piece appeared, critics attacked the article as insensitive and irresponsible.[14] They charged that Hannan (and his editors at *Grantland*) had no right to call attention to Vanderbilt's sexuality—even posthumously—without her blessing, that her sexuality was incidental to the story and used purely to sensationalize, and, most damningly, that Hannan's reportage may have contributed to her suicide. ESPN ombudsman Robert Lipsyte reiterated these charges. He claimed the piece "lacked understanding, empathy and in-

trospection" and that it constituted an "inexcusable instance of how the con-
ditioned drive to get to the core of a story can block the better angles of a journalist's nature and possibly lead to tragic consequences." Moreover, he asserted
the piece evinces *Grantland*'s tendency to privilege the fashionable long-form
genre over rigorous and ethical reportage. He called it "bloated" and part of
an alarming wave of unnecessarily elongated works that "clog the arteries of
sports-lit these days."[15] The piece would have been better, Lipsyte implies, if it
paid less attention to length and more to content. Lipsyte's critique implicates
Grantland in the "quantity over quality trap" that Simmons promised his site
would avoid.

Simmons published a mea culpa that acknowledged *Grantland*'s "collective
ignorance about the issues facing the transgender community in general, as well
as our biggest mistake: not educating ourselves on that front before seriously
considering whether to run the piece."[16] Though Simmons takes responsibility for the article's oversights, he also claims the costly mistake occurred in the
service of *Grantland*'s grandiose creative and journalistic ambitions. He frames
his apology with a quote from legendary University of California at Los Angeles basketball coach John Wooden—"If you're not making mistakes, you're
not doing anything"—and suggests Hannan's article was a slipup that would
result in even better work. Simmons thus uses the negligent piece to appeal to
Grantland's general quality; it is a careless aberration that proves the thoughtful
norm.

Beyond its appeals to and production of long form, *Grantland* constructs
its image by engaging well-known aesthetic traditions, specifically the sports
journalism and literature canons. Shortly after *Grantland*'s launch, *Slate*'s Tom
Scocca poked fun at the website's posturing. "Simmons's podcast," he quipped,
"will henceforth be known as *Mercury Theater on the Air* [the title of Orson
Welles's 1938 radio series] and his football gambling picks columns will be
retitled *A Fan's Notes* [the name of Frederick Exley's 1968 novel]." *Grantland*'s
Triangle blog actually includes a recurring column titled "A Fan's Notes"—a
direct reference to Exley's book. Along these lines, in 2011 Simmons featured
John Walsh on his podcast to discuss Hunter S. Thompson's life and brief stint
at *Page 2*. Walsh maintained that "Hunter would have loved Grantland."[17] The
website, he suggests, embodies Thompson's diverse tastes and iconoclastic
literary sophistication.

Like its editor, *Grantland* balances its appeals to highbrow culture with a
steadfast resistance to pomposity. In 2012 Amos Barshad posted a brief commentary on a recently discovered 1985 letter David Foster Wallace wrote to
the Amherst College newspaper while attending the school. In the dispatch,

Wallace rebuts another student's grievance that the college's restrictions against playing loud music—in this case, the Australian hard rock band AC/DC—were unduly authoritarian. In the process, he smugly dismisses AC/DC as puerile garbage. Perplexed by this discovery, Barshad observes that Wallace "never particularly seemed like a snob. . . . His tastes were catholic—and yet, he had no room in his heart for the simple joy of a sweat-drenched, beshorted Angus Young shredding on his Gibson SG." Barshad's piece demonstrates *Grantland's* familiarity with and appreciation for Wallace while affirming the populism upon which Simmons built his readership. The website, Barshad indicates, forges a unique space that satisfies readers interested in contemporary literature, avoids alienating rock fans, and reaches out to those who enjoy both Wallace and AC/DC. Similarly, John Brandon's commentary on George Plimpton's *Paper Lion* (1966) humorously and long-windedly reviews the famous volume as a "book for dudes (and non-dudes?) who are smart but don't have the time and/or inclination to sift through the offerings of literary fiction and who could use a solid recommendation or two and who, if they ignore that recommendation, will feel guilty and think a little less of themselves because they know that quality reading improves the quality of the individual."[18] Like Barshad's discussion, Brandon suggests *Grantland* satisfies a variety of reader that does not readily identify with stereotypes surrounding book culture and those who populate it. It is an implied male reader who enjoys books but is not bookish.

Echoing *SportsCentury's* and *30 for 30's* historical interventions, *Grantland* suggests that ESPN possesses the authority to organize the American sportswriting canon. In July 2011, it created the "Sports Book Hall of Fame," a series wherein its writers "induct" works into this elite group. The articles provide synopses that situate the selected books within the history of sportswriting and offer context for readers unfamiliar with their authors and subject matter. For instance, Jane Leavy's discussion of *Ball Four* outlines Bouton's literary predecessors, the many works he influenced, and his broader impact on investigative sports journalism. Moreover, Leavy maintains that *Grantland* would not exist without the road *Ball Four's* subversive style paved—a statement that both emphasizes the memoir's crucial significance and positions *Grantland* as a direct descendant of it.

Three months after *Grantland* inducted the Sports Book Hall of Fame's "inaugural class," it developed the similar "Director's Cut" series. Edited by Michael MacCambridge, the series provides new takes on "classic works of sports journalism." MacCambridge writes a brief introduction to each article that profiles its author, explains its importance to the history of sports journalism, and outlines the cultural and institutional contexts surrounding it. His introduction to Gay Talese's "The Silent Season of a Hero"—a 1966 *Esquire* profile of the notoriously private retired baseball star Joe DiMaggio—explains Talese's role in the 1960s "New Journalism" and outlines the measures he took to secure DiMaggio's reluctant cooperation. The "Director's Cut" pieces also include footnotes that provide additional information about the featured works, their production, and their legacy—much of which derives from interviews MacCambridge conducts with the still-living authors and others involved in the articles' publication. In a footnote to Talese's piece, MacCambridge mentions that *Grantland* briefly used George Lois's cover photograph from the *Esquire* issue in which it appeared—a man swinging a baseball bat in an empty ballpark—as its banner image prior to the website's official launch. The factoid both offers context impossible to glean from simply reading Talese's piece and, like Leavy's discussion of *Ball Four*, asserts *Grantland*'s relationship to this classic work of sportswriting and the magazine that published it.

Extending the credibility *Grantland*'s affirmation and illumination of sportswriting's established canon cultivate, the website introduces new and lesser-known works into this group. In 2012 Simmons teamed with Hock to produce an article and *30 for 30 Short*—part of a subseries of Hock-directed shorts branded as "Hockumentaries" to emphasize the filmmaker's distinct voice and to locate ESPN as its home—on the obscure children's sports fiction writer Alfred Slote and his 1971 novel, *Jake*. Slote's book, which had been out of print since 1981, tells the story of a tough and world-weary African American boy who finds joy in baseball despite his troubled home life. In his article, Simmons outlines his lifelong affection for Slote, whom he counts along with Halberstam as a key literary influence, and laments the novelist's exclusion from a canon dominated by the similar author Matt Christopher. "For whatever reason, Matt Christopher grabbed the 'readable sports books for little kids' corner in the late '70s and never relinquished it. In my mind, Slote was filet mignon and Christopher was ground beef." Simmons asserts Slote's important place in the history of children's sports literature and encourages renewed interest in his undervalued work. As he wistfully writes, "Maybe someday *Jake* will be back in print and the world will make sense again."[19]

Hock's companion documentary expands on Simmons's argument for Slote's literary merits. It does so by representing Slote as a creature of print. The film includes graphic sequences and intertitles that use the sound and font of a typewriter—a technology Slote prefers to computers. Moreover, it features the elderly writer's commentary on the creative advantages of writing on a typewriter as opposed to a computer: "A typewriter is a writing machine and a computer is an editing machine; and the books that come out of a typewriter are very different from the books that come out of a computer. The process changes the product because you have a chance to make things perfect as you go with the computer and there's a real loss of innocence." Hock's nostalgic tribute—similar to *Grantland*'s anachronistic evocation of Rice's pen—links Slote's unique artistry to the outmoded writing technology he employs. The film combines with Simmons's article to indicate that *Grantland* protects Slote's underappreciated typewritten books and gives them the credit they deserve.

In fact, Simmons and Hock's transmedia package compelled Slote to republish his baseball books in 2013. Slote used the endorsement as the centerpiece of his efforts to publicize the books via his personal website.[20] *Grantland*'s celebration of Slote suggests that Simmons's website breathes new life into the history of sportswriting—online and on bookshelves. It takes inspiration from sportswriting's canon, asserts the authority to decide which works belong in that exclusive group, and preserves, elucidates, and even reinvents the genre's print heritage.

Soon after Simmons left *Page 2* to start *Grantland*, his former *ESPN.com* home rebranded as *Playbook*, a short-lived venture geared toward young readers that emphasized gaming and social media. As *ESPN.com* senior director Lynn Hoppes—the employee Craggs heckled while in preliminary negotiations with *Grantland*—noted, "With *ESPN.com* you already have the main news side, you have the long-form site in *Grantland* and now you have *Playbook*, which focuses on entertaining you in a short-attention span way."[21] *Grantland*'s highbrow aspirations compelled *ESPN.com* to produce content that, by Hoppes's admission, is intentionally shallow. Moreover, the website's engagements with sportswriting's print heritage motivated *ESPN the Magazine* to integrate *Playbook*'s Web-specific design into its opening section to form an even closer relationship to its youthful audience. As *Page 2*, in John Skipper's words, "magazine'd" *ESPN.com*, *Grantland*'s emergence motivated the media outlet to "website" its magazine. These practices suggest that *Grantland*—despite its digital status—in some ways has more in common with traditional print magazines than does *ESPN the Magazine*. Beyond demonstrating how media convergence muddies the technological and ideological divisions that traditionally separate media, these developments illuminate how ESPN uses practices and attitudes commonly tied to particular media to build valuable niches in other contexts.

Grantland combines its engagements with sportswriting's print tradition with appeals to its cutting edge online. In December 2012, the *New York Times* published John Branch's "Snow Fall: The Avalanche at Tunnel Creek" as a multimedia feature conducive to the increasingly popular tablet technology. The piece integrates Branch's long-form article on a group of skiers caught in a deadly avalanche in the Cascade Mountains with video content, interactive maps, and biographical profiles on the main subjects that are animated by users scrolling through the article. It was immediately heralded as a beacon of online journalism's future, garnered a Pulitzer, and inspired other Web outlets to create similarly glitzy and tablet-friendly products. *New York Times* executive editor Jill Abramson boasts that *snow fall* quickly became a verb in the journalism industry that signals the act of transforming long-form features into immersive multimedia pieces. "Everyone wants to snow fall now," she remarked.[22] *Grantland* was among the first to do so. In May 2013, the website packaged Brian Phillips's account of the Alaskan Iditarod Trail Sled Dog Race, "Out in the Great Alone," as a multimedia feature. The piece's wintry aesthetic and focus on dangerous extreme sports place it into dialogue with "Snow Fall" and, just as important, assert that *Grantland*, like the *New York Times*, can "snow fall" content.

Grantland's initial success compelled other established sports media outlets to create similar boutique offshoots that feature celebrity staff and focus on long-form content. Most similar to *Grantland*'s personality-driven format, in 2013 *Sports Illustrated* NFL reporter Peter King used his expiring contract to negotiate a stand-alone website spin-off of his popular "Monday Morning Quarterback" column that features a handpicked collection of writers. As *Grantland* is organized around and expands on Simmons's pop cultural sensibility, King's *MMQB* focuses entirely on the NFL, trades on the decorated sportswriter's "insider" access, and gives its figurehead the editorial autonomy to indulge his interests in what he describes as less "filtered" and longer forms than *Sports Illustrated*'s regular magazine and website generally permit.[23]

Several more broadly focused specialty sports websites emerged to inflect their parent organizations with the type of respectability *Grantland* cultivates for ESPN. The Vox Media–owned sports blog network SB Nation created *SB Nation Longform* to coincide with its September 2012 redesign. Prior to the revamp, SB Nation's member blogs had dispersed looks. The network's long-form division endeavored to fashion a brand that would unite its many affiliates and offset their typically immediate focus on game reports and gossip. To build and market *SB Nation Longform*'s quality, Vox hired *Best American Sports Writing* series editor Glenn Stout—a recognized gatekeeper of quality long-form sportswriting—as its editor in chief. Stout claims that "it was easy to confuse what [SB Nation] was doing with *Bleacher Report* or *Buzzfeed*" before the redesign. "The long-form program was started," he explains, "to say 'Look, this is a site that wants to do good writing. We're not those other sites.'"[24] SB

Nation used Stout's reputation and long form's stylishness to make clear that it is more than a hub for brief updates or "listicles."

One month before *SB Nation Longform*'s launch, *USA Today* and MLB Advanced Media, a subsidiary of Major League Baseball, teamed to create *Sports on Earth*. Helmed by former *Inside Sports* and *Sports Illustrated* senior editor Larry Burke, the site recruited a collection of nationally recognized writers that included Dave Kindred, Gwen Knapp, Leigh Montville, Joe Posnanski, and Will Leitch in an effort to, as MLB Advanced Media vice president Dinn Mann put it, "restore the great tradition of sports writing and great storytelling." *Sports on Earth*'s comparative freedom from an established sports media organ like ESPN or SB Nation, Posnanski claimed, would propel these audacious journalistic strides. "Perhaps the best thing," he commented, "is that we're not saddled with any legacy issues. We literally had a blank board on what we wanted this to be."[25] By contrast, *Sports Illustrated*'s "Longform since 1954" initiative, which launched in October 2013 and spans the publication's print and digital platforms, suggests the legacy magazine has been producing this complex brand of journalism all along. In an introduction to the project, *Sports Illustrated* managing editor Matt Bean avers that long form is in the publication's "very DNA."[26] *Sports Illustrated* uses the genre's symbolic value to emphasize its quality while claiming status as the fashionable journalistic form's foundation.

Though adopting slightly different styles and concentrations, these boutique sites share a focus on long form, prominent staff, and minimized advertising. More important, they all have corporate backing. Despite the sites' sponsorship deals—most of which are tied to larger agreements made with their parent organizations—critics suggest these specialized outlets would not last independent of their attachment to powerful and diversified media conglomerates.[27] These corporate parents principally invest in the sites' potential to build a refined image. "*Grantland* is a prestige product," writes *Deadspin*'s Tim Marchman, "meant less to run quality work (though it does do that) than to run work that's perceived to be quality. It's no secret at *Grantland* that ESPN president John Skipper wants his tasteful loss leader to win awards and to play on the same field as the slicks [print magazines]." Similarly, Vox CEO Jim Bankoff admits that *SB Nation Longform* "is less about traffic generation than it is about creating brands."[28] These already wealthy outlets do not need their boutique websites to generate revenue. Instead, they invest in these sites' potential to deliver respectability—and the relatively upscale audiences it attracts—that their more immediately lucrative and mainstream properties do not relay. As *Grantland* used Phillips's "Out in the Great Alone" to show that it—like the *New*

York Times—could "Snow Fall," SB Nation, *USA Today* and MLB Advanced Media, and *Sports Illustrated* employed their boutique websites to suggest that they—like ESPN—can "*Grantland.*"

There are independent sites that offer content similar to, and even edgier than, *Grantland* and the specialty outlets it inspired. For instance, a group of writers and editors from the popular basketball-focused blog *FreeDarko* (2005–11) began a Kickstarter fund-raising campaign to create *The Classical* in 2011. Cofounder Nathaniel Friedman, who writes under the pseudonym Bethlehem Shoals, describes the website as "a DIY version of a large-scale project" and a "post-punk" approach to sportswriting that, like its predecessor, would not include advertisements.[29] The site takes its name, in fact, from a song by the postpunk band the Fall. This countercultural sensibility and DIY ethos prompted *Business Insider's* Noah Davis to describe *The Classical* as the "Anti-*Grantland.*"[30] But, and as corporate entities are wont to do, *Grantland* and its big-budget peers hired away several of *FreeDarko's* and *The Classical's* best-known contributors. Upon leaving, these writers often do not have the time to continue writing as frequently for the indie website and in some cases are contractually forbidden from doing so. *Classical* editor David Roth, who oversees the site while earning his principal income by serving as an SB Nation staffer, claims he "would have liked to keep" those writers who left. He does not, however, hold a grudge against these corporate outlets for poaching his staff, nor does he blame those writers—most of whom contributed to *The Classical* for little or no compensation—for joining well-paying sites. Despite *The Classical's* independence and punk spirit, Roth admits that "the exigencies of the [cash-strapped] position we're in are not very liberating." These difficulties, he contends, effectively transformed *The Classical* into a "farm team" that corporate sites use to scout talent.[31]

Even though *The Classical* seldom pays its writers and despite its successful Kickstarter campaign, the website cannot afford the sleek design that well-funded outlets like *Grantland* adopt, aesthetics they use in part to construct—however dubiously—an aura of artisanal independence similar to how ESPN Films codes its Disney-funded productions as indie. While *The Classical* is unencumbered by the larger institutional pressures that weigh on its corporate competitors, it is ironically unable to adopt their look. *Grantland* and the boutique sites it spawned showcase big media outlets building credibility by filtering their content through a framework that signals independence, but is impossible—or at least highly unlikely—for truly independent sites to afford. In doing so, they foster an online sportswriting industry that makes it increasingly difficult for independent voices to subsist without corporate assistance and the many institutional strings attached to it.

McSweeney's for Sports Geeks

Grantland arose amid ESPN's brief flirtation with sports fiction. In 2009 *ESPN the Magazine* profiled the Web-based literary sports journal *Stymie*, a little-known publication that began as a print item devoted entirely to golf fiction in 2008 and folded in 2014. The profile evolved into a cosponsored sports fiction contest—the winner of which would appear in *ESPN the Magazine*.[32] After its contest with *Stymie*, *ESPN the Magazine* teamed with the higher-profile independent publisher McSweeney's—an organization founded by Dave Eggers that produces the literary journal *Timothy McSweeney's Quarterly Concern* as well as books, magazines, and a website—to curate an issue devoted to sports fiction. Published in March 2011, "The Fiction Issue" included a collection of stories ranging from Eggers's "My Life in Baseball," a wacky surrealist memoir written from the perspective of San Francisco Giants relief pitcher Brian Wilson's signature beard, to Jess Walter's "Bleacher Couch Man," a darkly humorous story about an underachieving middle-aged divorcé who decides to turn his languishing life around after getting in a fight during a rec-league basketball game. Walter, a finalist for the 2006 National Book Award, observes that there are few popular outlets that publish short fiction and jokes that "writing fiction with men as an audience is a good way to starve to death." "The Fiction Issue," he explains, exposed his work to readers who otherwise would have been unlikely to encounter it.[33]

ESPN the Magazine editor Gary Belsky claims "The Fiction Issue" exemplifies ESPN's "mission to push the boundaries of sports media." "The merger of sports and fiction," the magazine's editors contend in the issue's introduction, "is as ancient as the *Iliad* (wrestling) and as contemporary as *Twilight* (baseball). But we think we're the first sports magazine to publish an issue dedicated to made-up stuff."[34] They thought wrong. The well-known weekly magazine *Golf World* has produced several fiction issues. Given *Golf World*'s renown and the fact that famous sportswriters like Dan Jenkins, Leigh Montville, and ESPN's own Rick Reilly had published fiction in its special issues, it is unlikely that *ESPN the Magazine*'s editors were, as they suggest, unaware of it. Other publications, like *Stymie*, are wholly devoted to sports fiction, poetry, and art, such as *Spitball: The Literary Baseball Magazine* (1981–), *Elysian Fields Quarterly* (1981–95, 1998–2009), *Aethlon: The Journal of Sport Literature* (1983–), and *Sport*

Literate (1995–).³⁵ These venues evidence a vibrant—if obscure—tradition of sports fiction out of which "The Fiction Issue" grows. *ESPN the Magazine*, however, ignores this heritage en route to positioning itself as an innovator in this marginal genre of sports media—a role that its partnership with a trendy outfit like McSweeney's broadcasts.

Grantland expanded on *ESPN the Magazine* and McSweeney's partnership with *Grantland Quarterly*, a hardcover product that repackages *Grantland's* best work along with previously unpublished articles, original artwork, and accoutrements like stickers, paper dolls, and postcards that require material form to serve their designed purpose. Volume 2, for instance, features a book cover that folds out into a reproduction of a retro Nike poster of San Antonio Spurs star George "Iceman" Gervin. The *Quarterly's* first four volumes include McSweeney's-curated stories that did not previously appear on *Grantland*, such as Walter's "Hadel's Wife," a continuation of the fictional world he created for "Bleacher Couch Man" wherein the same characters wrestle with existential and moral dilemmas over beers after a basketball game. David Cho claims the *Quarterly* and its showy accessories "differentiate [*Grantland*] from other sports websites." Moreover, its bonus material is sometimes edgier than *Grantland's* already relatively risqué content. For example, Jamie Allen's short story "Reunion" presents an awkward reconnection between two male friends that includes the memory of their adolescent sexual encounter. The stories also contain headier references to art and culture than *Grantland's* mostly mainstream evocations. The eponymous protagonist of "Hadel's Wife," a community college philosophy instructor, shares meandering theories on life that reference Aquinas, Augustine, Hegel, Kant, and Nietzsche. Thomas Mullen's "The Art of a Basketball" concerns a hapless young art conservator tasked with restoring an installation based on Jeff Koons's "One Ball Total Equilibrium Tank" (1985). *Grantland Quarterly's* ornate design and apparent willingness to test ESPN's normal creative boundaries provoked the *Los Angeles Times'* David Ulin to describe it as "an issue of *McSweeney's* [*Quarterly Concern*] for the sports geek in all of us."³⁶

While using ESPN Books would have allowed ESPN to recoup a greater percentage of *Grantland Quarterly's* profits, McSweeney's, the winner of two National Magazine Awards, has more aesthetic credibility than this mainstream corporate imprint. Beyond benefiting from McSweeney's brand, *Grantland's* collaboration with Eggers's publishing house allowed ESPN to infiltrate new markets and commercial settings. *Grantland Quarterly*, for example, is routinely sold at the independent bookstores that carry McSweeney's other products. ESPN's partnership with McSweeney's—which ended after just one year—placed this corporate item

into association with independently published products, a status ESPN Books'
titles do not enjoy that enables the company to court consumers who are less
likely to patronize its more mainstream products.[37]

Beyond its initial alliance with McSweeney's, the *Quarterly* mimics other
independent websites' forays into print culture. *FreeDarko*, for example, published two books: *The Macrophenomenal Pro Basketball Almanac* (2008) and *The
Undisputed Guide to Pro Basketball* (2010). They combined *FreeDarko*'s take on
NBA history and statistics with its graphic novel–inspired artistic renderings
of the sport, most of which were designed by Jacob Weinstein. *The Classical*
has continued *FreeDarko*'s aesthetic by commissioning artists to create illustra-
tions to accompany its articles. While this Web-based artwork contributes to
FreeDarko's and *The Classical*'s indie aesthetic, it is also a product of financial
necessity. These sites do not possess the resources to purchase the rights to
reproduce photographs from outlets like Getty Images. To sidestep this constraint, they recruit illustrators, who, like their writers, typically work gratis.[38]
Grantland Quarterly's artwork imitates *FreeDarko*'s and *The Classical*'s aesthetic,
and it often hires the artists these websites feature. The *Quarterly* no doubt
provides these illustrators with resources and visibility that the independent
websites, and the books they produce, cannot furnish. In the process—and
reflecting its incorporation of *FreeDarko*'s and *The Classical*'s writers—it claims
these creative templates as its signature look.

The *Quarterly* extends "Sports Book Hall of Fame" and "Director's Cut" series'
efforts to mediate the sportswriting canon by suggesting that *Grantland*'s content
deserves canonization. It continues a tradition of well-known magazines—a list
that includes *Sports Illustrated*, the *New Yorker*, and *Harper's*—anthologizing their
sportswriting in book form. In doing so, it places ESPN on par with these legacy
print publications. Volume 1 even evokes *Harper's* by including a list of sports
factoids in the ironic style of the magazine's "Harper's Index."

Similarly, the *Quarterly* suggests *Grantland*'s content possesses literary value
that necessitates print publication. "If our site has a problem," Dan Fierman
explains, "it's that we move so fast that readers miss stuff. The print journal
serves up the site's greatest hits in a medium better suited to long-form journalism." Despite *Grantland*'s digital status, Fierman claims the website's literary content is best appreciated via print, books in particular. Simmons even
argues the print product has the potential to "bring boring Internet columns
to life."[39] The *Quarterly*, they indicate, provides the sort of reading experience
that *Grantland*'s uniquely polished content demands.

In fact, the *Quarterly* takes pains to announce its materiality. Its first volume
boasted a faux-leather cover made to look and feel like a basketball with Sim-

mons's signature etched into it—a feature that mimics the placement of the NBA commissioner's autograph on official league balls and further reinforces Simmons's status as *Grantland*'s leader. Shortly after *Grantland Quarterly*'s debut, *Deadspin* created a snarky video that lampooned the publication as a gratuitous repackaging of mediocre content that was already available for free online. Titled "What Is the Grantland Book Good For?," the video features a ragtag group of young *Deadspin* interns putting an issue of the *Quarterly* through a battery of comic tests to make light of its materiality and to determine what purpose this print product could possibly serve that its website does not. The *Quarterly* cannot, they conclude, be used to play badminton, clean up a spill, or shoot baskets. It does, however, float, can serve as a bong, and extinguishes fires. In their most clever and condemning critique, the interns drop the *Quarterly* onto a computer keyboard and decide the nonsensical jumble of letters its impact generates qualifies it to write for Simmons's publication. The video ends by dismissing the *Quarterly* as a gimmick—a crass way for Simmons and ESPN to squeeze additional profits out of the website—and then blowing it up with fireworks.

Grantland Quarterly's use of the book, however, is more calculated than *Deadspin*'s sarcastic video suggests. Beyond employing the older medium to recirculate online content, the *Quarterly* exploits its cultural meanings to sculpt a refined image. Volume 8, for instance, features a burgundy imitation-leather cover with gold-leaf lettering. Though ironic, the classic storybook-style cover signals the *Quarterly*'s entrenchment and investment in book culture. Volume 10's cover continues this sentiment by adopting the look of a bookshelf. Simmons uses books' stereotypical repute as objects uninterested in commercial gain to market *Grantland Quarterly* as a labor of love. "Just know that we didn't create these to make money," he assured readers prior to the journal's initial publication (and directly before urging them to purchase it as a holiday gift for friends and family). Simmons frames the *Quarterly* as a result of his and his staff's creative inspiration rather than a commercially driven brand extension. Complementing *Grantland*'s constructed independence, Simmons uses the book's image as a "sacred product" unconcerned with generating revenue to dissociate *Grantland Quarterly* from the monetary motives that guide mainstream sports media, and, consequently, to brand it as morally and aesthetically superior to its competition. "The makers and marketers of works of art," Bourdieu asserts, "are adversaries in collusion, who each abide by the same law which demands the repression of direct manifestations of personal interest, at least in its overtly 'economic' form."[40] Accordingly, Simmons's disavowal of the *Quarterly*'s commercial dimensions builds symbolic value that bolsters the product's economic potential.

The *Quarterly* also illustrates digital media's capacity to create new artistic and economic uses for the book. This curious print item would not exist independent of Simmons's website and other online endeavors. Moreover, its design often adopts and evokes online aesthetics and culture. Volume 4, for instance, includes Rembert Browne's humorous commentary on the 1985 American Music Awards, which was originally published online as a series of responses to YouTube videos of the event. The repackaged print version features impressionistic drawings of the videos that imitate YouTube's look. Other issues include artistically rendered tweets and transcribed excerpts from Simmons's podcast. These inclusions suggest the *Quarterly* does not simply grow out of digital culture, but speaks back to it. *Grantland Quarterly* thus exploits the book's traditional value to build credibility while expanding the older medium's aesthetic and commercial uses. In this way, the *Quarterly* demonstrates how digital media create novel uses for the book—a medium many critics suggest they are rendering obsolete.[41] "If books survive as a vital information technology," writes media historian David J. Staley, "it will be because it is in the economic interests of authors and publishers to maintain books in tangible, physical form." These interests, as the *Quarterly*'s original partnership with McSweeney's and Simmons's assurances that the print product is not commercially motivated indicate, are also cultural. *Grantland Quarterly*'s development and promotion participate in the construction of books as "hallowed objects"—a value Ted Striphas claims has intensified along with digital media's ascendancy during the so-called late age of print—while inflecting *Grantland*, its personnel, and its parent with this significance.[42]

"A Little Bit of a Network"

In a 2009 review of *The Book of Basketball* published in *Deadspin*, decorated sportswriter Charles P. Pierce attacked Bill Simmons as self-important and unworthy of the prominence he so rapidly gained. Simmons, Pierce charges, "did very little that was new, but he did it on the Internet. . . . He is not a transformational figure. He did not reinvent sportswriting, or even the way people write about sports, which is not the same thing." Pierce suggests Simmons's style is not particularly skillful or intelligent. Rather, it is sloppy work that is often naively mistaken for Web-driven innovation. "You are not the cosmos, son," he dismissively writes. "Get the fuck over yourself."[43] Simmons indignantly responded by removing Pierce's name from his book's paperback edition and critiquing the veteran sportswriter as jealous of his success. A series of petty blog posts and tweets ensued.

Pierce's critique, however, overlooks the complex process by which Simmons and ESPN build respectability. While the material Simmons produces—as Jonathan Mahler avers—may not seem literary or even particularly sophisticated when considered in isolation, he and ESPN carefully filter their work through symbolic channels that signal literary quality and innovation. Simmons and his corporate parent do not simply sell content. They also shop the painstakingly sculpted image in which their material is packaged. A testament to this strategy—and extending ESPN's tradition of co-opting respectable, independent, and oppositional voices like Simmons—*Grantland* hired Pierce as a staff writer. Pierce's first article for the website recounted his experience working for the *National Sports Daily*, a pioneering and short-lived sports newspaper that ran from January 1990 to June 1991. The piece was included in *Grantland Quarterly*'s first volume as an insert along with Alex French and Howie Kahn's oral history of the newspaper. Funded by eccentric Mexican media magnate Emilio Azcárraga, the *National* hired Frank Deford—arguably the United States' most popular sportswriter at the time—to serve as its editor in chief and figurehead, assembled a stable of prominent staff writers, and regularly included long-form features. The *National*'s profound ambition, however, "exceeded the technology available to produce it." The paper hemorrhaged money, frequently missed printing deadlines because of its reliance on satellite communication to shuttle its typewritten articles about the country, and was distributed only via newsstands. The *National*, French and Kahn observe, was "emblematic of the parts of culture and media that were not yet ready to converge."[44]

Beyond commemorating the *National* as a curious and important moment in the history of sports media, *Grantland* indicates that it grows out of and even realizes the defunct publication's grandiose aspirations. *Grantland*'s initial use of Simmons as its editorial and artistic leader, recruitment of renowned writers, and emphasis on long form mimic the *National*'s format and marketing strategy. The website, however, is untrammeled by the technological boundaries that triggered its untimely predecessor's demise. *Grantland* situates itself as a fulfillment of the *National*'s quixotic dream. It is an unprecedented multimedia project rooted in print but unburdened by the medium's technological constraints and possesses the resources to incorporate even its most vocal critics.

Simmons, as Pierce points out, is not the cosmos. He is, however, an undeniably powerful point around which much of ESPN's corporate universe at one time orbited. And his realm continued growing after *Grantland*'s creation until his eventual departure. In 2013 he joined ESPN/ABC's NBA studio program *NBA Countdown* as an analyst. The position—which he juggles along with his writing, producing, and editorial duties—marks a transition from Simmons as a quirky outsider to a privileged insider who literally rubbed elbows with the sportscasters and former players he sat alongside while commentating. The following year, Disney tapped him to serve as an associate producer on the feature film *Million Dollar Arm*, an uplifting drama based on the true story of a Major League Baseball scout who recruits two Indian cricket players. Promotions for Peter Berg's *Lone Survivor* (2013) included a blurb from Simmons—captioned as a representative of *Grantland*—that championed the production as "the most extraordinary war film since *Saving Private Ryan*." The ads, which made no reference to ESPN, situated Simmons and *Grantland* as mainstream cultural intermediaries on par with *Variety*, *Hollywood Reporter*, or *USA Today* and powerful enough for a big-budget Hollywood film to invest in their potential to woo its macho target audience.

Simmons was not originally enthused by the prospect of titling his website *Grantland*—a name his ESPN superiors liked but that he thought pretentious. He was more partial to *Wheelhouse* or *The GOAT* (*Greatest of All Time*) and purchased the domains for both while developing the project.[45] However, Simmons's boutique publication has transformed him into arguably the United States' most pervasive sportswriter since Rice, who published books, hosted a radio show, served as a celebrity endorser, and produced a series of one-reel sports documentaries—*Grantland Rice's Sportlights*.[46] Despite Simmons's initial reluctance to name his site after Rice, there is no better historical precedent to the networked sports personality he has become.

Reflecting its founding editor's steady expansion and *30 for 30*'s metamorphosis, *Grantland* continues to spawn multiplatform offshoots that broaden its style and reach. These extensions, such as *The Triangle*, *Hollywood Prospectus*, and Grantland Channel, produce material designed for niches of the already specialized variety of sports fan *Grantland* attracts. As John Skipper puts it, *Grantland* helps ESPN to "get at the edges of what sport touches" and the consumers who occupy those margins. Cho likens *Grantland*'s diversified format to *New York Magazine*, a general interest publication that hosts complementary websites on entertainment, fashion, local news, and food. He claims *The Triangle* and *Hollywood Prospectus* blogs are designed to be "destination pages that . . . feel like products of their own."[47] Extending this effort, the Grantland Channel produces original programming, such as the 2014 Jonathan Hock–directed documentary series *The Finish Line*, in which aging NBA player Steve Nash reflects on his waning career and prospects for life after basketball. More prominently, in October 2014 ESPN's flagship channel premiered *The "Grantland" Basketball Hour*, an

NBA-themed and Simmons-hosted talk show that marked the *Grantland* brand's entrance into television.

Simmons calls *Grantland* "a little bit of a network" with distinct but complementary parts that drive traffic independently while contributing to its hip subbrand.[48] It is a microcosm of ESPN's multiplatform model whose subsidiaries compose sometimes seemingly unlikely pathways into the Worldwide Leader's ambit. Though Simmons eventually left, ESPN retained the brands he built. *Grantland*, to be sure, productively widens sport's stereotypical meanings and audience by placing it into dialogue with and probing its relationship to film, music, fashion, and so forth. Likewise, its strategic engagements with potent signifiers—from Grantland Rice to McSweeney's—suggest mainstream sports media can provoke thought as well as entertain. But *Grantland*'s expansion of sports media's creative possibilities simultaneously narrows the range of institutional participants in this milieu beyond the parent company that the boutique website does not always resemble, but that it unyieldingly fuels.

ESPN has built on *Grantland*'s success by creating additional sport and culture content organized around market-tested personalities. In August 2013, it hired former *ESPN.com* columnist Jason Whitlock away from Fox Sports— a move prompted in part by Fox's launch of the national cable channel Fox Sports 1 that same month. Whitlock claimed he rejoined ESPN with the intention of creating and editing a "Black *Grantland*" that would focus on African American perspectives. The same month, ESPN hired Nate Silver, editor of the statistics-heavy blog *FiveThirtyEight* who gained renown by accurately predicting the outcomes of the 2008 and 2012 presidential elections. The *New York Times* licensed and hosted Silver's blog from 2010 to 2013. ESPN opted to purchase rather than host the site. Silver, who began his career with *Baseball Prospectus*, claimed his decision to join ESPN was motivated in large part by *Grantland*'s highbrow aspirations. "I like the idea that ESPN wants to be the smart [sports] network," he noted.[49] The precise brand of "nerdy badass" around which *Grantland* crafted its niche identity, Silver augments this brainy image while propelling ESPN's expansion. Mirroring Simmons's pervasiveness across Disney's properties, Silver would edit *FiveThirtyEight*, appear on ABC News during election season, and lend his statistical expertise to spice up the network's Academy Awards coverage. Silver's acquisition works to ensure that political junkies agonizing over the 2016 presidential race will visit a subsidiary of *ESPN.com* to ascertain who will most likely be the United States' next leader. This is a far cry indeed from the days when ESPN served sports junkies willing to watch Australian Rules football on tape delay.

While some of *Grantland*'s and *FiveThirtyEight*'s content has nothing to do with sports, it is guided by the same priorities that compelled ESPN to televise the 1980 NFL draft, cover the 1987 America's Cup, and launch a magazine: to intensify its relationship to sports fans—specifically adult men with money—and to attract new customers. These efforts bring into relief the degree to which commercial sports media do not simply represent sport, but exploit its uses. Sport, in this sense, is as much a demographic category as a competitive physical activity. ESPN has perhaps never been driven by sport in and of itself. It is instead motivated by an attempt to capture the audiences sport delivers by packaging it in ways that complement their tastes, which span beyond sport. These endeavors make *Grantland*'s engagements with fashion and *FiveThirtyEight*'s political analyses seem as natural within ESPN's branded domain as the athletic competitions the media outlet has featured since its inception.

CONCLUSION

From *Frontline* to the Bottom Line

Brand management is front and center, being protective with the brand and aggressive with the brand.
We're trying to always move things forward. There is
no status quo.

—Norby Williamson, ESPN senior executive vice
president[1]

I have a very simple rule of how you establish value.
It's whatever anyone will pay.

—John Skipper, ESPN president[2]

In 2012 ESPN investigative reporters, and brothers, Mark Fainaru-Wada and
Steve Fainaru set out to write a book on the National Football League's involvement in football's concussion crisis. Fainaru-Wada, whose book *Game of Shadows* probed Major League Baseball's performance-enhancing drug epidemic,
and Fainaru, who received a Pulitzer for his *Washington Post* reports on the Iraq
War, composed a high-profile team that promised to make a valuable contribution to the rising body of work on the topic. Unambiguously titled *League of
Denial*, the project exposes the NFL's efforts to suppress information that links
the concussions football players regularly suffer to neurodegenerative disorders
and to discredit research that has validated such links.

Soon after the Fainarus began researching, the PBS series *Frontline* expressed
interest in producing an accompanying documentary. ESPN then approved a
formal partnership between *Frontline* and *Outside the Lines* committed to sup-
porting and publicizing *League of Denial*. The Fainarus broke off stories from
their research for use on *Outside the Lines*, *ESPN.com*, and *Frontline*'s website.

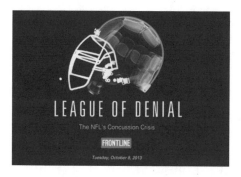

The title card from PBS *Frontline*'s 2014 documentary *League of Denial: The NFL's Concussion Crisis*. The documentary began as a collaboration between ESPN and PBS. ESPN curiously removed its brand from the project just weeks before its premiere.

ESPN and PBS also created the "Concussion Watch" website, which logged every concussion the NFL reported and classified them according to players, their position, and how many games they missed because of their injury. The project seemed an ideal journalistic endeavor wherein two qualified outlets pooled their respective expertise to investigate a powerful organization that was allegedly abusing its influence.

The partnership also neatly complemented ESPN's involvement in documentary and long-form journalism as well as its strategic alliances with institutions such as Tribeca, PEN, and McSweeney's. PBS has long been recognized as an "oasis" in the vast wasteland of TV that—even more so than "quality" outlets like HBO—fulfills the medium's civic potential.[3] Dwayne Bray, head of ESPN's investigative unit, called *Frontline* "the gold standard of longform investigative documentaries." "We're not the public trust that PBS is," admitted John Skipper, who suggested *Frontline*'s impeccable reputation would bring ESPN a new level of credibility. ESPN director of news Vince Doria called the journalistic coalition a "rare opportunity" that would "result in some ground breaking work."[4] Beyond its many benefits to ESPN, the partnership allowed PBS—an organization mired in perpetual fund-raising—to benefit from the traffic that ESPN's brand delivers.

Just weeks before *League of Denial*'s October 2013 premiere, ESPN abruptly removed its brand from the project and canceled its agreement with PBS. Skipper claimed *Frontline*'s trailer for the documentary—which ends with brain researcher Ann McKee claiming that she would not be surprised if every football player suffered some degree of brain trauma—was sensational and did not consider ESPN's editorial input. "Because ESPN is neither producing nor exercising editorial control over the *Frontline* documentaries," explained a company press release, "there will be no co-branding involving ESPN on the documentaries or their marketing materials. The use of ESPN's marks could incorrectly imply that we have editorial control." Mystified by ESPN's decision, *Frontline* executive producer Raney Aronson-Rath denied that PBS had complete control over the project and promised that *Frontline* "would definitely welcome [ESPN's] editorial thoughts." "We were about to share a cut with them and we welcomed their input," she explained. Moreover, Fainaru-Wada describes the partnership as "very collaborative," and both he and his brother note that their immediate ESPN supervisors were privy to the form the project was taking as it developed.[5]

Skipper's implication that *Frontline* lacks editorial scruples contradicts his celebration of PBS as a public trust (and is ironic coming from the media outlet responsible for *Bonds on Bonds* and *The Decision*). The Peabody Award *League of Denial* received in 2014—an accolade that recognizes works that deliver a valuable public service—further complicates Skipper's claim that the documentary was over the top. "It was not a good time for anyone who believed in journalism at ESPN," Fainaru-Wada explained of his employer's unexpected decision to remove its brand from the project.[6]

The *New York Times* reported that the National Football League pressured ESPN to dissociate from *Frontline* and its damning documentary—a charge the NFL and ESPN patently deny.[7] To be sure, ESPN's decision to remove its brand from *League of Denial* calls to mind *Playmakers'* NFL-driven cancellation. The corruption *League of Denial* uncovers, however, makes *Playmakers'* salacious plot points seem comparatively tame. But ESPN's detachment from *League of Denial* has far more troubling implications that suggest its business partnerships limit its journalistic capacities. To ESPN's credit, the Fainarus maintain that the media outlet's decision in no way impacted their reportage. The documentary was still permitted to caption the reporters as ESPN employees, and ESPN promoted the project via *ESPN.com*, *ESPN the Magazine*, *SportsCenter*, *Outside the Lines*, and *SportsNation*. ESPN also has not shied away from covering the concussion controversy since the documentary's release. For instance, soon after ESPN separated its brand from *League of Denial*, *Grantland* published Charles Pierce's critique of the $765 million settlement the NFL paid a group of retirees—a relative pittance, Pierce charges, designed to absolve the league from taking responsibility for negligence that spans decades and likely contributed to scores of untimely deaths. "This issue is about branding, not about journalism," Bray explained after ESPN ended the PBS partnership.[8] Though ESPN has continued to examine the topic, the media outlet's efforts to protect its brand restrict the precise form its reportage takes and how it is packaged.

ESPN senior vice president Norby Williamson describes the *League of Denial* incident as "a precedent situation where we did not want to co-brand with something that we did not have editorial control over." There are, however, many cases where ESPN proudly advertises its recusal of editorial control. It does not select which works are chosen for inclusion in the Tribeca/ESPN Film Festival, *Kobe Doin' Work* is a "Spike Lee Joint," and *30 for 30*'s documentaries are driven by "filmmaking originals" rather than ESPN. In each case, ESPN trumpets its lack of editorial governance to emphasize the undertakings' quality. When asked about this seeming inconsistency across ESPN's operations, Doria explained that ESPN Films documentaries can cede control to their respective directors because they are not "investigative in nature."[9] Contradictions again emerge, however. Billy Corben's *30 for 30* documentary *Broke* (2012), for example, is based on and extends investigative reporter Pablo Torre's examination of the alarming number of professional athletes who go bankrupt soon after their careers end. Moreover, *Outside the Lines* promoted *Broke*, along with several other ESPN Films productions, and provided the documentary with footage from a segment it produced on the same topic. Many other ESPN Films documentaries—such as *Let Them Wear Towels* and *Branded*—adopt the structure of investigative reports and are driven by interviews with reporters who have explored their themes and subjects. Doria's claims, then, like Skipper's and Williamson's remarks, are dubious.

Despite ESPN's vehement assertions to the contrary, its decision to end its partnership with PBS was almost certainly an effort to protect its relationship with the National Football League, which it pays roughly $2 billion a year for the rights to *Monday Night Football*. Several anonymous ESPN employees—presumably fearful of what would happen to their jobs if they spoke on the record—confirmed as much to the *New York Times*.[10] While ESPN builds prestige through diverse alliances with respected organizations and individuals, it will not, it seems, allow these efforts to compromise its partnership with the United States' most powerful sports league. With *League of Denial*, then, ESPN sacrificed a fifth Peabody to kowtow to its most valuable client. The incident usefully illustrates the limits of ESPN's cultural aspirations. It will attach its brand to a Hunter S. Thompson column that insults the president, but not to a PBS documentary that critiques the NFL.

A Branded Culture

Though very protective of it, ESPN continues to spread its brand as far as it will reasonably (and sometimes unreasonably) stretch. As of this writing, it owns twenty-four networks outside of the United States, and its TV programming is available in sixty-one countries. ESPN pairs its global expansion with a steady infiltration of regional markets. The SEC Network covers the American Southeast; the Longhorn Network, launched in 2011, is devoted entirely to the University of Texas; and ESPN Radio's hundreds of affiliates populate U.S. markets ranging from Millinocket, Maine, to Kennewick, Washington. ESPN accompanies its proliferation with an acquisition of commodities tied to distinct places and audiences. Within the span of several months straddling 2007–8, for example, ESPN purchased the cricket website *Cricinfo.com,* the rugby site *Scrum.com,* and the Formula 1 auto racing site *Racing-live.com*—all of which principally attract fans that dwell beyond U.S. borders and cover sports that ESPN's domestic coverage gives little attention. Guided by similar goals, the SEC Network hired Birmingham, Alabama–based sports talk radio icon Paul Finebaum as one of its main football commentators. Whether their primary appeal is global or regional, ESPN organizes these assets under its institutional banner and uses them as entry points into its ever-swelling empire. It works to create a state of affairs wherein Sri Lankan cricket fans and University of Alabama football supporters alike will get their sports news from ESPN.

ESPN fortifies its multiplatform colonialist project by exploiting the deregulated U.S. cable TV industry's amenability to corporate interests. Every cable subscriber—from sports junkies to sports averse—pays dearly for ESPN. According to the financial information firm SNL Kagan, ESPN charged an average of $6.04 per subscriber in 2014. Cable's next most costly channel, TNT, demanded $1.48. "I have a very simple rule of how you establish value," Skipper gloats. "It's whatever anyone will pay." Skipper's philosophy is aided by Disney lobbyists pressuring Congress to ensure that media conglomerates can sell their cable channels in bundles, a practice that enables them to use their most popular properties to force operators to carry their less prevalent channels.[11] The Disney bundle, for instance, leverages ESPN to ensure the many subscribers who purchase cable solely to watch the Worldwide Leader must also pay for ABC Family. It also constrains those subscribers principally interested in AMC's dramas and TLC's reality programs to pay for ESPN. Simultaneously, the substantial fees Disney demands for ESPN dissuade cable operators from adding new sports channels to their basic packages, which makes it difficult for ESPN competitors to enter the sports TV market and relegates most of the sports channels that do emerge to less visible—and more expensive—premium sports tiers. "ESPN is a virtual monopoly," claimed Charter Communications cofounder Jerry Kent. "Backed up by Disney, it has a gun to the heads of cable operators."[12] Sports TV—particularly live event coverage—has remained profitable amid industrial and technological changes that see consumers increasingly augmenting their cable television consumption with online content and in some cases even "cutting the cord" in favor of subscription streaming packages.[13] These shifts, which ESPN exploits with its streaming service Watch ESPN and its partnership with the Internet TV service Sling, have broadened ESPN's influence well beyond the specific context of sport media.

ESPN's steady expansion and fee increases would be impossible without its recognizable brand, which becomes more visible with each new property it acquires and space it enters. "Brands," reminds cultural critic Sarah Banet-Weiser, "are about culture as much as they are about economics."[14] They compose symbols through which everyday life is lived that transmit social and economic value. From the T-shirts it licenses to its decision to separate from *League of Denial*, ESPN molds the meanings its "magic name" signals and monitors where it roams. It creates and maintains a framework through which sport is experienced and interpreted—a culture—that suggests sport's existence and meanings are inseparable from and impossible without ESPN.

Along with many other critics, *Columbia Journalism Review*'s Sam Eifling recognizes this and complains that the branded culture ESPN fashions is a degraded one wherein the content it produces—much of which it passes off as legitimate journalism, rigorous historiography, and inspired art—is always secondary to its bottom line. ESPN's "M.O.," he argues, "is to favor the sanitized and shiny over the nuanced and disturbing; to promote profit over novelty; to carnival-bark athletes into celebrities, then siphon riches off the fame it fathers."[15] While such critiques have merit, there is still a lot to praise about ESPN. For all its predictability, *SportsCentury* is a rich historical resource, Ralph Wiley's *Page 2* columns stand among the most insightful commentaries on modern sport's racial politics, *Playmakers*' scandalous depictions of pro football have proved prophetic, ESPN Films has kindled a popular interest in the sports documentary, and *Grantland* has brought sportswriting into closer proximity with arts and cultural commentary. These creations institute sports media as a major player in the contemporary cultural industries—not merely a repository for event coverage, highlights, and updates.

Cultural value is built through what Bourdieu calls a "social alchemy" of symbolically potent traditions, institutions, and gatekeepers.[16] ESPN situates itself as a site of cultural production—an organization that fosters intellectual and artistic activity—by associating with, exploiting, and in some cases co-opting these powerful signifiers. Beyond inflecting ESPN with authority and authenticity, these activities position its brand as a recognizable symbol—like Apple, Harley-Davidson, and Nike—that sports fans employ to distinguish themselves.

Like Bourdieu claims of art, ESPN's varied efforts to build distinction are relatively high in symbolic capital and low in economic capital.[17] With few exceptions, the revenues ESPN's documentaries, books, and long-form journalism generate pale in comparison to its live event coverage and popular studio programs like *First Take* and *SportsNation*. But these comparatively highbrow productions—despite ESPN's frequent assertions to the contrary—are not art for art's sake. Their respectability deliberately offsets *First Take*'s and *SportsNation*'s comparative shallowness. Norby Williamson describes the scope of ESPN's content as a "pendulum" that strategically oscillates between the poles of sophistication and superficiality.[18] Programs like *SportsNation* attract large audiences of mostly young men, while ESPN Films' documentaries and *Grantland*'s long-form features assure smaller, but slightly broader, audiences that ESPN is not driven by the lowest common denominator. As Skipper remarks:

> We're ubiquitous. And there is a tendency in culture to think of big as bad: "The big bad Coca-Cola Company. Big bad Nike." Part of what we're trying to do is provide people with surprise and delight from places where they don't expect to see ESPN. So it becomes harder to say "big bad ESPN." Sometimes we get tarred: "They're everywhere. They drive me crazy." When someone like that sees a *30 for 30*, it forces them to stop and go "Wow. My thinking of ESPN as a soulless corporate entity is pretty hard to do when I watch a really smart, sensitive, nuanced examination of something."[19]

But more than simply appeasing those consumers with more refined sports media palates, ESPN's diverse efforts to build prestige suggest the organization governs sport's meanings, uses, and potential. These sometimes surprisingly classy activities have helped ESPN to produce a sports media landscape with more content than ever before. But they have also aided the company's efforts to claim this environment as its kingdom and to limit the presence of alternatives that might question or contest its reign. They make ESPN's carefully orchestrated and vigilantly guarded status as the Worldwide Leader in Sports seem a natural fact and filter all of the content it produces through this cultural and industrial common sense. This is precisely why it is vital to critique this brand—however artful, inventive, or inspiring its products may be—and to point out the motives that guide its construction and maintenance.

The Entertainment and Sports Programming Network's First Press Release, June 26, 1978

The Entertainment and Sports Programming Network

6/26/78

FOR IMMEDIATE RELEASE.......

   Ed Eagan, President of Cable Promotions, and Bob Beyus, President
of Live Video, today announced the consolidation and expansion of their
respective companies into the Entertainment and Sports Programming
Network. ESP, Inc. will provide a unique program service for cable
television systems throughout Connecticut. The initial program
offering will air in early September and encompass a wide variety of
LIVE televised professional and collegiate athletic events along with
a weekly sports magazine and many special sports events throughout the
state.

   Eagan also announced the appointment of Bill Rasmussen, formerly
Communications Director of the New England Whalers, to the post of
Vice President/Programming. Rasmussen will be responsible for
acquisition and development of local programming.

   Scott Rasmussen has also joined the ESP staff according to Eagan
and will serve as Director of Production for the Network.

   "Connecticut's sports fans deserve to see many of the outstanding
sports events played in their own state," said Eagan. "Working with
the cable systems, ESP, Inc. will make these events available to
subscribers statewide."

   Bill Rasmussen added, "Our target for Phase I is 150 local programs
with future expansion planned to over 1,000 local programs annually."

319 COOKE STREET □ PLAINVILLE, CONNECTICUT 06062 □ 203-747-6847

6/26/78   2   2   2   2   2

ESP, Inc. will utilize the talents of top professionals in a continuing effort to provide the best of Connecticut sports to cable system subscribers:

.....WTIC's Dean of Sports, Arnold Dean, and WTIC sports personality Lou Palmer, subject to WTIC schedule availibility, will handle the play-by-play and color commentary for many ESP originated events.

.....Gordie Howe, Hockey's Living Legend, will present an instructional series for youth hockey players of Connecticut.

.....Colleen Howe will host her own talk show that will cover the diversified spectrum of activities in which she is involved.

.....Tel Fax of Philadelphia will provide remote pickup facilities for many ESP events. Tel Fax performs similar services for the Philadelphia Flyers, St. Louis Blues, Pittsburgh Penguins and many college football and basketball teams.

The ESP staff:

.....Bill Rasmussen--16 years television in Massachusetts and Conn--
     several national network shows--sportscaster, newscaster, director
     and producer, WWLP-TV and WHCT-TV--Communications Director, Whalers.

.....Scott Rasmussen--8 years radio and TV--perhaps best known as Whalers
     PA man--produced and directed Whaler current highlight film--
     co-producer of Gordie Howe Birthday Night in Springfield and
     Happy Birthday Gordie magazine.

.....Ed Eagan--strong business background--very active in amateur sports
     with emphasis on youth hockey--former Armed Forces Network sports
     reporter--also free lance talent for CPTV auction and cable TV.

.....Bob Beyus--First Class engineer--11 years radio and TV in Conn--
     formerly chief engineer WFSB-TV & Channel 20, Waterbury & TV center
     at Central Connecticut State College.

APPENDIX B

SportsCentury Top One Hundred Athletes of the Twentieth Century

1	Michael Jordan	22	Joe DiMaggio
2	Babe Ruth	23	Jackie Joyner-Kersee[a]
3	Muhammad Ali	24	Sugar Ray Robinson
4	Jim Brown	25	Joe Montana
5	Wayne Gretzky	26	Kareem Abdul-Jabbar
6	Jesse Owens	27	Jerry Rice
7	Jim Thorpe	28	Red Grange
8	Willie Mays	29	Arnold Palmer
9	Jack Nicklaus	30	Larry Bird
10	Babe Didrikson[a]	31	Bobby Orr
11	Joe Louis	32	Johnny Unitas
12	Carl Lewis	33	Mark Spitz
13	Wilt Chamberlain	34	Lou Gehrig
14	Hank Aaron	35	Secretariat[b]
15	Jackie Robinson	36	Oscar Robertson
16	Ted Williams	37	Mickey Mantle
17	Magic Johnson	38	Ben Hogan
18	Bill Russell	39	Walter Payton
19	Martina Navratilova[a]	40	Lawrence Taylor
20	Ty Cobb	41	Wilma Rudolph[a]
21	Gordie Howe	42	Sandy Koufax

[a] Women
[b] Horses

43	Julius Erving		72	Bo Jackson
44	Bobby Jones		73	Josh Gibson
45	Bill Tilden		74	Deion Sanders
46	Eric Heiden		75	Dan Marino
47	Edwin Moses		76	Barry Sanders
48	Pete Sampras		77	Cy Young
49	O. J. Simpson		78	Bob Mathias
50	Chris Evert[a]		79	Gale Sayers
51	Rocky Marciano		80	A. J. Foyt
52	Jack Dempsey		81	Jimmy Connors
53	Rafer Johnson		82	Bobby Hull
54	Greg Louganis		83	Honus Wagner
55	Mario Lemieux		84	Man o' War[b]
56	Pete Rose		85	Maurice Richard
57	Willie Shoemaker		86	Otto Graham
58	Elgin Baylor		87	Henry Armstrong
59	Billie Jean King[a]		88	Joe Namath
60	Walter Johnson		89	Rogers Hornsby
61	Stan Musial		90	Richard Petty
62	Jerry West		91	Bob Beamon
63	Satchel Paige		92	Mario Andretti
64	Sammy Baugh		93	Don Hutson
65	Althea Gibson[a]		94	Bob Cousy
66	Eddie Arcaro		95	George Blanda
67	Bob Gibson		96	Michael Johnson
68	Al Oerter		97	Citation[b]
69	Bonnie Blair[a]		98	Don Budge
70	Dick Butkus		99	Sam Snead
71	Roberto Clemente		100	Jack Johnson

APPENDIX C

SportsCentury Panel

Mitch Albom[a]
Roone Arledge[a]
Chris Berman[a]
Steve Bornstein[a]
Ray Cave
Bill Conlin
Bob Costas
Lucy Danziger[b]
Frank Deford
Anita DeFrantz[b]
Mel Durslag
Harry Edwards
Dick Enberg
Roy Firestone[a]
Curt Gowdy[a]
Bud Greenspan[a]
Bryant Gumbel
David Halberstam[a]
Steve Hirdt[a]
Keith Jackson[a]
Sally Jenkins[b]
Tony Kornheiser[a]
Sam Lacy
Richard Lapchick

Bob Ley[a]
Robert Lipsyte[a]
Donna Lopiano[b]
Mike Lupica[a]
Jim McKay[a]
Al Michaels[a]
Jim Murray
Jim Nantz
Dan Patrick[a]
Shirley Povich
Robin Roberts[a,b]
Harold Rosenthal
Bob Ryan[a]
Dick Schaap[a]
Vin Scully
Blackie Sherrod
Jim Simpson[a]
Charley Steiner[a]
Bert Sugar
Pat Summerall
Mike Tirico[a]
Lesley Visser[a,b]
Michael Wilbon[a]
George Will[a]

[a] Had or has since worked for ABC or ESPN
[b] Women

Notes

Introduction

1. Qtd. in Waters and Wilson, "An All-Sports TV Network."
2. Qtd. in Martzke and Cherner, "Channeling How to View Sports."
3. Qtd. in Leavy, "New Cure for Insomnia."
4. Callahan, "Tuning Out the 24-Hour Sports Glut."
5. Qtd. in Hiestand, "Pioneer Steers ABC, ESPN."
6. ESPN had created similar services prior to Mobile ESPN. In 1992 it created a 900-number, 1–900–976-ESPN, which was updated every ten minutes and gave news and score updates for ninety-five cents per minute. In 1995 it launched ESPNet to Go with Motorola, a pager that delivered scores, schedules, and headlines.
7. Qtd. in Sandomir, "ESPN the Ring Tone."
8. Badenhausen, "Value of ESPN Surpasses $50 Billion."
9. Rowe, *Sport, Culture and the Media*, 23; McChesney, "Media Made Sport." See also Jhally, "Spectacle of Accumulation."
10. R. Williams, *Culture*, 13; R. Williams, *Keywords*, 87; Arnold, "Culture and Anarchy."
11. H. Jenkins, *Convergence Culture*, 15. Importantly, TV scholar Michelle Hilmes notes that "convergence is not a new phenomenon, [but rather] the hallmark of modern media" ("Nailing Mercury," 27).
12. Gershon, *Breakup 2.0*, 3. Gershon bases her theorization of media ideology in part on Silverstein, "Language Structure and Linguistic Ideology."
13. Bodenheimer, "Keynote Speech."
14. Bourdieu, *Field of Cultural Production*, 75.

15. For more specific discussions of middlebrow culture, see Radway, *Feeling for Books*; and J. Rubin, *The Making of Middlebrow Culture*.

16. R. Adams, "ESPN Gets $850 Million to Stay in the Game."

17. T. Adams and Tuggle, "ESPN's *SportsCenter* and Coverage of Women's Athletics"; Bryant, Comisky, and Zillmann, "Drama in Sports Commentary"; Cossar, "Televised Golf and the Creation of Narrative"; Duncan and Cooky, "Silence, Sports Bras, and Wrestling Porn"; Goldlust, *Playing for Keeps*; Kian, Mondello, and Vincent, "ESPN—the Women's Sports Network?"; Meân, "Sport Identities and Consumption"; Morse, "Sport on Television"; L. Mullen and Mazzocco, "Coaches, Drama, and Technology"; Real, "Super Bowl: Mythic Spectacle"; Tuggle, "Differences in Television Sports Reporting"; Turner, "Longitudinal Analysis of Gender and Ethnicity Portrayals"; Whannel, *Fields in Vision*; B. Williams, "Structure of Televised Football."

18. A notable exception is the work of Victoria E. Johnson; see "Everything New Is Old Again," "Historicizing TV Networking," and "*Monday Night Football.*"

19. Lotz, *Television Will Be Revolutionized*, 3; Spigel, introduction to *Television after TV*, 19.

Chapter 1. From the Entertainment and Sports Programming Network to ESPN

1. W. Johnson, "Sports Junkies of the U.S. Rejoice!"

2. Knott, "ESPN."

3. Bill Rasmussen, telephone interview with the author, August 29, 2013; Bob Beyus, telephone interview with the author, September 26, 2013. Beyus claimed to be the "father of ESPN" and to "own its birthright." He also said that he bankrolled the endeavor's initial operations—from phone bills to office supplies—and that he was "squeezed out" by partners who considered him a mere placeholder while they were searching for someone with deeper pockets and better technological resources. He claimed he wound up losing his home as a result of his investment in ESP. When asked why he had never pursued legal action, he said he worried that ESPN parent Getty Oil would have kept any lawyer he retained tied up in court until his resources ran dry.

4. Scott Rasmussen, telephone interview with the author, September 27, 2013.

5. Lublin, "Dogfight in Space." ESPN first used its satellite in early January 1979 for a test broadcast of a basketball game between Rutgers and the University of Connecticut. As a result, its first payment was not due until May, since it had ninety days from first use and then thirty days to issue the payment. Prior to this test broadcast on its channel, it had rented space for several experimental telecasts of University of Connecticut athletic events. The first was an October 1978 men's soccer match between the University of Connecticut and Athletes in Action. These initial telecasts, however, were part of separate onetime satellite space rentals and, consequently, had no effect on ESPN's agreement with RCA. S. Rasmussen interview.

6. B. Rasmussen, *Sports Junkies Rejoice!*, 23; Gunther and Carter, *Monday Night Mayhem*; Hyatt, *Kicking Off the Week*; Spence and Diles, *Up Close and Personal*; Sugar, "*The Thrill of*

Victory"; V. Johnson, "*Monday Night Football*"; Whannel, "Pregnant with Anticipation," 415.

7. Edgerton, *Columbia History of American Television*, 286.

8. "Television: The Big Daddy of Nearly All Sports."

9. The Sloan Commission on Cable Communications, *On the Cable*; Ralph Smith, *Wired Nation*; Streeter, "Cable Fable Revisited"; Maddox, *Beyond Babel*, 145.

10. M. Mullen, *Rise of Cable Programming*, 7; McChesney, "Global Media, Neoliberalism, and Imperialism," 1. See also Aufderheide, "Cable Television and the Public Interest"; Le Duc, *Beyond Broadcasting*; and Winston, "Rejecting the Jehovah's Witness Gambit."

11. The Madison Square Garden Network is different from the regional MSG Network.

12. See Edgerton, "Brief History of HBO"; and T. Miller and Kim, "Overview."

13. Montgomery, "Super Station." Turner briefly flirted with the idea of creating an all-sports cable channel in 1997. See Parsons, *Blue Skies*, 389.

14. B. Rasmussen, *Sports Junkies Rejoice!*, 77.

15. In *Just a Guy*, Bill Rasmussen's brother Don explains their family's early investment in ESPN. Similar to Beyus's account, Don Rasmussen claims Bill used deceptive measures to manipulate family members and to ensure that they did not receive the amount their ESPN stocks were worth after the ABC purchase. Don actually quit his job as a middle school principal to work as an ESPN sales representative until January 1981. Don Rasmussen, telephone interview with the author, October 6, 2013.

16. "Proposal to the National Collegiate Athletic Association," September 1, 1978, Don Rasmussen personal papers.

17. Goldenson and Wolf, *Beating the Odds*, 434.

18. Stuart Evey, telephone interview with the author, June 28, 2013.

19. Ibid.; B. Rasmussen interview.

20. B. Rasmussen interview; S. Rasmussen interview.

21. Evey interview.

22. Ourand, "Champions."

23. "Seven Ways to Be an Agency Hero."

24. B. Miller, "Television Goes (Even More) Sports Crazy."

25. Since so few affiliates are independent, it is now exceedingly rare for broadcast networks to pay them. This was the dominant model, however, when ESPN emerged.

26. Qtd. in Leavy, "New Cure for Insomnia."

27. Harris, "Getty Hopes for a Gusher"; "Fate of Sports Rights."

28. Qtd. in Leavy, "New Cure for Insomnia."

29. Qtd. in W. Johnson, "Sports Junkies of the U.S. Rejoice!"

30. The higher-profile Jim Simpson did not introduce ESPN's first moments because he was fulfilling his contractual obligation to NBC. He did not join ESPN until several days after its premiere.

31. Qtd. in J. Miller and Shales, *Those Guys Have All the Fun*, 47.

32. The precise time ESPN signed off each night varied slightly depending on the programming scheduled during a given morning.

33. Leavy, "New Cure for Insomnia."

34. Hill, "Building a Sports TV Empire."

35. B. Rasmussen interview.

36. Red Smith, "Cable TV for Sports Junkies"; Isaacs, "24 Hours of Plainville." In 1988 the *Wall Street Journal*'s William M. Bulkeley conducted a similar, and equally sardonic, experiment with an entire weekend of uninterrupted viewing. See Bulkeley, "Sports Potato."

37. Freeman, *ESPN: The Uncensored History*, 98. Shortly after Scott Rasmussen left ESPN, he, along with his father, started a short-lived twenty-four-hour radio network called Enterprise Radio. See Shapiro, "'Son of ESPN' Launches New Satellite 'Enterprise'"; and Birchard, *Jock around the Clock*. The radio network, which launched on January 1, 1981, was off the air within a year on the brink of bankruptcy. Scott Rasmussen was eventually arrested for failing to pay more than one hundred employees for five weeks. Bill Rasmussen stayed on ESPN's payroll as a consultant until Texaco purchased Getty in 1984.

38. Goldenson and Wolf, *Beating the Odds*, 434. Not long after ESPN's launch, Getty teamed with several Hollywood studios to develop Premiere—a pay-cable network that aimed to compete with HBO, Showtime, and Cinemax. Getty's contribution consisted primarily of transponder space. Though its launch was scheduled for January 1981, Premiere's distribution model—which gave it exclusive pay-cable rights to certain films owned by its Hollywood partners—was ruled a violation of antitrust regulations.

39. Lindquist, "Not a Stretch"; Rosen, "NFL Aims Draft at Real Fans."

40. "Watch the NFL Draft Live Only on ESPN."

41. Weinreb, *Bigger than the Game*, 174.

42. Simmons qtd. in Shapiro, "Say ESPN and You've Said It All"; Leavy, "New Cure for Insomnia"; Grimes qtd. in Furlotte, "USFL: Made-for-TV," 22.

43. Evey, *Creating an Empire*, 174; "New Video's New Bedfellows."

44. "ESPN Blacks Out Black Colleges."

45. "Pitch the Rich"; "We're #1."

46. "Men Who Don't Watch TV Watch ESPN"; Simmons qtd. in Shapiro, "Say ESPN and You've Said It All"; Aufderheide, "Cable Television and the Public Interest"; Streeter, *Selling the Air*; Winston, "Rejecting the Jehovah's Witness Gambit."

47. Carvell, "Prime Time Player"; Keating, *Cutthroat*, 3; Landro, "ESPN Says Losses for Year Could Reach $20 Million."

48. J. Miller and Shales, *Those Guys Have All the Fun*, 543. Bill Rasmussen claims that he initially sought to adopt a funding model similar to the one ESPN instituted in 1983. Before Chet Simmons was hired, Rasmussen charged the first cable providers he secured. Simmons, however, insisted on the network-inspired funding structure with which he was so familiar from his experience at ABC and NBC. Those operators with whom Rasmussen originally struck deals renegotiated their contracts according to Simmons's criteria. B. Rasmussen interview.

49. "ABC to Buy 15% Stake in ESPN." Prior to the purchase, ABC subsidiary ABC Video Enterprises and ESPN pursued a joint venture to create a pay programming service.

50. *NCAA v. Board of the Regents of the University of Oklahoma*, 468 U.S. 85 (1984). See also Dunnavant, *Fifty-Year Seduction*, 165–66; Oriard, *Bowled Over*, 157–60; Ronald Smith, *Play-by-Play*, 162–70; White, "Colleges May Find TV's Golden Egg Is Tarnished"; "ABC, ESPN Win CFA Rights," 32; "Turner Pondering ESPN Purchase"; and "ABC Buys ESPN for $202 Million."

51. Nabisco sold its 20 percent interest to the Hearst Corporation in 1990 after Capital Cities opted not to acquire it. Shortly after, ESPN purchased Ohlmeyer Communications Company, with which it had collaborated on different event packages. "Hearst to Buy 20% of ESPN"; "Ohlymeyer Deals Sports to ESPN."

52. ABC, however, would not permit its new property to share in its 1984 Olympics coverage—even though the network had access to, and even produced, far more content than it had space to showcase. Knoll, "More Coverage for Olympics Fans." ABC Sports president Roone Arledge and ESPN president Bill Grimes did begin conversations regarding how ESPN might complement ABC's 1988 Winter Olympics coverage, however, while the event was in the early stages of planning. Roone Arledge Papers, Box 36, Folder 8, Columbia University Rare Book & Manuscript Library, New York.

53. McCormick, "Cable TV's Cloudy Skies," 12; Schmuckler and Dean, "Cable TV Law"; W. Williams and Mahoney, "Perceived Impact of the Cable Policy Act."

54. Delaney, "Nabisco Gives ESPN New Program Taste"; N. Klein, *No Logo*, 3–4; Lash and Urry, *Economies of Signs and Space*; Lury, *Brands*; Sherry, *Servicescapes*.

55. Arvidsson, *Brands*; Elliott and Davies, "Symbolic Brands," 155.

56. Caldwell, "Critical Industrial Practice"; Turow, *Breaking Up America*, 105.

57. Qtd. in Graham, "*Bio* Gets New Lease on Lives."

58. "What to Look Forward to on Cable," 95.

59. "By the Time You Read about a Hostile Takeover." In 1985 *Business Times* was canceled and replaced by the similar program *Nation's Business Today*. Produced by the U.S. Chamber of Commerce's American Business Network, *Nation's Business Today* ran until 1991.

60. Berkow, "Those Soggy Sailors." See also Goodwin, "At Long Last, a Major Event for ESPN."

61. B. Lloyd, "After Years of Costly Efforts, the Race Is Finally On"; B. Lloyd, "America's Cup"; "What's What in the America's Cup."

62. Qtd. in Hiestand, "Did You Know?"; J. Miller and Shales, *Those Guys Have All the Fun*, 138.

63. Qtd. in Walley, "Some Clever Taking Buoyed a Listing Net."

64. Qtd. in Chad, "TV Sports Fans."

65. Chad, "Football on ESPN Is Good"; Chad, "Inaugural NFL Broadcast on ESPN"; Berman qtd. in Fortunato, *Commissioner*, 97; Grimes qtd. in Hewitt, "Rise of ESPN."

66. Walley, "ESPN Gets Chance"; "ESPN Scores with NFL Football."

67. Steve Bornstein, telephone interview with the author, August 29, 2013; John A. Walsh, telephone interview with the author, July 23, 2013; Bornstein interview.

68. Vitale qtd. in Taaffe, "Hey, DV, Lower the Volume!"; ESPN colleague qtd. in Lidz, "Yabba Dabba Doo."

69. Shapiro, "With World Watching"; Walsh qtd. in Fleischman, "ESPNation Rules the Sports World"; Skipper qtd. in Greenfeld, "ESPN."

70. Shanahan qtd. in Hirshberg, *ESPN25*, 56; Olbermann qtd. in Ourand, "ESPN's Storytelling Draws in Exec"; Barton qtd. in Keating, *Cutthroat*, 193; Fabrikant, "For Cable Networks."

71. Bornstein qtd. in J. Miller and Shales, *Those Guys Have All the Fun*, 217; Turcsik, "Profiles in Excellence," 22; Nelson, "ESPN Builds Cult Following."

72. Olbermann and Patrick leveraged their celebrity into the 1997 coauthored book *The Big Show*.

73. See Goldman and Papson, *Nike Culture*. Weiden + Kennedy's first ad campaign for *SportsCenter* was 1993's "It Could Happen So You Better Watch," which suggested that *SportsCenter* provided instant access to the sports world's unpredictable events. As ESPN vice president for marketing Harriet Seitler claimed regarding the campaign, "We want people to know that they have to watch *SportsCenter* or they may miss something great" (qtd. in Cooper, "*SportsCenter* Gets Promotion Push").

74. Qtd. in M. Rubin, "Network."

75. Beyond the "This is *SportsCenter*" and "It's Not Crazy, It's Sports" campaigns, Weiden + Kennedy also produced a series of campy commercials for ESPN's NCAA men's basketball coverage featuring Robert Goulet singing adaptations of lounge songs that incorporate references to the sport. In 2012 ESPN Deportes launched its own Weiden + Kennedy–produced variation of "This is *SportsCenter*" called "Esto es *SportsCenter*," which adopts the same template.

76. John Lack, telephone interview with the author, August 8, 2013; Frager, "Whether You Get It or Not." Semiao claims ESPN's original idea for ESPN2 was to make it more of a secondary outlet for sporting events and news than a niche-driven channel that skews toward younger viewers. However, and like Bornstein, he noted that cable operators would consent to add the channel only if it was clearly differentiated from ESPN's flagship channel. Ron Semiao, telephone interview with the author, November 7, 2013.

77. Sandomir, "ESPN Adding Channel and Attitude." ESPN did carry the daily afternoon extreme sports-focused program *Max Out* prior to ESPN2's launch. It moved *Max Out* to ESPN2 once the new channel began operations.

78. Qtd. in Browne, *Amped*, 235.

79. "Cable Nets Line Up for Fall"; Browne, *Amped*, 237; Hiestand, "Sports Rock." Olbermann left ESPN2 in 1994 to return to ESPN's *SportsCenter*. He left the network entirely in 1997 to host a series of cable news programs. In August 2013, he returned to ESPN to host the sports news program *Olbermann*.

80. Lack interview; Hiestand, "ESPN at 15."

81. Oriard, *Brand NFL*, 175; Crepeau, *NFL Football*, 164–65. Similar to ESPN's decision to hire John Lack and Harriet Seitler, the NFL hired former MTV copresident Sarah Levinson in 1994 to run NFL Properties.

82. Wise, "X Games"; Browne, *Amped*, 232–52; Hiestand, "ESPN Extreme Games." Ron Semiao points out that ESPN's ownership of the X-Games enabled the media outlet to promise advertisers on-site signage as well as commercial time. The X-Games allowed

ESPN to attract new sponsors that found the X-Games to be a fitting complement to their brands. Semiao interview. The X-Games was originally conceived as an event that would take place in both the summer and the winter. It began with the summer version because ESPN was in greater need of content during that season.

83. Wolf, "Middle-Aged Need Their Extremes, Too"; Semiao interview.

84. Lukes, "I'm Not Really a Doctor," 81. Farred makes a similar argument in "Cool as the Other Side of the Pillow."

85. Disney agreed to purchase Capital Cities Communications in the late summer of 1995, but the FCC did not clear the acquisition until early 1996. See Fabrikant, "2 Boards Approve."

86. Shapiro, "With World Watching"; Carter and Sandomir, "Trophy in Eisner's Big Deal."

87. Qtd. in Walley, "The Colossal Combos." See also Wasko, *Understanding Disney*; and Levine, "Fractured Fairy Tales and Fragmented Markets."

88. The Walt Disney Company sold its interests in both the Angels and the Ducks in 2005.

89. Freeman, *ESPN: The Uncensored History*, 269.

90. Qtd. in Jensen, "Cable TV Marketer of the Year."

91. In 1998 Sears department store also opened one hundred ESPN shops within its stores. These shops, as well as the ESPN Stores, were all closed by 1999. In 2010 ESPN closed all of its ESPN Zone restaurants except those in Los Angeles and Anaheim.

92. The previous year ESPN produced a ninety-minute special entitled *ESPN Town Meeting: Sports in Black & White*, which was hosted by ABC News' Ted Koppel and held at Howard University. Though not nearly as high profile as Clinton's town hall meeting, the 1997 special no doubt helped to position ESPN as an outlet that could produce serious and civic-minded content.

93. Kent, "*SportsCenter* Highlight"; Thiel, "*SportsCenter* Proves It Has Legs."

94. Walsh interview; Doria qtd. in Leonard Shapiro, "With World Watching"; Vitale and Weiss, *Living a Dream*, 5; Knott, "ESPN."

95. W. Johnson, "Sports Junkies of the U.S. Rejoice!"

96. Greenfeld, "ESPN."

Chapter 2. *SportsCentury*

1. Qtd. in Raissman, "New Look for ESPN Classic."

2. Halbwachs, *On Collective Memory*, 43.

3. Hagel qtd. in "*SportsCentury* Tour in N.Y."; A. Smith and Hollihan, *ESPN the Company*, 152.

4. Nichols, *Representing Reality*, 3; Corner, "Television Documentary and the Category of the Aesthetic," 93; Minow, "Address to the 39th Annual Convention."

5. See Curtin, *Redeeming the Wasteland*; Murray, "'I Think We Need a New Name for It'"; Vogan, "Chronicling Sport, Branding Institutions"; and Watson, *Expanding Vista*.

6. Original historical sports documentaries ESPN produced prior to *SportsCentury* include *Breaking the Line: The Legacy of Jackie Robinson* (1997), which won a Cable Ace

Award and Sport in Society Award; *Roger Maris: Reluctant Hero* (1998); and *Babe Ruth's Larger than Life Legacy* (1998). ESPN also produced the National Geographic–inspired documentary adventure series *Expedition Earth* from 1990 to 1995.

7. See C. Anderson, "Producing an Aristocracy of Culture in American Television"; Feuer, Kerr, and Vahimagi, *MTM: "Quality Television"*; and McCabe and Akass, *Quality TV*.

8. Most of this scholarship focuses on cinematic texts. See Ingle and Sutera, *Gender and Genre in Sports Documentaries* and *Identity and Myth in Sports Documentaries*; and McDonald, "Situating the Sport Documentary." An exception is Poulton, "'I Predict a Riot.'"

9. Billings, "In Search of Women Athletes." Ironically, *SportsCentury* eventually won a "Tribute Accolade" from Women in Cable & Telecommunications in 2002.

10. Spencer, "'America's Sweetheart' and 'Czech-Mate,'" 19. Incidentally, the 2010 ESPN Films *30 for 30* documentary *Unmatched* examines Evert and Navratilova's friendship and rivalry, along with the sexual politics that mark them.

11. Billings, "In Search of Women Athletes," 416; Nathan, "Sometimes, ESPN Seems Ubiquitous," 530; Hunt, "Reality, Identity, and Empathy."

12. Caldwell, "Convergence Television."

13. The only other sports documentary to win the Academy Award for Best Documentary Feature prior to *When We Were Kings* was Bruce Nyznik and Lawrence Schiller's *The Man Who Skied Down Everest* (1975).

14. See Taaffe, "Legends in Their Own Time"; and Vogan, *Keepers of the Flame.*

15. Based on *When It Was a Game*'s success, HBO released a second installment of the documentary in 1992 and a third in 2000.

16. Edgerton, *Ken Burns's America*, 111.

17. Ibid., 113.

18. Shapiro, "ESPN's *SportsCentury* Goes Back-Back-Back"; Bodenheimer qtd. in J. Miller and Shales, *Those Guys Have All the Fun*, 417; Mark Shapiro, interview with the author, October 4, 2013; Sandomir, "Top Athletes Countdown"; Bianculli, "Put 'Top 50' in Winner's Circle," 116.

19. *SportsCentury*'s participating sponsors included Anheuser-Busch, Burger King, Lincoln Financial Group, Mastercard, Nike, and Wheaties.

20. Qtd. in J. Miller and Shales, *Those Guys Have All the Fun*, 418. Shapiro amassed several crews led by directors of photography that would travel about the country to conduct interviews. Franchella trained each crew to reproduce the interviews' aesthetic by providing detailed specifications for lighting, shadows, microphone, and audio.

21. Twenty-six of the forty-eight panelists either had or would later work for ABC or ESPN. See appendix C.

22. In *Televisuality* Caldwell explains how TV networks during the 1980s would organize lavish and heavily promoted "television events" to distinguish themselves from the influx of cable channels. Though Caldwell discusses network TV in particular, ESPN uses a similar strategy with *SportsCentury*. See also Roscoe, "Multi-platform Event Television."

23. Ryan qtd. in Vecsey, "Wilt or Kareem? Chris or Martina?"; Deford qtd. in Cavanaugh, "Play It Again"; Kornheiser cited in Kimball, "One Last List to Incite Debate"; Roberts qtd. in Sherman, "Viewers Lap Up *SportsCentury.*"

24. Sugar, "Patriots' Turnaround"; Kimball, "One Last List to Incite Debate."

25. ESPN's online activities seek to facilitate communities similar to those Robert Kozinets calls "brand communities," wherein consumers gather to discuss and debate content related to the brand. See Kozinets, "E-Tribalized Marketing?" While this process gives consumers a degree of agency and voice, it is important to note that ESPN exerts control over the horizons by which *ESPN.com* users can participate.

26. John Dahl, telephone interview with the author, March 21, 2014.

27. Qtd. in "*SportsCentury* Tour in N.Y." Nick at Nite actually staged a national "TV Land Mall Tour" in 1989 designed to publicize the addition of the sitcom *Green Acres* to its programming schedule. See Murray, "'TV Satisfaction Guaranteed!,'" 75. Shortly after the *SportsCentury* mall tour, ESPN unveiled ESPN the Truck, a branded truck with various video monitors that makes appearances at events and trade shows.

28. Sandomir, "Top Athletes Countdown"; J. Miller and Shales, *Those Guys Have All the Fun*, 420; Roone Arledge Papers, Box 21, Folder 4, Columbia University Rare Book & Manuscript Library, New York.

29. Shapiro qtd. in Cavanaugh, "Play It Again"; "Family Film Rebuts Ruth's 'Called Shot'"; Shapiro, "ESPN's *SportsCentury* Goes Back-Back-Back."

30. A&E's documentary uses only voice-over narration and archive footage.

31. *SportsCentury*'s use of this effect is more ornamental than Burns's employment of it. It pans more quickly and arranges photographs near objects and memorabilia that evoke the featured subjects. The sequence used in the profile for Chicago Bears linebacker Dick Butkus, for example, places photographs alongside shoulder pads and other football gear. The shots thus signal memorabilia's potential to—much like photographs—stir memories and emotions, a point Nathan explores in "John Unitas's Jacket and Other Objects of Importance."

32. See R. Creamer, *Babe.*

33. Kent, "ESPN Shows Un-Ruthian Effort"; Shapiro interview.

34. Fulfilling the role Halberstam played for the *SportsCentury* book, Robert W. Creamer penned the foreword to *Sports Illustrated*'s commemorative book, which was also divided into chapters devoted to each decade.

35. ESPN further built its position as a public broker of sport's meaning in 1999 through its *SportsFigures* series, an educational collection of programming made for the Cable in the Classroom initiative. Through a sponsorship with Infoseek's Go Network, ESPN distributed video sets of the series to each of the United States' public and private high schools. The charitable endeavor doubled as a public relations and marketing ploy that cast ESPN as invested in education and exposed its brand to young audiences.

36. Sherman, "Viewers Lap Up *SportsCentury.*"

37. Kompare, *Rerun Nation*, 172. See also Holt, *Empires of Entertainment.*

38. Richmond, "Let's Go to the Videotape."

39. Qtd. in Maurstad, "Classic Sports TV around the Clock."

40. Qtd. in "Classic Sports Network Stings Like a Bee"; Brian Bedol, telephone interview with the author, May 16, 2014.

41. Qtd. in "Classic Sports Network Stings Like a Bee."

42. Kompare, "Reruns 2.0"; Kompare, *Rerun Nation*, 171.

43. In "Concept of Live Television," Feuer notes that sports broadcasts rely on and put on display TV's capacity for liveness more forcefully than other genres.

44. Qtd. in Sandomir, "Channel for Lovers of Athletic Nostalgia."

45. It is commonplace for MSOs to require cable outlets to grant them equity in exchange for carriage. See Turow, *Breaking Up America*, 102.

46. In opposition to CSN's gripe, Cablevision charged that the cable channel lodged the FCC complaint in an attempt to derail its launch of American Sports Classics. Cablevision and CSN ended up settling out of court. See A. King, "Classic Battle"; and Mannes, "Classic Sport Spat."

47. Qtd. in Dempsey, "ESPN Game for Classic Sports Net."

48. In some ways, ESPN's foray into regional programming mirrors the niche it established in the historical programming market. In 1994 it purchased the syndicator Creative Sports and rebranded it as ESPN Regional Television, which focuses on college programming tailored to regional markets. In 1997, shortly after Disney purchased Capital Cities, ERT merged with Ohlmeyer Communications Company. ESPN rebranded ERT programming as ESPN Plus in 2001. ESPN Plus is based out of Charlotte, North Carolina. It served as the foundation from which ESPNU launched, and it houses the channel's production facilities.

49. Elsen, "ESPN Steps into the Ring." The Big Fights, Inc., library also had footage from several Olympic Games and various events held at Madison Square Garden. Disney also hired Big Fights cofounder Bill Cayton to serve as a consultant after the purchase.

50. Semiao qtd. in Schlosser, "Lineup Changes for ESPN Classic"; Shapiro qtd. in Raissman, "New Look for ESPN Classic."

51. Shapiro interview. Joseph Turow claims developing signature programs became increasingly important for cable TV outlets to maintain a competitive edge during the mid-1990s. See Turow, *Breaking Up America*, 105–6.

52. Fleming, "ESPN Ups Shapiro to Sr. VP"; Hinckley, "Anna's Made an Impact."

53. A. Smith and Hollihan, *ESPN the Company*, 189.

54. Qtd. in Ginn, "News Shows Must Retain ESPN's Reputation for Quality." Shapiro's statement on women audiences reflects a common industrial assumption that women viewers are more interested in story-driven content and will be more likely to watch sports content if they are presented in this manner. These same attitudes informed the "Up Close and Personal" approach Roone Arledge developed for ABC Sports. David Remnick explains these assumptions and the production practices that grew out of them in "The Inside-Out Olympics."

55. Caldwell, "Convergence Television," 49. John Dahl notes that *SportsCentury's* interview process anticipated these potential combinations. Crews would ask interviewees about a variety of topics—some of which were only indirectly relevant to their careers

and experiences—with the expectation that it might prove useful in other profiles. Dahl interview.

56. Bornstein, telephone interview with the author, August 29, 2013. "I'm a big believer in 'the long tail,'" Bornstein elaborated, referencing journalist Chris Anderson's observation that contemporary businesses increasingly privilege investing in less expensive and immediately salable content that will generate greater long-term yields over devoting resources to more costly popular material with a shorter shelf life.

57. Trouillot, *Silencing the Past*, 51.

58. Sandomir, "Games (and Ghosts) of Yesteryear."

59. Schwartz and Cook, "Archives, Records, and Power," 1; Foucault, *The Archaeology of Knowledge*, 129.

60. I use the term *history* here in the way that Keith Jenkins employs it in *Rethinking History*. Jenkins defines history as a narrative about "the past," or the events, artifacts, and memories out of which that history is built.

61. Sandomir, "ESPN Plays Games with Its Digital Ads."

62. Taaffe, "Legends in Their Own Time." *Greatest Sports Legends* defrayed its production costs by taping at La Costa Resort and showcasing it in the program's introductory sequences and interviews. In exchange for the publicity, La Costa would provide its facility and lodging for the featured athletes, interviewees, and Rotfeld's production staff.

63. D. Anderson, "The Sports Legendizer." Rotfeld made a *Greatest Sports Legends* piece on the notoriously shady boxing promoter Don King in 1986 in exchange for access to his film library—a collection he used to create segments on several boxers. At one point, Rotfeld sued NFL Films for violating an agreement they had made to provide his company with footage. In response, NFL Films charged that Rotfeld had used its footage without permission. See Taaffe, "Legends in Their Own Time"; and Wood, "Giving Heroes a New Look."

64. In 1997 TNT repackaged this special as a six-hour documentary released exclusively on DVD.

65. Sekula, "Reading an Archive," 116.

66. ESPN/Disney charges a per-second rate for commercial use of its archived footage. Some footage, such as video of Howard Cosell, must also be cleared by the individuals it features or by their estates.

67. A 2005 episode actually includes a cameo wherein the *Mystery Science Theatre 3000* personalities briefly give *Cheap Seats* the ironic treatment they provide to the old movies. Cohost Randy Sklar likened the cameo to "a giant M. C. Escher painting of commentary." Qtd. in Crane, "TV Sports Show."

68. See Kompare, "I've Seen This One Before," 27; Murray, "'TV Satisfaction Guaranteed!'"; and M. Mullen, *Rise of Cable Programming*, 169–72.

69. Schwartz and Cook, "Archives, Records, and Power," 4; Derrida, *Archive Fever*, 4.

70. Qtd. in Marchand, "NFL Network Wants Super Bowl Series."

71. From 2001 to 2006, ESPN competitor Fox Sports Net produced *Beyond the Glory* that presents visually jarring and edgy profiles consistent with the bold brand Fox

cultivates. Along these lines, in 2006 the Fox-owned Madison Square Garden channel created *50 Greatest Moments at Madison Square Garden*, which counted down the famous moments with documentary profiles. In 2013 the National Baseball Hall of Fame produced *Boys in the Hall*, a biographical documentary series based on former MLB commissioner Fay Vincent's Baseball Oral History Project. Fox Sports Net purchased the syndicated program's first season. Along these lines, in 2002 the nascent Yankees Entertainment and Sports Network (YES)—a cable outlet owned in part by Fox and the New York Yankees—sought to reclaim the franchise's history by creating the biographical documentary series *Yankeeography*. The series imitates *SportsCentury*'s set design, lighting, and graphics—while also evoking A&E's *Biography*—to profile prominent Yankees. Also reflecting *SportsCentury*, its generic documentaries offer little new insight on familiar figures like Babe Ruth, Joe DiMaggio, and Mickey Mantle. In fact, they employ many of the same interviewees, photographs, and archival footage that *SportsCentury* used in its varied profiles of current and former Yankees. However, and again like its predecessor, *Yankeeography* brands YES and the Yankees organization as the team's official historians.

72. Crepeau, "There Seems to Be No End in Sight," 525.

Chapter 3. *ESPN the Magazine* and *Page 2*

1. Qtd. in "Media Notes."

2. Qtd. in Cohen, "Writing a Sports Column."

3. Qtd. in Shea, "How ESPN Changes Everything," 46.

4. Rowe, "Sports Journalism," 385. In his comprehensive history of American journalism, Frank Luther Mott claims early-twentieth-century sports journalism was characterized by a "slangy and facetious style" (*American Journalism*, 579).

5. Evensen, "Jazz Age Journalism's Battle," 230; Evensen, *When Dempsey Fought Tunney*, xiv; Oriard, *King Football*, 25; Woodward, *Sports Page*, 35.

6. Precedents to CNN/SI's cable sports news channel include Sports News Network (1989–90) and Newsport (1993–97).

7. Cave qtd. in MacCambridge, *Franchise*, 5; Michener, *Sports in America*, 323.

8. *Sports Illustrated* has continued to produce some content for television after CNN/SI's folding in 2002. Most notably, it coproduces short pieces for HBO's *Real Sports with Bryant Gumbel*. It also teamed with HBO for the 2013 documentary *Sports in America: Our Defining Stories*.

9. Qtd. in Raissman, "Cable Nets Plugs News to the Max."

10. CNN stopped producing *Sports Tonight* upon CNN/SI's 2002 dissolution.

11. "Another Bounce from ESPN."

12. Eisner qtd. in J. Miller and Shales, *Those Guys Have All the Fun*, 404; Steve Bornstein, telephone interview with the author, August 29, 2013; Pedersen, "Interview with John Papanek," 286; R. Adams, "Top Sports Titles Find There's Room for Two."

13. Qtd. in Stilson, "A-List Profile." John Skipper, who joined ESPN from the Disney Publishing Group in 1997 to serve as *ESPN the Magazine*'s senior vice president and gen-

eral manager, worked at *Rolling Stone* and *Spin* before joining the Walt Disney Company. He claims the new magazine's resonances with *Rolling Stone* were an outgrowth of his experience at the magazine. He even contracted *Rolling Stone*'s printer and had it use the same type of paper on which the popular music and culture magazine was produced. John Skipper, telephone interview with the author, July 18, 2014.

14. Looney, "ESPN Invites Itself to *SI*'s Table."

15. Woolsey, "Not Your Father's Sports Magazine"; Poniewozik, "*ESPN the Magazine* Kicks Sand"; Walsh qtd. in Ryan, "ESPN vs. *Sports Illustrated*," 64.

16. Qtd. in Whitmire, "New ESPN Leads Mini-boom of Sports Magazines"; Ryan, "ESPN vs. *Sports Illustrated*," 64. In 2008 *ESPN the Magazine* shifted almost entirely to a themed issue format—"The Money Issue," "The Fan Issue," "The Photo Issue," and so forth. Though this format still engages the sports calendar and sports news, it is less reliant on these time-sensitive factors.

17. Qtd. in Looney, "ESPN Invites Itself to *SI*'s Table."

18. Pogrebin, "ESPN Rivals Set for Fight." While ESPN hired Reilly in 2007, he did not begin writing for the media outlet until June 2008. Upon Reilly's arrival, *ESPN the Magazine* replaced "0:01" with the sportswriter's "Life of Reilly" column, which overtook *Sports Illustrated*'s "Point After" back-page column from 1998 until 2007. *Sports Illustrated* hired Dan Patrick, who left ESPN in 2007, soon after ESPN recruited Reilly and began to include a weekly interview segment similar to "Outtakes."

19. When he was editing *Inside Sports*, Walsh developed a "Swimsuit Spectacular" special issue to compete with the "Swimsuit Issue."

20. "*ESPN the Magazine, SI* Lead All Publications."

21. ESPN Books initially published most of its titles in collaboration with Hyperion, another Walt Disney Company property. It became a stand-alone subsidiary, with its own management team and mission statement, in 2004. See McClintock, "ESPN Sports Bigger Books."

22. Trachtenberg, "ESPN's Next Hurdle."

23. In 2008 ESPN launched a magazine in cooperation with Mexican publisher Grupo GW that focuses specifically on Mexican readers.

24. *ESPN.com*'s actual URL as of this writing is *ESPN.go.com*. Its original URL was *ESPNet.SportsZone.com*. ESPN hosted the National Football League's website from 1996 to 2001, when the NFL realized the immense value of controlling its own Web presence and content.

25. Carr, *Shallows*, 108. Bauerlein echoes Carr's argument in *Dumbest Generation*.

26. Koppett, *Rise and Fall of the Press Box*, 3. See Schultz and Sheffer, "Sports Journalists Who Blog"; Siapera and Spyridou, "Field of Online Journalism"; and Singer, "Who Are These Guys?"

27. Qtd. in B. Jackson, "Sports Blogs Weave Tangled Web."

28. Leitch, *Life as a Loser*, 14.

29. K. Jackson, "Lasting Lessons of a *Page 2* Editor"; Halberstam, "In Admiration of Iverson."

30. A friend of John Walsh from their days at *Rolling Stone,* Thompson briefly wrote a back-page column for *Inside Sports* titled "The Good Doctor."

31. Thompson, *Hey Rube,* xx. Walsh also unsuccessfully courted *Sports Illustrated*'s Sally Jenkins in an effort to attract female readers.

32. Foucault, "What Is an Author?," 106.

33. *Sports Illustrated* repackaged Faulkner's piece as part of a 1994 series wherein the magazine celebrated its fortieth anniversary by revisiting some of its best-ever works. Other canonical novelists who have written for *Sports Illustrated* include John Dos Passos, John Steinbeck, and Don DeLillo.

34. Thompson, "State of Disgrace"; Thompson, introduction to *The Gospel according to ESPN,* 6.

35. Walsh qtd. in Simmons, "B.S. Report," October 27, 2011; Thompson, "The Bush League"; Thompson, "Sad Week in America."

36. Qtd. in J. Miller and Shales, *Those Guys Have All the Fun,* 646.

37. Qtd. in Mahler, "Can Bill Simmons Win the Big One?" See also Tannenbaum, "Bill Simmons' Big Score."

38. Simmons qtd. in Berman et al., "Bill Simmons"; Curtis, "Bill Simmons"; Simmons qtd. in Cohen, "Writing a Sports Column."

39. Simmons qtd. in Berman et al., "Bill Simmons"; Curtis, "Adrift on the Sea," 42; Shoals, "Court of Opinion."

40. Walsh qtd. in Ballard, "Writing Up a Storm," 60; Lovink, *Zero Comments,* 13; Ballard, "Writing Up a Storm," 60; H. Jenkins, *Convergence Culture,* 73; Lessig, *Free Culture;* and Pearson, "Fandom in the Digital Era."

41. A pre–*Page 2* column from 2000, "Grading the Wimbledon Babes," for instance, issues a prefatory warning to potential female readers of its overt sexism before proceeding to explain who he thinks are the tournament's most desirable female participants.

42. Simmons qtd. in Curtis, "Bill Simmons"; Leitch qtd. in St. John, "Sports Guy Thrives Online."

43. Simmons reinforced his position as the ringmaster of an online sports subculture by posting a glossary of his sayings in 2007. Simmons, "Welcome to the Glossary." Olbermann and Patrick open their 1997 book spin-off, *The Big Show,* with a glossary of their popular catchphrases.

44. Wall, "Blogs of War," 165; Simmons, "Going Toe-to-Toe with 'Ali.'"

45. John Walsh, telephone interview with the author, July 23, 2013.

46. Mahler, "Can Bill Simmons Win the Big One?," 42.

47. Simmons, "Sports Guy Goes Hollywood."

48. Simmons's podcast was originally titled *Eye of the Sports Guy.* It was retitled the *B.S. Report* just one month after its May 2007 debut.

49. Greenfeld, "ESPN."

50. See Lemke, "Worldwide Leader in Sports." For a discussion of "subcultural capital," see Thornton, *Club Cultures.*

51. Webb, "New Magazine on Sports Culture"; D. King, "What Fans Can Find Online."

52. Merron, "Letter to the Editor"; O'Keefe, "Sports Salon"; Cummings, "*SportsJones* Offers Alternative."

53. S. Klein, "*SportsJones.*"

54. Simmons, "Best Sports Book Series." *SportsJones* incidentally posted a critique of the *Best American Sports Writing's* 1998 edition that claimed its contents were far too mainstream.

55. Simmons, "Mailbag Returns after a Long Summer's Nap."

56. Simmons, *Book of Basketball*, 23; Simmons, "Mailbag Returns after a Long Summer's Nap"; Simmons, "Tribute to the Ultimate Teacher."

57. Qtd. in Mahler, "Can Bill Simmons Win the Big One?," 43. Halberstam—who, according to Kevin Jackson, would ironically fax his online columns to *Page 2's* editors—admitted his lack of familiarity with the Internet when he took the position. "I'm delighted to be part of something new like the Internet, which I don't yet understand," he said shortly after being hired. See K. Jackson, "Lasting Lessons of a *Page 2* Editor"; and "Pulitzer Prize–Winning Columnist David Halberstam."

58. Bourdieu, *Distinction*, 3; Simmons qtd. in Cohen, "Writing a Sports Column."

59. Leitch, "Bill Simmons, Establishment."

60. Simmons, *Now I Can Die in Peace*, 18; Simmons, *Book of Basketball*, x.

61. Simmons qtd. in Cohen, "Writing a Sports Column"; L. Miller, *Reluctant Capitalists*, 6, 19; Striphas, *Late Age of Print*, 6; Simmons, "Sports Guy's Thanksgiving Picks."

62. Simmons, "Curious Guy: Chuck Klosterman"; Simmons, "Now That Jocks Talk to Us Directly."

63. H. Jenkins, *Convergence Culture*, 3.

Chapter 4. ESPN Original Entertainment

1. Qtd. in Umstead, "ESPN Makes New Unit for Original Programs."

2. Qtd. in "ESPN Execs Discuss Network's Plan for Growth."

3. Waters and Wilson, "An All-Sports TV Network."

4. ESPN packaged the X-Games, Winter X-Games, and ESPYs under the EOE banner even though they preceded the subsidiary's development. EOE became a category under which the majority of the nonevent or news content ESPN produced "in-house" was organized. Ron Semiao, telephone interview with the author, November 7, 2013.

5. Qtd. in McConville, "ESPN Juicing Up Sun with Block of Originals."

6. Mark Shapiro, interview with the author, October 4, 2013; Erhardt qtd. in Chunovic, "ESPN2 Gets Its Friday Night 'Block Party' On." Victoria E. Johnson discusses the demographic choices that guided ESPN's development of the *Friday Night Block Party* in "Historicizing TV Networking."

7. Ballard, "Say It Ain't So"; Shapiro interview.

8. Qtd. in Frutkin, "ESPN Hikes Football Drama."

9. Shapiro qtd. in "ESPN Execs Discuss Network's Plan for Growth." Boxing great Sugar Ray Leonard and actor Sylvester Stallone—capitalizing on the program's similarities to the plot of *Rocky* (1976)—initially hosted *The Contender*. Stallone left the show after its first season. After ESPN canceled *The Contender* in 2008, the cable channel Versus picked it up for another season, hiring actor Tony Danza, who had a brief stint as a professional boxer prior to his dramatic career, to host.

10. In 2007 EOE also made a pilot episode for a sports-themed program similar to *Unsolved Mysteries* titled *Unsettled Scores*. The pilot focused on Bison Dele, a former NBA player (previously named Brian Williams) who disappeared at sea under mysterious circumstances.

11. Wallace qtd. in Sandomir, "Reality Bites Back"; Roberts, "Move over Anna Nicole"; Hoffarth, "Creating a Bond with Bonds"; Tollin qtd. in Flint, "ESPN's Bonds Program Doesn't Taint the Network"; Walsh qtd. in Solomon, "Plan for Bonds Reality Show."

12. Sanello, *Reel v. Real*, xiii; Sorlin, *Film in History*, 21; Rosenstone, *History on Film/Film on History*, 160. See also Rosenstone, *Visions of the Past*.

13. Paget, *No Other Way to Tell It*, 6; Lipkin, *Real Emotional Logic*, 55.

14. ABC produced a largely unsuccessful remake of *Brian's Song* in 2001 to capitalize on the film's thirtieth anniversary.

15. Gomery, *"Brian's Song,"* 96. The U.S. Steel Hour made a TV production of *Bang the Drum Slowly* in 1956 starring Paul Newman. While Harris's book had already been adapted, the profound success of *Brian's Song* certainly prompted its remake as a theatrical feature.

16. Fuller, "Dangerous Fictions," 62.

17. Qtd. in "ESPN Execs Discuss Network's Plan for Growth."

18. Lipkin, "Defining Docudrama," 372; Melvin qtd. in "ESPN to Produce TV Movie"; Feinstein qtd. in Sandomir, "Story behind *Brink*."

19. Qtd. in Schaffer, "4-Minute Mile, Plus a Girlfriend."

20. Ibid.; Toplin, *Reel History*, 60.

21. Lipkin, *Real Emotional Logic*, 69.

22. Ibid., 81.

23. Lipkin, *Docudrama Performs the Past*, 91.

24. Beatty, "ESPN Buys B.A.S.S. Fishing Society."

25. Shapiro qtd. in Larson, "ESPN Calls Up Sports Dramas"; Sandomir, "Story behind *Brink*." EOE and ESPN Films often program productions around events like the Heisman Trophy presentation and "Selection Sunday" because these events run for definite durations. Unlike a sporting event, which can go into overtime, these types of events are organized to fit into discrete time slots, and their content will not necessitate greater airtime. They are therefore conducive to premiering EOE and ESPN Films productions because ESPN can be certain these programs will air at the precise time when they are scheduled.

26. Dempsey, "Auds Swear by Knight Bio."

27. Qtd. in Merron, "Reel Life."

28. H. Jenkins, *Convergence Culture*, 97.

29. Nack, *Ruffian: A Racetrack Romance*, 9. *ESPN.com* also included Nack's *Ruffian* in a short-lived "Book Club" series it hosted, which unsurprisingly featured many ESPN Books titles.

30. Shapiro qtd. in Grossman, "ESPN Signals Drama Game Plan"; Kaufman, "King Kaufman's Sports Daily." As with *Playmakers*, the NFL would not allow *Any Given Sunday* to use its logos or employ league stadia as locations. Stone's film did, however, feature several former NFL players and coaches as characters, including Jim Brown, Dick Butkus, Lawrence Taylor, and Johnny Unitas.

31. Qtd. in Estrin, "Fielding a Hit Drama."

32. Bernstein, "ESPN Writes New Script."

33. Keisser, "Hollywood Beat for ESPN," 16.

34. Sandomir, "ESPN Reaches New Low"; Tagliabue qtd. in Ballard, "Under Review"; Sandomir, "Citing NFL, ESPN Cancels *Playmakers*."

35. Qtd. in Dempsey, "Will ESPN Play Hardball"; Sherman, "Drama On, Off Screen for *Playmakers*." Along these lines, Keith Strudler and Maxwell Schnurer critique *Playmakers'* racial politics in "Race to the Bottom." The controversy over *Playmakers* occurred as ESPN was dealing with another racially charged NFL-related incident. Shapiro hired conservative radio personality Rush Limbaugh as an NFL analyst on *NFL Sunday Countdown* in hopes that the polarizing commentator would broaden the pregame program's audience. Limbaugh claimed Philadelphia Eagles quarterback Donovan McNabb received more attention than warranted because "the liberal media" wanted to see an African American succeed at his position. The comment sparked a brouhaha that resulted in Limbaugh's removal. While *Playmakers* did not limit itself to reproducing racial stereotypes, Tagliabue and Upshaw used the incident to buttress their complaints.

36. Shapiro qtd. in Sandomir, "Bad Boys, Bad Boys"; Semiao qtd. in Bechtel and Kennedy, "One and Done."

37. Semiao qtd. in Fryer, "*Playmakers* Drawing Ire across the NFL"; Shapiro qtd. in Sandomir, "Citing NFL, ESPN Cancels *Playmakers*." Prior to its cancellation, and in response to the NFL's complaints, ESPN stopped promoting *Playmakers* on *Sunday Night Football*. From 1984 to 1991, HBO produced the football-themed comedy *1st and Ten*. The program, about the fictional California Bulls franchise owned by a glamorous female heiress, dealt with some of the same tawdry themes that *Playmakers* engaged. *1st and Ten*, which often gave active NFL players cameos, took full advantage of HBO's ability to present nudity and foul language. What's more, HBO was producing the highlight and magazine program *Inside the NFL* in cooperation with NFL Films at the time. Despite HBO's partnership with the NFL, the league did not view the premium cable comedy as a threat to its image. While the NFL certainly did not allow *1st and Ten* to use its brand or logos, it did not ask HBO to discontinue the series, a decision it likely could have prompted given *Inside the NFL's* importance to the media outlet.

38. Shapiro interview. ESPN Films made a *30 for 30 Short* on this topic titled *The Deal* in early 2014. EOE briefly stated plans to produce a scripted series called *Hit Men* about an inner-city men's boxing club that it believed might complement *The Contender*. Spike Lee

also prepared a pilot for a series based on his basketball film *He Got Game*. Other abandoned films included a biopic on boxer Jack Johnson, a film on the 1927 Jack Dempsey–Gene Tunney "long count," and a docudrama on Joe DiMaggio and Marilyn Monroe's relationship with the working title *Mr. and Mrs. America*.

39. Qtd. in Hibberd, "ESPN Plans Summer Film Offensive."

40. Shapiro interview. Though not an EOE production, ESPN Deportes continued these brand placements with its 2011 series *El Diez*, which focused on a Mexican professional soccer league's combined glamour and seediness. Like *Playmakers* and *Tilt*, the eight-episode series integrated commentary from ESPN Deportes' soccer news program *Fútbol Picante* on its fictional characters.

41. Shapiro qtd. in Ballard, "Say It Ain't So," 20; Michael Antinoro, telephone interview with the author, March 21, 2014; Will Leitch, telephone interview with the author, December 17, 2013. Leitch also details the ESPN-based frustrations that inspired him to start *Deadspin* in *God Save the Fan*.

42. Paulsen, "Decade in Review."

Chapter 5. ESPN Films

1. Qtd. in Deitsch, "Stories of Their Time."

2. Dan Silver, telephone interview with the author, April 7, 2014.

3. Qtd. in Spanberg, "Field of Dreammakers."

4. Hirshberg, *ESPN25*, 12.

5. This was particularly important in 2004 because *Sports Illustrated* celebrated its fiftieth anniversary the same year. Thought not as lavish or extensive as *ESPN25*, *Sports Illustrated* fashioned a special issue that emphasized its centrality to sport's previous half century.

6. Gatti qtd. in M. Creamer, "ESPN Honors Fans"; Sandomir, "At ESPN, after 25 Years"; Steinberg, "Philly's Favorite Colt on Another Magazine Cover."

7. John Dahl, telephone interview with the author, March 27, 2014.

8. Qtd. in Bayer, "Tackling Sports History."

9. John Dahl, telephone interview with the author, March 21, 2014.

10. Prior to discovering *Through the Fire*, ESPN attempted to license Dana Adam Shapiro, Jeff Mandel, and Henry Alex Rubin's *Murderball* after ESPN Content Development's Ron Wechsler saw it at the 2005 Sundance Film Festival. Though ESPN did not get *Murderball*'s rights, Wechsler contends that the company's interest in the film prompted it to continue pursuing independent documentaries and led to *Through the Fire*'s purchase later that year. Ron Wechsler, telephone interview with the author, April 9, 2014.

11. Jonathan Hock, telephone interview with the author, March 14, 2014.

12. Dahl interview, March 21, 2014; Connor Schell, telephone interview with the author, April 3, 2014; De Valck, *Film Festivals*, 106; Elsaesser, "Images for Sale," 61. See also Wong, *Film Festivals*.

13. Rosenthal cited in Zeitchik, "ESPN in Film Festival Game"; Dan Silver interview, April 7, 2014.

14. Zeitchik, "ESPN Films Suits Up for Pair of Theatricals."

15. Ron Semiao, telephone interview with the author, November 7, 2014; Skipper qtd. in Consoli, "Throwing Out the Script," 6.

16. Windolf, "With *Black Magic,* Dan Klores Shoots and Scores."

17. Qtd. in Hoffarth, "*Kobe Doin' Work* Shoots and . . ."

18. Lee, "Behind the Lens." *Zidane* was inspired by Hellmuth Costard's *Football Like Never Before* (1971), an experimental film that trained several cameras on English soccer star George Best during a single game.

19. Lee quoted in Touré, "Spike Shoots, Kobe Scores."

20. Dahl interview, March 21, 2014.

21. Schell interview.

22. Simmons, "Bill Simmons on *30 for 30*"; Schell interview; Simmons qtd. in Sandomir, "ESPN Film Series Hands Camera to Someone Else." Schell claims that ESPN was planning to create a branded documentary series regardless of ESPN's thirtieth anniversary. The anniversary, however, provided an opportune occasion to do so.

23. Clinkskales qtd. in Lemke, "Len Bias' Death"; Lynch qtd. in Lidz, "Big Picture, for Real, Behind Sports."

24. Simmons, "Bill Simmons on *30 for 30*."

25. Ibid.

26. ESPN producer Mark Durand notes that Morgen actually had a difficult time selling his unconventional approach in *June 17, 1994* to ESPN Films' management. Durand, telephone interview with the author, June 27, 2014.

27. R. Lloyd, "ESPN's *June 17, 1994* Recalls a Fateful Day in Sports"; Schell interview.

28. Simmons, "Interview with Dahl and Schell"; Sandomir, "ESPN Film Series Hands Camera to Someone Else"; Simmons, "Bill Simmons on *30 for 30*."

29. Qtd. in Umstead, "Interview with Ross Greenburg."

30. Qtd. in Hiestand, "HBO Sports."

31. Ellis, *Visible Fictions,* 25; Caldwell, *Televisuality,* 84–88.

32. Dahl interview, March 21, 2014.

33. Simmons, "Bill Simmons on *30 for 30*."

34. Simmons, "Interview with Brett Morgen."

35. Qtd. in Coyle, "ESPN Hands Off to *30 for 30* Filmmakers." ESPN adapted ESPN Films' decision to hire famous directors by commissioning Errol Morris in 2012 to produce an eight-minute documentary as part of the network's "It's Not Crazy, It's Sports" publicity campaign. The documentary, which examines sports-themed funerals, emphasizes Morris's participation and includes interviews with eccentric characters that echo his feature-length films. Morris also created a series of short documentaries on eccentric topics for the "It's Not Crazy" campaign in the winter of 2015. The shorts were launched on *Grantland.com* as part of "Erroll Morris Week" that highlighted the Academy Award–winning director's involvement with the media outlet.

36. Hock interview; "Chat with Bill Simmons."

37. Qtd. in Sandomir, "ESPN Film Series Hands Camera to Someone Else."

38. Qtd. in Coyle, "ESPN Hands Off to *30 for 30* Filmmakers."

39. Bordwell, "Art Cinema as a Mode of Practice," 59; Caldwell, *Televisuality*, 105.

40. An exception is Spike Lee's *Jim Brown: All-American* (2003), which HBO branded as a "Spike Lee Joint."

41. Simmons, "Interview with Barry Levinson."

42. Schell interview; Dan Silver, interview with the author, April 25, 2014. Though ESPN does not participate in the selection of festival films, it can choose to omit a documentary from the Tribeca/ESPN Sports Film Festival if it does not think the production is a suitable fit. The omitted film, however, will still be included in Tribeca's regular festival. Moreover, Dan Silver notes that Tribeca has denied ESPN submissions, though he did not disclose which ones. Silver interview, April 7, 2014.

43. Hale, "River Surfing, Rugby Bonding, and Bicycle Soaring"; Simmons, "Interview with Dahl and Schell."

44. Finn, "It's Hard to Resist Bombast of Jets"; Sepinwall, "ESPN Scores Big."

45. Dahl interview, March 21, 2014.

46. Simmons, "Interview with Dahl and Schell"; John Skipper, interview with the author, July 18, 2014.

47. Schell qtd. in Bayer, "Tackling Sports History"; Clinkscales qtd. in Szalai, "ESPN Films Scores Regular Weekend Home"; Schell qtd. in "ESPN Announces 'ESPN Films on Classic.'"

48. Schell interview.

49. Dahl interview, March 21, 2014. ESPN Films also produced a series of "I Scored a Goal" vignettes that appeared throughout ESPN's and ABC's 2010 World Cup coverage. Each vignette featured a player who scored a goal in a World Cup final match discussing the experience and his memories of it.

50. Libby Geist, telephone interview with the author, April 4, 2014; Dahl interview, March 21, 2014; Geist interview.

51. The three *30 for 30* documentaries on women's sports prior to *Nine for IX*'s premiere are Lisa Lax and Nancy Stern Winters's *Unmatched*, John Singleton's *Marion Jones: Press Pause*, and Eric Drath's *Renée*. Those that included at least one female director were *Unmatched*, Barbara Kopple's *House of Steinbrenner*, and Maura Mandt and Josh Swade's *There's No Place Like Home*.

52. Geist interview; Laura Gentile, telephone interview with the author, April 30, 2014.

53. Arthur, "LeBron's Distasteful Decision"; Deitsch, "Media Power Rankings for June/July"; Shapiro, "Coverage of LeBron James's Decision."

54. Stinson, "LeBachelor Gives His Heart to Miami"; Simpson, "LeBron James and the Rise of Sports Reality TV"; Bissinger, "LeBron's 'Decision'?"

55. Deitsch, "Stories of Their Time"; Simmons, "Interview with Dahl and Schell."

Chapter 6. *Grantland*

1. Mahler, "Lone Horseman of the Sportspocalypse."

2. Marchman, "How *Grantland* Screwed Up the Story."

3. Steve Isenberg, telephone interview with the author, September 19, 2013. Similar to the PEN/ESPN Award, *ESPN the Magazine* founded the *ESPN the Magazine* College Journalism Award in 2004 to recognize aspiring sportswriters.

4. Mahler, "Can Bill Simmons Win the Big One?," 43.

5. Qtd. in Greenfeld, "ESPN."

6. Simmons qtd. in Stableford, "ESPN Lines Up Big Names"; Parrish, "Have Bill Simmons and *Grantland* Made It Cool?"; Simmons qtd. in Crupi, "Simmons Banks *Grantland* Success"; Simmons qtd. in Mahler, "Can Bill Simmons Win the Big One?," 42.

7. Simmons, "Welcome to *Grantland*."

8. See Ballard, "The Last Happy Man"; Morris, "The Tao of Gronk."

9. Simmons, "Sports Book Hall of Fame."

10. Schell qtd. in Sandomir, "ESPN Doubles Up"; Silver, "Growth of Short Content." Silver appeared on this panel with documentarian Morgan Spurlock and *New York Times* op-doc producer Jason Springarn-Koff.

11. Qtd. in Leitch, "Tommy Craggs, Tom Scocca Talk." Craggs claims his botched hire was complicated by a combination of his continual criticism of ESPN after he had informally agreed to join *Grantland*, ESPN's internal politics, and his worry that his work might be impacted by those politics. For instance, he knew *Grantland*'s name well before it leaked—an obvious story for *Deadspin*—but he was ambivalent about publishing it because of his nascent relationship with ESPN. "We were in a position of compromise," he says, "that *Deadspin* doesn't like to be in." He eventually decided to run the story regardless and rationalized his decision by surmising that ESPN hired him because of his work at *Deadspin* and would presumably want him to continue this work—however insensitive it might be toward his future employer—while he was still at the website. "Wouldn't a prospective employer think less of me if I were derelict in my duties at my present job?" he asks. His view that ESPN's "internal politics have an effect on everyone there and harm the work" prompted him to abandon the opportunity for good. Tommy Craggs, telephone interview with the author, February 11, 2014.

12. Boynton, "Notes toward a Supreme Nonfiction," 130. See also Folkenflik, "Great Long-Form Journalism, Just Clicks Away."

13. Mahler, "When Long-Form Is Bad Form"; Mahler qtd. in Del Ray, "*Grantland* Grows Up."

14. Levin, "Digging Too Deep"; Marchman, "How *Grantland* Screwed Up the Story"; Zeigler, "How ESPN and *Grantland* Desperately Failed the Trans Community."

15. Lipsyte, "Dr. V Story Understandable, Inexcusable."

16. Simmons, "The Dr. V Story."

17. Scocca, "Bill Simmons's Internet Tendency"; Simmons, "Interview with John Walsh."

18. Barshad, "Wait, David Foster Wallace Didn't Like AC/DC?"; Brandon, "Texas' TV Troubles."

19. Simmons, "Alfred Slote Fan Club."

20. Slote admits that he had not considered republishing his out-of-print books prior to the production of Hock's documentary. His grandson, in fact, recognized the opportunity

and helped the octogenarian to build a website to promote and sell his books. Alfred Slote, telephone interview with the author, June 9, 2014.

21. Qtd. in Chong-Adler, "*Page 2* Is Now *Playbook*." ESPN abandoned *Playbook* by the end of 2013.

22. Qtd. in Pompeo, "*Times* Editor Jill Abramson Likes 'Snowfalling.'" See also Dowling and Vogan, "Can We Snowfall This?"

23. Peter King, telephone interview with the author, February 13, 2014. Also like Simmons, King had repackaged his column into a book, *Monday Morning Quarterback*, published by the *Sports Illustrated* subsidiary Sports Illustrated Books in 2009.

24. Glenn Stout, telephone interview with the author, January 26, 2014.

25. Qtd. in Fisher, "MLBAM, *USA Today* to Launch Site." Posnanski left *Sports on Earth* in January 2013 to join NBC Sports.

26. "Beyond the Box Score," 2.

27. Duffy, "*Grantland* at Two."

28. Marchman, "How *Grantland* Screwed Up the Story"; Bankoff qtd. in Dubois, "Evolution of Sports Blog Nation."

29. Shoals, "DIY Version of a Large-Scale Project."

30. Davis, "Anti-*Grantland*." A kindred spirit, *Deadspin* supported *The Classical* as it was getting off the ground by providing it with space for a column.

31. David Roth, telephone interview with the author, February 4, 2014. *SB Nation* allowed Roth to continue his work at *The Classical* upon his hiring. However, he has to get permission from Vox Media if he plans to publish sportswriting elsewhere in print or online.

32. Michael Bible's "The Bow Tie Miracle," a youthful romp about two drunken high schoolers who sneak into the Carolina Panthers owner's luxury box during a game, won the *Stymie* and *ESPN the Magazine* contest. *ESPN the Magazine* printed it alongside the McSweeney's-curated pieces in "The Fiction Issue." *Stymie* published the runners-up in its Spring–Summer 2011 issue.

33. Jess Walter, telephone interview with the author, January 24, 2014. ESPN packaged additional works of sports fiction online and reissued the entire collection as a book, *ESPN Quick Pitches*, released immediately after the issue. *ESPN the Magazine* reinforced "The Fiction Issue's" presumptions about its sports-minded male audience: "You're undoubtedly about to read more fiction than you have since high school English (Good news: No quiz!)." Like *Grantland*'s assurances against elitism, "The Fiction Issue" promises its readership that it is presenting a brand of fiction that will satisfy those who do not commonly read fiction and who may even feel threatened by literary culture. See "Contents: Elsewhere," 12.

34. Belsky, introduction to *ESPN Quick Pitches*, 2; "The Fiction Issue."

35. *Elysian Fields Quarterly* started as the *Minneapolis Review of Baseball* and changed its name along with a 1998 relaunch. *Aethlon* launched as *Arete: The Journal of Sport Literature* and changed its title in 1988.

36. Cho qtd. in McDermott, "Web-Focused Spinmedia"; Ulin, "*Grantland* Takes on the Bigger World of Sports."

37. Once *Grantland* and McSweeney's ended their partnership, the *Quarterly* stopped including fiction.

38. Roth interview.

39. Fierman qtd. in Stoeffel, "McSweeney's Publishes *Grantland Quarterly*"; Simmons, "Sports Guy's Thanksgiving Picks."

40. Simmons, "Sports Guy's Thanksgiving Picks"; Bourdieu, *Field of Cultural Production*, 79. See also Bourdieu, "Production of Belief."

41. See Birkerts, *Gutenberg Elegies*; and Darnton, *Case for Books*.

42. Staley, "Future of the Book," 21; Striphas, *Late Age of Print*, 9. See also Gomez, *Print Is Dead*; and Eco and Carriere, *This Is Not the End of the Book*. Striphas borrows the phrase "late age of print" from Bolter's discussion in *Writing Space*.

43. Pierce, "You Are Not the Cosmos."

44. French and Kahn, "Greatest Paper That Ever Died," 4, 3.

45. Leitch, "Exclusive Interview with Tommy Craggs."

46. Fountain, *Sportswriter*, 196–97; Harper, *How You Played the Game*, 313–14. Rice earned an Academy Award for *Amphibious Fighters* (1943), a *Sportslight* on underwater military combat.

47. John Skipper, telephone interview with the author, July 18, 2014; Cho qtd. in Del Ray, "*Grantland* Grows Up."

48. Qtd. in Ourand, "Simmons Likes *30 for 30* Sponsorship."

49. Qtd. in Sherman, "Personally-Branded Websites Key." Whitlock's website, *The Undefeated,* launched in the summer of 2015.

Conclusion

1. Norby Williamson, telephone interview with the author, October 3, 2013.

2. Qtd. in Greenfeld, "ESPN."

3. See Ouellette, *Viewers Like You.*

4. Qtd. in "ESPN Drops Out of Project of NFL Head Injuries"; Lipsyte, "Was ESPN Sloppy, Naïve, or Compromised?"; "*Frontline* & ESPN's *Outside the Lines* Team Up."

5. Associated Press, "ESPN Drops Out of PBS Project on NFL Head Injuries"; Aronson-Rath qtd. in Sandomir, "ESPN Quits Film Project"; Mark Fainaru-Wada, telephone interview with the author, April 30, 2014; Steve Fainaru, telephone interview with the author, June 9, 2014.

6. Fainaru-Wada interview. ESPN's removal of its brand from *League of Denial* coincided with the network's decision to move its Sunday edition of *Outside the Lines*—the network's most acclaimed journalistic program—from 9:00 a.m. on ESPN to 8:00 a.m. on ESPN2. It replaced the 9:00 a.m. edition with additional NFL-related programming leading up to the league's Sunday-afternoon games. Critics understandably charge that the scheduling shift further illustrates ESPN's long history of prioritizing its promotion of the NFL over its commitment to journalism.

7. J. Miller and Belson, "NFL Pressure."

8. Fainaru-Wada interview; Fainaru interview; Bray qtd. in Lipsyte, "Was ESPN Sloppy, Naïve, or Compromised?"

9. Williamson interview; Doria qtd. in Lipsyte, "Winning Ugly."

10. J. Miller and Belson, "NFL Pressure."

11. See Sandomir, Miller, and Eder, "To Protect Its Empire."

12. Qtd. in Lowry, "ESPN's Full Court Press."

13. See Hutchins and Rowe, *Sport beyond Television*.

14. Banet-Weiser, *Authentic™*, 5.

15. Eifling, "*Grantland* Rises."

16. Bourdieu, *Field of Cultural Production*, 81.

17. Ibid. See also Bourdieu, *Rules of Art*.

18. Williamson interview.

19. John Skipper, telephone interview with the author, July 18, 2014.

Bibliography

"ABC, ESPN with CFA Rights." *Broadcasting* (July 30, 1984): 32.

"ABC Buys ESPN for $202 Million." *Broadcasting* (May 7, 1984): 65.

"ABC to Buy 15% Stake in ESPN." *Wall Street Journal*, January 4, 1984, 40.

Adams, Russell. "ESPN Gets $850 Million to Stay in the Game." *SportsBusiness Daily* (January 24, 2005). http://www.sportsbusinessdaily.com/Journal/Issues/2005/01/20050124/This-Weeks-Issue/ESPN-Gets-$850-Million-To-Stay-In-The-Game.aspx.

———. "Top Sports Titles Find There's Room for Two." *SportsBusiness Daily* (September 22, 2003). http://m.sportsbusinessdaily.com/Journal/Issues/2003/09/20030922/Media/Top-Sports-Titles-Find-Theres-Room-For-Two.aspx.

Adams, Terry, and C. A. Tuggle. "ESPN's *SportsCenter* and Coverage of Women's Athletics: It's a Boy's Club." *Mass Communication & Society* 7, no. 2 (2004): 237–48.

Anderson, Christopher. "Producing an Aristocracy of Culture in American Television." In *The Essential HBO Reader*, edited by Gary R. Edgerton and Jeffrey P. Jones, 23–41. Lexington: University Press of Kentucky, 2008.

Anderson, Dave. "The Sports Legendizer." *New York Times*, March 31, 1983, B22.

"Another Bounce from ESPN: A New Sports-News Channel." *New York Daily News*, June 11, 1996, 82.

Arledge, Roone. *Roone: A Memoir*. New York: HarperCollins, 2003.

Arnold, Matthew. "Culture and Anarchy: An Essay in Political and Social Criticism." Oxford: Oxford University Press, 2006.

Arthur, Bruce. "LeBron's Distasteful Decision." *National Post*, December 27, 2010. http://news.nationalpost.com/2010/12/27/2010-in-sport-lebrons-distasteful-decision/.

Arvidsson, Adam. *Brands: Meaning and Value in Media Culture.* New York: Routledge, 2006.

Associated Press. "ESPN Drops Out of PBS Project on NFL Head Injuries." *ESPN.com,* August 23, 2013. http://sports.espn.go.com/espn/wire?section=nfl&id=9594860.

———. *The Sports 100: The 20th Century's Greatest Athletes.* Champaign, Ill.: Sports, 1999.

Aufderheide, Patricia. "Cable Television and the Public Interest." *Journal of Communication* 42, no. 1 (1992): 52–65.

Badenhausen, Kurt. "The Value of ESPN Surpasses $50 Billion." *Forbes.com,* April 29, 2014. http://www.forbes.com/sites/kurtbadenhausen/2014/04/29/the-value-of-espn-surpasses-50-billion/.

Ballard, Chris. "The Last Happy Man." *Sports Illustrated,* September 3, 2012, 54–56.

———. "Say It Ain't So." *Sports Illustrated,* July 30, 2001, 20.

———. "Under Review." *Sports Illustrated,* September 15, 2003, 30.

———. "Writing Up a Storm." *Sports Illustrated,* March 27, 2006, 58–65.

Banet-Weiser, Sarah. *Authentic™: The Politics of Ambivalence in a Brand Culture.* New York: New York University Press, 2013.

Barshad, Amos. "Wait, David Foster Wallace Didn't Like AC/DC? This Changes Everything." *Grantland.com,* February 22, 2012. http://grantland.com/hollywood-prospectus/wait-david-foster-wallace-didnt-like-acdc-this-changes-everything/.

Bauerlein, Mark. *The Dumbest Generation: How the Digital Age Stupefies Young Americans and Jeopardizes Our Future (or, Don't Trust Anyone under 30).* New York: Penguin, 2008.

Bayer, H. Scott. "Tackling Sport History: ESPN's *30 for 30.*" *Documentary.org* (Fall 2010). http://www.documentary.org/magazine/documentarians-tackle-sports-history-espns-30-30.

Beatty, Sally. "ESPN Buys B.A.S.S. Fishing Society, May Launch Outdoor Sports Channel." *Wall Street Journal,* April 5, 2001. http://online.wsj.com/news/articles/SB986417804406622833.

Bechtel, Mark, and Kostya Kennedy. "One and Done." *Sports Illustrated,* November 24, 2003, 26.

Belsky, Gary. Introduction to *ESPN Quick Pitches: A Star-Studded Lineup of Original Sports Fiction,* 1–2. New York: ESPN Books, 2011.

Berkow, Ira. "Those Soggy Sailors." *New York Times,* February 10, 1987, D32.

Berman, John, et al. "Bill Simmons: The Sports Guy Talks about His New Website." *ABCNews.com,* June 9, 2011. http://abcnews.go.com/Entertainment/bill-simmons-sports-guy-talks-website-basketball-jesus/story?id=13801530.

Bernstein, Andy. "ESPN Writes New Script with *Playmakers* Drama Series." *Sports Business Journal* (August 18, 2003). http://m.sportsbusinessdaily.com/Journal/Issues/2003/08/20030818/Media/ESPN-Writes-New-Script-With-Playmakers-Drama-Series.aspx.

"Beyond the Box Score." *Sports Illustrated,* October 14, 2013, 2.

Bianculli, David. "Put 'Top 50' in Winner's Circle." *New York Daily News,* January 22, 1999. http://www.nydailynews.com/archives/entertainment/put-top-50-winner-circle-article-1.821975.

Billings, Andrew. "In Search of Women Athletes: ESPN's List of the Top 100 Athletes of the Century." *Journal of Sport & Social Issues* 24, no. 4 (2000): 415–21.

Birchard, John. *Jock around the Clock: The Story of History's First All-Sports Radio Network.* N.p.: Xlibris, 2010.

Birkerts, Sven. *The Gutenberg Elegies: The Fate of Reading in an Electronic Age.* New York: Faber and Faber, 1994.

Bissinger, Buzz. "LeBron's 'Decision'? To Avoid the Path of Greatness." *VanityFair.com,* July 9, 2010. http://www.vanityfair.com/news/2010/07/lebrons-decision-to-avoid-the-path-of-greatness.

Bodenheimer, George. "Keynote Speech." UBS Conference 33rd Annual Conference, New York, December 5, 2005.

Bolter, Jay David. *Writing Space: The Computer, Hypertext, and the History of Writing.* Hillsdale, N.J.: Lawrence Erlbaum Associates, 1991.

Bordwell, David. "The Art Cinema as a Mode of Practice." *Film Criticism* 4, no. 1 (1979): 56–64.

Bourdieu, Pierre. *Distinction: A Social Critique of the Judgment of Taste.* Translated by Richard Nice. Cambridge, Mass.: Harvard University Press, 1984.

———. *The Field of Cultural Production.* Translated by Randal Johnson. New York: Columbia University Press, 1993.

———. "The Production of Belief: Contribution to an Economy of Symbolic Goods." Translated by Richard Nice. *Media, Culture & Society* 2 (1980): 261–93.

———. *Rules of Art: Genesis and Structure of the Literary Field.* Translated by Susan Emanuel. Stanford, Calif.: Stanford University Press, 1992.

Bouton, Jim. *Ball Four: My Life and Hard Times Throwing the Knuckleball in the Big Leagues.* New York: Dell, 1970.

Boynton, Robert. "Notes toward a Supreme Nonfiction: Teaching Literary Reportage in the Twenty-First Century." *Literary Journalism Studies* 5, no. 2 (2013): 125–31.

Brandon, John. "Texas' TV Troubles, Bama/LSU, and the Best Football Book Ever." *Grantland.com,* November 1, 2012. http://grantland.com/features/mack-brown-texas-tv-troubles-alabama-lsu-best-football-book-ever/.

Browne, David. *Amped: How Big Air, Big Dollars, and a New Generation Took Sports to the Extreme.* New York: Bloomsbury, 2004.

Bryant, Jennings, Paul Comisky, and Dolph Zillmann. "Drama in Sports Commentary." *Journal of Communication* 27 (1977): 140–49.

Bulkeley, William M. "Sports Potato." *Wall Street Journal,* February 26, 1988, D13.

"By the Time You Read about a Hostile Takeover It Could Be Too Late." *Wall Street Journal,* May 9, 1985, 5.

"Cable Nets Line Up for Fall." *Broadcasting* (July 19, 1993): 14.

Caldwell, John T. "Convergence Television: Aggregating Form and Repurposing Content in the Culture of Conglomeration." In *Television after TV: Essays on a Medium in Transition*, edited by Lynn Spigel and Jan Olsson, 41–74. Durham, N.C.: Duke University Press, 2004.

———. "Critical Industrial Practice: Branding, Repurposing, and the Migratory Patterns of Industrial Texts." *Television & New Media* 7, no. 2 (2006): 99–134.

———. *Televisuality: Style, Crisis, and Authority in American Television*. New Brunswick, N.J.: Rutgers University Press, 1995.

Callahan, Tom. "Tuning Out the 24-Hour Sports Glut: A Viewer's Lament." *Newsweek*, December 11, 1989, 68.

Carr, Nicholas. *The Shallows: What the Internet Is Doing to Our Brains*. New York: W. W. Norton, 2010.

Carter, Bill, and Richard Sandomir. "The Trophy in Eisner's Big Deal." *New York Times*, August 6, 1995, F1.

Carvell, Tim. "Prime Time Player." *Fortune*, March 2, 1998, 134–44.

Cavanaugh, Jack. "Play It Again: Choosing the Best Athletes of the Century." *New York Times*, March 21, 1999, 651.

Chad, Norman. "Football Is Good on ESPN . . . Except." *Washington Post*, November 10, 1987, E2.

———. "Inaugural NFL Broadcast on ESPN Gets High Ratings, but Thumbs Down." *Washington Post*, August 27, 1987, B5.

———. "To TV Sports Fans, ESPN Grows from Novelty to Necessity." *Washington Post*, October 18, 1987, 41.

"Chat with Bill Simmons." *ESPN.com*, November 28, 2010. http://m.espn.go.com/general/ chat/chat?eventId=35710&page=4&hcId=3755252&wjb=.

Chong-Adler, Kristie. "*Page 2* Is Now *Playbook*: *ESPN.com*, the *Magazine's* Collaboration." *ESPN.com*, October 5, 2012. http://frontrow.espn.go.com/2012/04/page-2-is-now -playbook-espn-com-the-magazines-collaboration/.

Chunovic, Louis. "ESPN2 Gets Its Friday Night 'Block Party' On." *Television Week* (May 5, 2003). http://www.tvweek.com/news/2003/05/espn2_gets_its_friday_night_bl.php.

"Classic Sports Network Becomes Sole Nostalgia Outlet of NFL." Associated Press, May 20, 1997.

"Classic Sports Network Stings Like a Bee." *PR Newswire* (April 25, 1995).

Cohen, Noam. "Writing a Sports Column Far from Print, and the Game." *New York Times*, November 16, 2009, B1.

Consoli, John. "Throwing Out the Script." *Mediaweek* (September 29, 2008): 6–8.

Cooper, Jim. "*SportsCenter* Gets Promotion Push." *Broadcasting & Cable* (August 2, 1993): 44.

Corner, John. "Television Documentary and the Category of the Aesthetic." *Screen* 44, no. 1 (2003): 92–100.

Cossar, Harper. "Televised Golf and the Creation of Narrative." *Film & History* 35, no. 1 (2005): 52–59.

Coyle, Jake. "ESPN Hands Off to *30 for 30* Filmmakers, and They Run with It." Associated Press, June 21, 2010.

Crane, Dan. "A TV Sports Show That's More about Chuckles than Cheers." *New York Times*, March 12, 2005, B9.

Creamer, Matthew. "ESPN Honors Fans to Celebrate 25th Year." *PRWeek* (April 19, 2004). http://www.prweek.com/article/1246102/espn-honors-fans-celebrate-25th-year.

Creamer, Robert W. *Babe: The Legend Comes to Life*. New York: Simon & Schuster, 1974.

Crepeau, Richard C. *NFL Football: A History of America's New National Pastime*. Urbana: University of Illinois Press, 2014.

———. "There Seems to Be No End in Sight." *Journal of Sport History* 27, no. 3 (Fall 2000): 525–27.

Crupi, Anthony. "Bill Simmons Banks *Grantland* Success on Sponsorships." *Adweek* (June 9, 2011). http://www.adweek.com/news/advertising-branding/bill-simmons-banks -grantland-success-sponsorships-132376.

Cummings, Tommy. "*SportsJones* Offers Alternative from Mainstream." *Fort Worth Star Telegraph*, May 11, 1999, 2.

Curtin, Michael. *Redeeming the Wasteland: Television Documentary and Cold War Politics*. New Brunswick, N.J.: Rutgers University Press, 1995.

Curtis, Bryan. "Adrift on the Sea of *ESPN.com*." *New York Times*, June 4, 2006. http:// www.nytimes.com/2006/06/04/sports/playmagazine/04espn.com.html?pagewante -=all&_r=0.

———. "Bill Simmons: Bard of the Red Sox." *Slate.com*, October 5, 2005. http://www .slate.com/articles/news_and_politics/the_middlebrow/2005/10/bill_simmons .html.

Darnton, Robert. *The Case for Books: Past, Present, and Future*. New York: PublicAffairs, 2009.

Davis, Noah. "The Anti-*Grantland*: The Rest of the Best in Sportswriting Are Starting a New Website." *Business Insider*, August 15, 2011. http://www.businessinsider.com/here -are-the-details-of-that-awesome-new-sports-publication-youve-been-hearing-about -2011–8.

Deitsch, Richard. "Media Power Rankings for June/July." *Sports Illustrated*, July 15, 2010. http://www.si.com/more-sports/2010/07/15/junemedia-power?eref=sihp.

———. "The Stories of Their Time: ESPN's *30 for 30* Fields a Rich Lineup of Documentaries." *Sports Illustrated*, December 20, 2010, 26.

Delaney, Tom. "Nabisco Gives ESPN New Program Taste." *Adweek*, September 17, 1984.

Del Ray, Jason. "As *Grantland* Grows Up, It Looks to *New York Magazine* as a Model." *Ad Age* (January 10, 2013). http://adage.com/article/digital/grantland-grows-york -magazine-a-model/239098/.

Dempsey, John. "Auds Swear by Knight Bio." *Daily Variety*, March 12, 2002, 8.

———. "ESPN Game for Classic Sports Net." *Daily Variety*, September 4, 1997, 1.

———. "Will ESPN Play Hardball?" *Daily Variety*, November 10, 2003, 22.

Derrida, Jacques. *Archive Fever: A Freudian Impression*. Translated by Eric Prenowitz. Chicago: University of Chicago Press, 1996.

De Valck, Marijke. *Film Festivals: From European Geopolitics to Global Cinephilia*. Amsterdam: Amsterdam University Press, 2007.

Dowling, David, and Travis Vogan. "'Can We Snow Fall This? Digital Longform and the Race for the Tablet Market." *Digital Journalism*. doi: 10.1080/21670811.2014.930250.

Dubois, Lou. "The Evolution of Sports Blog Nation." *Inc.com*, August 20, 2010. http://www.inc.com/news/articles/2010/08/interview-with-jim-bankoff-ceo-of-sbnation.html.

Dubow, Josh. "Bonds Tells Media No More Interviews without Release Waivers." Associated Press, February 24, 2006.

———. "No Waiver Needed for Normal Group Interviews with Bonds." Associated Press, February 25, 2006.

Duffy, Ty. "*Grantland* at Two: What Has Bill Simmons Built?" *The Big Lead*, June 12, 2013. http://thebiglead.com/2013/06/12/grantland-at-two-what-has-bill-simmons-built/.

Duncan, Margaret Carlisle, and Cheryl Cooky. "Silence, Sports Bras, and Wrestling Porn: Women in Televised Sports News and Highlight Shows." *Journal of Sport and Social Issues* 27, no. 1 (February 2003): 38–51.

Dunnavant, Keith. *The Fifty-Year Seduction: How Television Manipulated College Football, from the Birth of the Modern NCAA to the Creation of the BCS*. New York: Thomas Dunne Books, 2004.

Eco, Umberto, and Jean-Claude Carriere. *This Is Not the End of the Book*. Evanston, Ill.: Northwestern University Press, 2012.

Edgerton, Gary R. "A Brief History of HBO." In *The Essential HBO Reader*, edited by Gary R. Edgerton and Jeffrey P. Jones, 1–22. Lexington: University Press of Kentucky, 2009.

———. *The Columbia History of American Television*. New York: Columbia University Press, 2007.

———. *Ken Burns's America*. New York: Palgrave, 2001.

Eifling, Sam. "*Grantland* Rises." *Columbia Journalism Review* (June 10, 2011). http://www.cjr.org/the_news_frontier/grantland_rises.php?page=all.

Eisner, Michael. *Work in Progress: Risking Failure, Surviving Success*. New York: Hyperion, 1998.

Elliott, Richard, and Andrea Davies. "Symbolic Brands and Authenticity of Identity Performance." In *Brand Culture*, edited by Jonathan E. Schroeder and Miriam Salzer Mörling, 155–71. London: Routledge, 2006.

Ellis, John. *Visible Fictions: Cinema, Television, Video*. London: Routledge, 1992.

Elsaesser, Thomas. "Images for Sale: The 'New' British Cinema." In *Fires Were Started: British Cinema and Thatcherism*, edited by Lester D. Friedman, 52–69. Minneapolis: University of Minnesota Press, 1993.

Elsen, Jon. "ESPN Steps into the Ring with Big Fights." *New York Post*, May 13, 1998, 32.

ESPN. *ESPN Quick Pitches: A Star-Studded Lineup of Original Sports Fiction*. New York: ESPN Books, 2011.

"ESPN Announces 'ESPN Films on Classic.'" *Sports Video Group* (June 14, 2011). http://sportsvideo.org/main/blog/2011/06/espn-announces-espn-films-on-classic/.

"ESPN Blacks Out Black Colleges." *New Pittsburgh Courier,* November 7, 1981, 9.

"ESPN Execs Discuss Network's Plan for Growth." *SportsBusiness Daily* (August 28, 2002). http://www.sportsbusinessdaily.com/Daily/Issues/2002/08/Issue-236/Sports-Media/ESPN-Execs-Discuss-Networks-Plan-For-Growth.aspx?hl=Colleges&sc=0.

"ESPN Scores with NFL Football." *Broadcasting* (January 4, 1988): 98.

"*ESPN the Magazine, SI* Lead All Publications in Male 18–34 Readership." *SportsBusiness Daily* (November 18, 2011). http://www.sportsbusinessdaily.com/Daily/Issues/2011/11/18/Research-and-Ratings/Fall-Mags.aspx.

"ESPN to Produce TV Movie on Indiana Basketball Team." *U-Wire* (July 16, 2001).

Estrin, Eric. "Fielding a Hit Drama." *TelevisionWeek* (October 27, 2003): 26.

Evensen, Bruce J. "Jazz Age Journalism's Battle over Professionalism, Circulation, and the Sports Page." *Journal of Sport History* 20, no. 3 (1993): 229–46.

———. *When Dempsey Fought Tunney: Heroes, Hokum, and Storytelling in the Jazz Age.* Knoxville: University of Tennessee Press, 1996.

Evey, Stuart. *Creating an Empire: The No-Holds-Barred Story of Power, Ego, Money, and Vision That Transformed a Culture.* Chicago: Triumph, 2004.

Fabrikant, Geraldine. "For Cable Networks, the Road Gets a Little Steeper." *New York Times,* February 26, 1989, F6.

———. "2 Boards Approve." *New York Times,* August 1, 1995, A1.

Fainaru-Wada, Mark, and Steve Fainaru. *League of Denial: The NFL, Concussions and the Battle for Truth.* New York: Crown, 2013.

"Family Film Rebuts Ruth's 'Called Shot.'" *St. Petersburg Times,* December 25, 1999, C3.

Farred, Grant. "Cool as the Other Side of the Pillow: How ESPN's *SportsCenter* Has Changed Television Sports Talk." *Journal of Sport & Social Issues* 24, no. 2 (2000): 96–117.

"The Fate of Sports Rights." *Broadcasting* (January 11, 1982): 55.

Feuer, Jane. "The Concept of Live Television: Ontology as Ideology." In *Regarding Television,* edited by E. Ann Kaplan, 12–22. Frederick, Md.: University Publications of America, 1982.

Feuer, Jane, Paul Kerr, and Tise Vahimagi, eds. *MTM: "Quality Television."* London: BFI, 1984.

"The Fiction Issue." *ESPN the Magazine,* March 7, 2011, 55.

Finn, Chad. "It's Hard to Resist Bombast of Jets." *Boston Globe,* August 27, 2010. http://www.boston.com/sports/football/articles/2010/08/27/its_hard_to_resist_bombast_of_jets/.

Fisher, Eric. "MLBAM, *USA Today* to Launch Site." *SportsBusiness Daily* (July 16, 2012): 5.

Fleischman, Bill. "ESPNation Rules the Sports World." *Philadelphia Daily News,* September 7, 2001, 142.

Fleming, Michael. "ESPN Ups Shapiro to Sr. VP." *Daily Variety,* July 12, 2001, 5.

Flint, Joe. "ESPN Bonds Program Doesn't Taint the Network." *Wall Street Journal*, April 12, 2006. http://www.wsj.com/articles/SB114467953669721802.

Folkenflik, David. "Great Long-Form Journalism, Just Clicks Away." *All Things Considered*, podcast audio, April 12, 2013.

Fortunato, John. *Commissioner: The Legacy of Pete Rozelle*. Lanham, Md.: Taylor Trade, 2006.

Foucault, Michel. *The Archaeology of Knowledge*. Translated by A. M. Sheridan Smith. New York: Pantheon, 1972.

———. "What Is an Author?" In *The Foucault Reader*, edited by Paul Rabinow, 101–12. New York: Pantheon, 1984.

Fountain, Charles. *Sportswriter: The Life and Times of Grantland Rice*. Oxford: Oxford University Press, 1993.

"Four Sports Channels among Top 10 for Cable Net Monthly Subscriber Fees." *SportsBusiness Daily* (February 29, 2012). http://www.sportsbusinessdaily.com/Daily/Issues/2012/02/29/Research-and-Ratings/Sub-fees.aspx.

Frager, Ray. "Whether You Get It or Not, ESPN Has No Tie to the Tried and True." *Baltimore Sun*, October 1, 1993. http://articles.baltimoresun.com/1993-10-01/sports/1993274121_1_sportsnight-sportscenter-olbermann.

Freeman, Michael. *ESPN: The Uncensored History*. Dallas: Taylor, 2000.

French, Alex, and Howie Kahn. "The Greatest Paper That Ever Died." *Grantland Quarterly* 1 (2011): 3–48.

"*Frontline* & ESPN's *Outside the Lines* Team Up to Examine NFL Concussions." *PBS.org*, November 16, 2012. http://www.pbs.org/wgbh/pages/frontline/sports/concussion-watch/frontline-espns-outside-the-lines-team-up-to-examine-nfl-concussions/.

Frutkin, A. J. "ESPN Hikes Football Drama." *Mediaweek* (August 11, 2003): 6.

Fryer, Jenna. "*Playmakers* Drawing Ire across the NFL." Associated Press, September 12, 2003.

Fuller, Jennifer. "Dangerous Fictions: Race, History, and *King*." *Cinema Journal* 49, no. 2 (2010): 40–62.

Furlotte, Nicolas. "USFL: Made-for-TV." *Cable Marketing* (February 1983): 22, 40–41.

Gershon, Ilana. *The Breakup 2.0: Disconnecting over New Media*. Ithaca, N.Y.: Cornell University Press, 2010.

Ginn, Sharon. "News Shows Must Retain ESPN's Reputation for Quality." *St. Petersburg Times*, July 20, 2001, C3.

Goldenson, Leonard H., and Marvin J. Wolf. *Beating the Odds: The Untold Story behind the Rise of ABC*. New York: Scribner, 1991.

Goldlust, John. *Playing for Keeps: Sport, the Media and Society*. Melbourne: Longman Cheshire, 1987.

Goldman, Robert, and Stephen Papson. *Nike Culture: The Sign of the Swoosh*. London: Sage, 1998.

Gomery, Douglas. "*Brian's Song*: Television, Hollywood, and the Evolution of the Movie Made for TV." In *Why Docudrama? Fact-Fiction on Film and TV*, edited by Allan Rosenthal, 78–100. Carbondale: Southern Illinois University Press, 1999.

Gomez, Scott. *Print Is Dead: Books in Our Digital Age.* New York: Macmillan, 2008.

Goodwin, Michael. "At Long Last, a Major Event for ESPN." *New York Times*, January 30, 1987, D20.

Graham, Jefferson. "*Bio* Gets New Lease on Lives." *USA Today*, June 13, 1994, D3.

Greenfeld, Karl Taro. "ESPN: The Everywhere Sports Profit Network." *Bloomburg Businessweek* (August 30, 2012). http://www.businessweek.com/articles/2012-08-30/espn-everywhere-sports-profit-network.

Grossman, Andrew. "ESPN Signals Drama Game Plan." *Hollywood Reporter*, September 13, 2002.

Gunther, Marc, and Bill Carter. *Monday Night Mayhem: The Inside Story of ABC's "Monday Night Football."* New York: Beech Tree Books, 1988.

Halberstam, David. "In Admiration of Iverson." *ESPN.com*, June 12, 2001. http://espn.go.com/page2/s/halberstam/010611.html.

Halbwachs, Maurice. *On Collective Memory.* Translated by Lewis A. Cosner. Chicago: University of Chicago Press, 1992.

Hale, Mike. "River Surfing, Rugby Bonding, and Bicycle Soaring." *New York Times*, April 16, 2010, C8.

Harper, William. *How You Played the Game: The Life of Grantland Rice.* Columbia: University of Missouri Press, 1999.

Harris, Kathryn. "Getty Hopes for a Gusher in All-Sports Cable Network." *Los Angeles Times*, March 16, 1980, F3.

"Hearst to Buy 20% of ESPN from Nabisco." *Broadcasting* (September 17, 1990): 46.

Hesmondhalgh, David. *The Cultural Industries.* London: Sage, 2002.

Hewitt, Brian. "Rise of ESPN Is Cultural Explosion in a Nutshell." *Chicago Sun-Times*, March 26, 1995, 21.

Hibberd, James. "ESPN Plans Summer Film Offensive." *Television Week* (May 16, 2005): 8.

Hiestand, Michael. "Did You Know? ESPN Is 20 Today." *USA Today*, September 7, 1999, C3.

———. "ESPN at 15, Eyes the 21st Century." *USA Today*, August 31, 1994, C3.

———. "ESPN Extreme Games Give Less in Marketing." *USA Today*, June 22, 1995, C3.

———. "HBO Sports Stakes Out Documentary Turf." *USA Today*, April 28, 2010, C3.

———. "Pioneer Steers ABC, ESPN to Top of Game." *USA Today*, December 10, 1997, C1.

———. "Sports Rock." *USA Today*, September 29, 1993, C1.

Hill, Lee Alan. "Building a Sport TV Empire." *TelevisionWeek* (September 6, 2004): 11.

Hilmes, Michelle. "Nailing Mercury: The Problem of Media Industry Historiography." In *Media Industries: History, Theory, Method*, edited by Jennifer Holt and Alisa Perren, 21–33. Malden, Mass.: Blackwell, 2009.

Hinckley, David. "Anna's Made an Impact, but What Kind?" *New York Daily News*, November 24, 2002, 11.

Hirshberg, Charles. *ESPN25: 25 Mind-Bending, Eye-Popping, Culture-Morphing Years of Highlights.* New York: ESPN Books, 2004.

Hoffarth, Tom. "Creating a Bond with Bonds." *Los Angeles Daily News*, March 3, 2006, S2.

———. "*Kobe Doin' Work* Shoots and . . ." *Los Angeles Daily News*, May 15, 2009, C2.

Holt, Jennifer. *Empires of Entertainment: Media Industries and the Politics of Deregulation, 1980–1996.* New Brunswick, N.J.: Rutgers University Press, 2011.

Hunt, Tristram. "Reality, Identity and Empathy: The Changing Face of Social History Television." *Journal of Social History* 39, no. 3 (2006): 843–58.

Hutchins, Brett, and David Rowe. *Sport beyond Television: The Internet, Digital Media, and the Rise of Networked Media.* New York: Routledge, 2012.

Hyatt, Wesley. *Kicking Off the Week: A History of "Monday Night Football" on ABC Television, 1970–2005.* Jefferson, N.C.: McFarland, 2007.

Inabinett, Mark. *Grantland Rice and His Heroes: The Sportswriter as Mythmaker in the 1920s.* Knoxville: University of Tennessee Press, 1994.

Ingle, Zachary, and David M. Sutera, eds. *Gender and Genre in Sports Documentaries: Critical Essays.* Lanham, Md.: Scarecrow Press, 2012.

———. *Identity and Myth in Sports Documentaries: Critical Essays.* Lanham, Md.: Scarecrow Press, 2012.

Isaacs, Stan. "24 Hours of Plainville." *Sports Illustrated*, January 7, 1980, 43.

Jackson, Barry. "Sports Blogs Weave a Tangled Web." *Miami Herald*, March 14, 2008, D7.

Jackson, Kevin. "Lasting Lessons of a *Page 2* Editor." *ESPN.com*, April 13, 2012. http://espn .go.com/espn/page2/story/_/id/7797078/page-2-founding-editor-kevin-jackson -shares-lasting-memories-section.

Jenkins, Henry. *Convergence Culture: Where Old and New Media Collide.* New York: New York University Press, 2006.

Jenkins, Keith. *Rethinking History.* New York: Routledge, 1991.

Jensen, Jeff. "Cable TV Marketer of the Year." *Advertising Age* (December 9, 1996): S1.

Jhally, Sut. "The Spectacle of Accumulation: Material and Cultural Factors in the Evolution of the Sports/Media Complex." *Insurgent Sociologist* 12, no. 3 (1984): 41–57.

Johnson, Victoria E. "Everything New Is Old Again: Sport Television, Innovation, and Tradition for a Multi-platform Era." In *Beyond Prime-Time: Television Programming in the Post-network Era*, edited by Amanda Lotz, 114–37. New York Routledge, 2009.

———. "Historicizing TV Networking: Broadcasting, Cable, and the Case of ESPN." In *Media Industries: History, Theory, and Method*, edited by Jennifer Holt and Alisa Perren, 57–68. Malden, Mass.: Wiley-Blackwell, 2009.

———. "*Monday Night Football*: Brand Identity." In *How to Watch Television*, edited by Ethan Thompson and Jason Mittell, 262–70. New York: New York University Press, 2013.

Johnson, William O. "Sports Junkies of the U.S. Rejoice!" *Sports Illustrated*, July 23, 1979, 43.

Kaufman, King. "King Kaufman's Sports Daily." *Salon.com*, August 26, 2003. http://www .salon.com/2003/08/26/tuesday_89/.

Keating, Stephen. *Cutthroat: High Stakes & Killer Movies on the Electronic Frontier.* Boulder, Colo.: Johnson Books, 1999.

Keisser, Bob. "The Hollywood Beat for ESPN." *TelevisionWeek* (November 7, 2005): 15–16.

Kent, Milton. "ESPN Shows Un-Ruthian Effort in Its Jerry-Built Documentary." *Baltimore Sun*, July 21, 1998. http://articles.baltimoresun.com/1998–07–21/sports/1998202115_1_ruth -babe-joe-don-baker.

———. "*SportsCenter* Highlight: 20,000 Milestone Show Prompts Smithsonian Honor for ESPN TV Sports Landmark." *Baltimore Sun*, May 19, 1998. http://articles.baltimoresun.com/1998-05-19/sports/1998139024_1_espn-sportscenter-sportscenter-theme-da-da-da.

Kerwin, Ann Marie. "Promo Muscle of Cable Net Will Back 'ESPN Magazine.'" *Advertising Age* (October 13, 1997): 6.

Kian, Edward M., Michael Mondello, and John Vincent. "ESPN—the Women's Sports Network? A Content Analysis of Internet Coverage of March Madness." *Journal of Broadcasting & Electronic Media* 53, no. 3 (2009): 477–95.

Kimball, George. "One Last List to Incite Debate." *Irish Times*, December 30, 1999, 21.

King, Angela G. "Classic Battle: Cable Fight over Old TV Sports Shows Is Not a Game." *New York Daily News*, March 23, 1997, 22.

King, David. "What Fans Can Find Online." *Link-Up* 16, no. 4 (1999): 7.

King, Peter. *Monday Morning Quarterback: A Fully Caffeinated Guide to Everything You Need to Know about the NFL.* New York: Sports Illustrated Books, 2010.

Klatell, David A., and Norman Marcus. *Inside Big Time Sports: A Behind the Scenes Look at Television, Money & the Fans.* Boring, Ore.: Mastermedia, 1996.

———. *Sports for Sale: Television, Money, and the Fans.* Oxford: Oxford University Press, 1988.

Klein, Naomi. *No Logo.* New York: Picador, 1999.

Klein, Steve. "*SportsJones*: Say It Ain't So; Another Indie Gets Swallowed." *Content Exchange* (August 27, 2001). http://mason.gmu.edu/~sklein1/index_files/contentexchange columns/column1.htm.

Knoll, Steve. "More Coverage for Olympics Fans." *New York Times*, July 22, 1984, H22.

Knott, Tom. "ESPN: The Wal-Mart of Sports." *Washington Times*, September 14, 1999, B1.

Kompare, Derek. "I've Seen This One Before: The Construction of 'Classic TV' on Cable Television." In *Small Screens, Big Ideas: Television in the 1950s*, edited by Janet Thumin, 19–34. London: I. B. Taurus, 2002.

———. *Rerun Nation: How Repeats Invented American Television.* New York: Routledge, 2005.

———. "Reruns 2.0: Revising Repetition for Multi-platform Television Distribution." *Journal of Popular Film and Television* 38, no. 2 (2010): 79–83.

Koppett, Leonard. *The Rise and Fall of the Press Box.* Toronto: Sports Classic Books, 2003.

Kozinets, Robert. "E-Tribalized Marketing? The Strategic Implications of Virtual Communities of Consumption." *European Management Journal* 17, no. 3 (1999): 252–63.

Landro, Laura. "ESPN Says Losses for Year Could Reach $20 Million as Advertising Sales Falter." *Wall Street Journal*, October 22, 1982, 8.

Larson, Megan. "ESPN Calls Up Sports Dramas." *MediaWeek* (February 18, 2002): 5.

Lash, Scott, and John Urry. *Economies of Signs and Space.* London: Sage, 1994.

Leavy, Jane. "A New Cure for Insomnia—Jocks around the Clock." *Washington Post*, September 30, 1979, T8.

Le Duc, Don R. *Beyond Broadcasting: Patterns in Policy and Law.* New York: Longman, 1987.

Lee, Spike. "Behind the Lens." *ESPN.com*, May 11, 2009. http://sports.espn.go.com/espn/page2/features/kobedoinwork.

Lefton, Terry. "Classic Sports Courts Families via Eateries." *Brandweek* (November 25, 1996): 5.

Leitch, Will. "Bill Simmons, Establishment." *Deadspin*, November 10, 2009. http://deadspin.com/5401300/bill-simmons-establishment.

———. "An Exclusive Interview with Tommy Craggs about the Bill Simmons *Grantland* Project." *Deadspin*, April 28, 2011. http://deadspin.com/5796720/an-exclusive-interview-with-tommy-craggs-about-the-bill-simmons-grantland-project.

———. *God Save the Fan: How Steroid Hypocrites, Soul-Sucking Suits, and a Worldwide Leader Not Named Bush Have Taken the Fun Out of Sports*. New York: HarperCollins, 2008.

———. *Life as a Loser*. Boston: Arriviste Press, 2004.

———. "Tommy Craggs, Tom Scocca Talk *Deadspin, Grantland,* and Pink Gorillas." *New York Magazine*, June 7, 2011. http://nymag.com/daily/sports/2011/06/tommy_craggs_tom_scocca_talk_d.html.

Lemke, Tim. "Len Bias' Death Part of Major ESPN Series." *Washington Times*, October 6, 2011, C1.

———. "Worldwide Leader in Sports Expands Its Web." *Washington Times*, April 11, 2001, C1.

Lessig, Lawrence. *Free Culture: How Big Media Uses Technology and the Law to Lock Down Culture and Control Creativity*. New York: Penguin, 2004.

Levin, Josh. "Digging Too Deep." *Slate.com*, January 19, 2014. http://www.slate.com/articles/life/culturebox/2014/01/essay_anne_vanderbilt_dr_v_s_magical_putter_grantland_s_expos_of_a_trans.html.

Levine, Elana. "Fractured Fairy Tales and Fragmented Markets: Disney's Weddings of a Lifetime and the Cultural Politics of Media Conglomeration." *Television & New Media* 6, no. 1 (2005): 71–88.

Lewis, Paul. "'Ulysses' at Top as Panel Picks 100 Best Novels." *New York Times*, July 20, 1991, E1.

Lidz, Franz. "The Big Picture, for Real, Behind Sports." *New York Times*, September 30, 2009, AR25.

———. "Yabba Dabba Doo." *Sports Illustrated*, March 26, 1990, 38.

Lindquist, Jerry. "Not a Stretch: Kiper's No NFL Draft Dodger." *Richmond Times-Dispatch*, April 15, 1999, C4.

Lipkin, Steven N. "Defining Docudrama: *In the Name of the Father, Schindler's List,* and *JFK*." In *Why Docudrama: Fact-Fiction on Film and TV*, edited by Allan Rosenthal, 370–84. Carbondale: Southern Illinois University Press, 1999.

———. *Docudrama Performs the Past: Arenas of Argument in Films Based on True Stories*. Newcastle, UK: Cambridge Scholars, 2011.

———. *Real Emotional Logic: Film and Television Melodrama as Persuasive Practice*. Carbondale: Southern Illinois University Press, 2002.

Lipsyte, Robert. "Dr. V Story Understandable, Inexcusable." *ESPN.com*, January 27, 2014. http://espn.go.com/blog/ombudsman/post/_/id/305/dr-v-story-understandable -inexcusable.

———. "Was ESPN Sloppy, Naïve, or Compromised?" *ESPN.com*, August 25, 2013. http://espn.go.com/blog/ombudsman/post/_/id/96/was-espn-sloppy-naive-or -compromised.

———. "Winning Ugly: ESPN Journalism Prevails." *ESPN.com*, October 15, 2013. http:// espn.go.com/blog/ombudsman/post/_/id/176/winning-ugly-espn-journalism-prevails.

Lloyd, Barbara. "After Years of Costly Efforts, the Race Is Finally On." *New York Times*, January 30, 1987, A1.

———. "America's Cup: A Victory for *Stars & Stripes*." *New York Times*, January 14, 1987, A1.

Lloyd, Robert. "ESPN's *June 17, 1994* Recalls Fateful Day in Sports." *Los Angeles Times*, June 16, 2010. http://articles.latimes.com/2010/jun/16/entertainment/la-et-espn-film-20100616.

Looney, Douglas. "ESPN Invites Itself to *SI*'s Table." *Christian Science Monitor*, March 13, 1998, B8.

Lotz, Amanda D. *The Television Will Be Revolutionized*. New York: New York University Press, 2007.

Lovink, Geert. *Zero Comments: Blogging and Critical Internet Culture*. New York: Routledge, 2008.

Lowes, Mark Douglas. *Inside the Sports Pages: Work Routines, Professional Ideologies, and the Manufacture of Sports News*. Toronto: University of Toronto Press, 2000.

Lowry, Tom. "ESPN's Full Court Press." *Bloomburg Businessweek* (February 10, 2002). http://www.businessweek.com/stories/2002-02-10/espns-full-court-press.

Lublin, Joann S. "Dogfight in Space." *Wall Street Journal*, September 8, 1978, 1.

Lukes, Timothy J. "I'm Not Really a Doctor, but I Play One on TV: Glibness in America." *Journal of Sport & Social Issues* 24, no. 1 (2000): 78–83.

Lury, Celia. *Brands: The Logos of the Global Economy*. London: Routledge, 2004.

MacCambridge, Michael. *The Franchise: A History of "Sports Illustrated" Magazine*. New York: Hyperion, 1997.

Maddox, Brenda. *Beyond Babel: New Directions in Communications*. Boston: Beacon Press, 1972.

Mahler, Jonathan. "Can Bill Simmons Win the Big One?" *New York Times Magazine*, June 5, 2011, 40–43, 52–53.

———. "The Lone Horseman of the Sportspocalypse." *New York Times*, June 2, 2011. http:// 6thfloor.blogs.nytimes.com/2011/06/02/the-lone-horseman-of-the-sportspocalypse/ ?_php=true&_type=blogs&_r=0.

———. "When Long-Form Is Bad Form." *New York Times*, January 24, 2014. http:// www.nytimes.com/2014/01/25/opinion/when-long-form-is-bad-form.html?_r=0.

Mannes, George. "Classic Sport Spat: Cablevision Channel Has Rival Riled." *New York Daily News*, March 18, 1997, 46.

Marchand, Andrew. "NFL Network Wants Super Bowl Series to Be Signature Show." *SportsBusiness Daily* (October 23, 2006). http://www.sportsbusinessdaily.com/Journal/Issues/2006/10/20061023/Media/NFL-Network-Wants-Super-Bowl-Series-To-Be-Signature-Show.aspx?hl=Indianapolis%20Colts&sc=0.

Marchman, Tim. "How *Grantland* Screwed Up the Story of Essay Anne Vanderbilt, Inventor." *Deadspin*, January 20, 2014. http://deadspin.com/how-grantland-screwed-up-the-story-of-essay-anne-vander-1505368906.

Martzke, Rudy, and Reid Cherner. "Channeling How to View Sports." *USA Today*, August 17, 2004, C1.

Maurstad, Tom. "Classic Sports TV around the Clock." *St. Louis Post-Dispatch*, June 8, 1996, D8.

McCabe, Janet, and Kim Akass, eds. *Quality TV: Contemporary American Television and Beyond*. New York: I. B. Taurus, 2007.

McChesney, Robert W. "Global Media, Neoliberalism, and Imperialism." *Monthly Review* 52, no. 10 (2001): 1–16.

———. "Media Made Sport: A History of Sports Coverage in the United States." In *Media, Sports, and Society*, edited by Lawrence A. Wenner, 49–69. London: Sage, 1989.

McClintock, Pamela. "ESPN Sports Bigger Books." *Variety*, May 13, 2004, 31.

McConville, Jim. "ESPN Juicing Up Sun with Block of Originals." *Hollywood Reporter*, August 23, 2001, 2.

McCormick, Lynde D. "Cable TV's Cloudy Skies Could Brighten." *Christian Science Monitor*, December 31, 1984, 12.

McDermott, John. "Web-Focused Spinmedia Plotting a Second Go-round with Print." *Advertising Age* (September 23, 2013): 19.

McDonald, Ian. "Situating the Sport Documentary." *Journal of Sport & Social Issues* 31, no. 3 (2007): 208–25.

Meān, Lindsey J. "Sport Identities and Consumption: The Construction of Sport at *ESPN.com*." In *Sports Media: Transformation, Integration, Consumption*, edited by Andrew C. Billings, 162–80. New York: Routledge, 2011.

"Media Notes." *SportsBusiness Journal* (March 24, 1998). http://www.sportsbusinessdaily.com/Daily/Issues/1998/03/24/Sports-Media/MEDIA-NOTES.aspx?hl=Showtime&sc=0.

"Men Who Don't Watch TV Watch ESPN." *Wall Street Journal*, April 29, 1985, 19.

Merron, Jeff. "Letter to the Editor." *Columbia Journalism Review* 38 (2000): 6.

———. "Reel Life: Lowdown on *Junction*." *ESPN.com*, December 17, 2002. http://espn.go.com/page2/s/merron/021217.html.

Michener, James A. *Sports in America*. New York: Random House, 1976.

Miller, Bryan. "Television Goes (Even More) Sports Crazy." *Connecticut Magazine* 42, no. 9 (1979): 52–64.

Miller, James Andrew, and Ken Belson. "NFL Pressure Said to Lead ESPN to Quit Film Project." *New York Times*, August 23, 2013, D1.

Miller, James Andrew, and Tom Shales. *Those Guys Have All the Fun: Inside the World of ESPN*. New York: Little, Brown, 2011.

Miller, Laura U. *Reluctant Capitalists: Bookselling and the Culture of Consumption*. Chicago: University of Chicago Press, 2006.

Miller, Toby, and Linda J. Kim. "Overview: It Isn't TV, It's the 'Real King of the Ring.'" In *The Essential HBO Reader*, edited by Gary R. Edgerton and Jeffrey P. Jones, 217–38. Lexington: University Press of Kentucky, 2009.

Minkoff, Randy. "SportsCast." United Press International, January 28, 1987.

Minow, Newton N. "Address to the 39th Annual Convention of the National Association of Broadcasters." In *Equal Time: The Private Broadcaster and the Public Interest*, by Newton Minow, 45–69. New York: Atheneum, 1964.

Montgomery, Jim. "Super Station." *Wall Street Journal*, January 9, 1979, 1.

Morris, Wesley. "The Tao of Gronk." *Grantland.com*, September 18, 2012. http://grantland.com/features/rob-gronkowski-new-england-patriots-party-style/.

Morse, Margaret. "Sport on Television: Replay and Display." In *Regarding Television*, edited by E. Ann Kaplan, 44–66. Frederick, Md.: University Publications of America, 1983.

Mott, Frank Luther. *American Journalism: A History, 1690–1960*. New York: Macmillan, 1962.

Mullen, Lawrence J., and Dennis W. Mazzocco. "Coaches, Drama, and Technology: Mediation of Super Bowl Broadcasts from 1969 to 1997." *Critical Studies in Media Communication* 17, no. 3 (2000): 347–63.

Mullen, Megan. *The Rise of Cable Programming in the United States*. Austin: University of Texas Press, 2003.

Murray, Susan. "'I Think We Need a New Name for It': The Meeting of Documentary and Reality TV." In *Reality TV: Remaking Television Culture*, edited by Susan Murray and Laurie Ouellete, 65–81. New York: New York University Press.

———. "'TV Satisfaction Guaranteed!': Nick at Nite and TV Land's 'Adult' Attractions." In *Nickelodeon Nation: The History, Politics, and Economics of America's Only TV Channel for Kids*, edited by Heather Hendershot, 69–84. New York: New York University Press, 2004.

Nack, William. *Ruffian: A Racetrack Romance*. New York: ESPN Books, 2007.

Nathan, Daniel A. "John Unitas's Jacket and Other Objects of Importance." *Rethinking History* 16, no. 4 (2012): 543–63.

———. "Sometimes, ESPN Seems Ubiquitous." *Journal of Sport History* 27, no. 3 (2000): 528–30.

Nelson, John. "ESPN Builds Cult Following in 16 Years of 'All Sports, All the Time.'" Associated Press, November 21, 1995.

"New Video's New Bedfellows." *Broadcasting* (September 28, 1981): 21.

Nichols, Bill. *Representing Reality: Issues and Concepts in Documentary*. Bloomington: Indiana University Press, 1991.

"Ohlymeyer Deals Sports to ESPN." *Broadcasting* (March 22, 1993): 24.

O'Keefe, John. "Sports Salon." *Sports Illustrated*, April 9, 2001, 22.

Olbermann, Keith, and Dan Patrick. *The Big Show: A Tribute to ESPN's "SportsCenter."* New York: Pocket Books, 1997.

Oriard, Michael. *Bowled Over: Big-Time College Football from the Sixties to the BCS Era*. Chapel Hill: University of North Carolina Press, 2009.

———. *Brand NFL: Making & Selling America's Favorite Sport*. Chapel Hill: University of North Carolina Press, 2007.

———. *King Football: Sport & Spectacle in the Golden Age of Radio & Newsreels, Movies & Magazines, the Weekly & the Daily Press*. Chapel Hill: University of North Carolina Press, 2001.

———. *Reading Football: How the Popular Press Created an American Spectacle*. Chapel Hill: University of North Carolina Press, 1993.

Orwall, Bruce. "ESPN Adds Entertainment Shows to Its Playbook." *Wall Street Journal*, March 6, 2002, B1.

Ouellette, Laurie. *Viewers Like You: How Public TV Failed the People*. New York: Columbia University Press, 2002.

Ourand, John. "Champions: Bill Rasmussen, ESPN Creator." *SportsBusiness Journal* (April 4, 2011): 29.

———. "ESPN's Storytelling Draws in Exec." *SportsBusiness Journal* (January 29, 2007): 10.

———. "Simmons Likes *30 for 30* Sponsorship Model for His New Website." *SportsBusiness Journal* (February 28, 2011): 8.

Paget, Derek. *No Other Way to Tell It: Docudrama on Film and Television*. Manchester: Manchester University Press, 1998.

Parrish, Matt. "Have Bill Simmons and *Grantland* Made It Cool for Geeks to Like Sports?" *Phoenix*, December 14, 2011. http://thephoenix.com/boston/recroom/131311-have-bill-simmons-and-grantland-made-it-cool-for-g/.

Parsons, Patrick R. *Blue Skies: A History of Cable Television*. Philadelphia: Temple University Press, 2008.

Paulsen. "Decade in Review: 10 Worst Sports Shows." *Sports Media Watch* (December 15, 2009). http://www.sportsmediawatch.com/2009/12/decade-in-review-10-worst-sports-shows/.

Pearson, Roberta. "Fandom in the Digital Era." *Popular Communication* 8, no. 1 (2010): 84–95.

Pedersen, Paul M. "Interview with Jon Papanek." *International Journal of Sport Communication* 3, no. 3 (2010): 284–87.

Pierce, Charles P. "You Are Not the Cosmos: A Review of Bill Simmons's *The Book of Basketball*." *Deadspin*, November 12, 2009. http://deadspin.com/5403430/you-are-not-the-cosmos-a-review-of-bill-simmonss-book-of-basketball.

"Pitch the Rich." *Broadcasting* (December 10, 1979): 81.

Pogrebin, Robin. "ESPN Rivals Set for Fight as Magazine Debut Draws Near." *New York Times*, January 19, 1998, D1.

Pompeo, Joe. "*Times* Editor Jill Abramson Likes 'Snowfalling' a Lot Better than 'Native Advertising.'" *Capital New York*, May 7, 2013. http://www.capitalnewyork.com/article/media/2013/05/8529791/times-editor-jill-abramson-likes-snowfalling-lot-better-native-adverti.

Poniewozik, James. "*ESPN the Magazine* Kicks Sand in *SI*: The Swimsuit Issue's Face." *Salon.com*, March 18, 1998. http://www.salon.com/1998/03/18/media_240/.

Poulton, Emma. "'I Predict a Riot': Forecasts, Facts and Fiction in 'Football Hooligan' Documentaries." *Sports in Society* 11, nos. 2–3 (2008): 330–48.

"Pulitzer Prize–Winning Journalist David Halberstam Joins *ESPN.com*'s *Page 2* as Regular Columnist." *Businesswire* (February 7, 2001).

Rader, Benjamin G. *In Its Own Image: How Television Has Transformed Sports*. New York: Free Press, 1984.

Radway, Janice. *A Feeling for Books: The Book-of-the-Month Club, Literary Taste, and Middle-Class Desire*. Chapel Hill: University of North Carolina Press, 1997.

Raissman, Bob. "Cable Nets Plug News to the Max." *New York Daily News*, October 27, 1996, 93.

———. "ESPN Losing Its Religion." *New York Daily News*, April 3, 1998, 108.

———. "New Look for ESPN Classic." *New York Daily News*, May 7, 2000, 69.

Rasmussen, Bill. *Sports Junkies Rejoice! The Birth of ESPN*. Hartsdale, N.Y.: QV, 1983.

Rasmussen, Don. *Just a Guy: An Autobiography by the Quiet Founder of ESPN*. North Charleston, S.C.: CreateSpace Independent, 2013.

Real, Michael. "Super Bowl: Mythic Spectacle." *Journal of Communication* 25, no. 1 (1975): 31–43.

Remnick, David. "The Inside-Out Olympics." *New Yorker*, August 5, 1996, 26–28.

Richmond, Ray. "ESPN's Sports-Apalooza." *Daily Variety*, October 29, 1997, 8.

———. "Let's Go to the Videotape: Nick at Nite Scores." *Variety*, March 10, 1997, 33.

Roberts, Selena. "Move over Anna Nicole, Here's Barry." *New York Times*, April 4, 2006, D7.

Roscoe, Jane. "Multi-platform Even Television: Reconceptualizing Our Relationship with Television." *Communication Review* 7 (2004): 363–69.

Rosen, Byron. "NFL Aims Draft at Real Fans." *Washington Post*, April 3, 1980, F6.

Rosenstone, Robert A. *History on Film/Film on History*. Harlow, UK: Pearson, 2006.

———. *Visions of the Past: The Challenge of Film to Our Idea of History*. Cambridge, Mass.: Harvard University Press, 1995.

Rowe, David. *Sport, Culture, and the Media: The Unruly Trinity*. Buckingham, UK: Open University Press, 1999.

———. "Sports Journalism: Still the 'Toy Department' of News Media?" *Journalism*, 8, no. 4 (2007): 385–405.

Rubin, Joan Shelley. *The Making of Middlebrow Culture*. Chapel Hill: University of North Carolina Press, 1992.

Rubin, Mike. "The Straw That Stirs the Shtick." *New York Times*, October 18, 1998, SM102.

Ryan, Pat. "ESPN vs. *Sports Illustrated*: The Game Is On." *Columbia Journalism Review* 37, no. 1 (1998): 64–66.

Sandomir, Richard. "At ESPN after 25 Years, Happy Birthday to Us." *New York Times*, September 7, 2004, D1.

———. "Bad Boys, Bad Boys, Whatcha Gonna Do?" *New York Times*, August 24, 2003, B4.

———. "A Channel for Lovers of Athletic Nostalgia." *New York Times*, April 4, 1994, D6.

———. "Citing NFL, ESPN Cancels *Playmakers*." *New York Times*, February 5, 2004, D1.

———. "ESPN Adding Channel and Attitude." *New York Times*, June 26, 1993, 35.

———. "ESPN Doubles Up on *30 for 30* Documentary Series." *New York Times*, May 15, 2012. http://mediadecoder.blogs.nytimes.com/2012/05/15/espn-doubles-up-on-30 -for-30-documentary-series/?_php=true&_type=blogs&_r=0.

———. "ESPN Film Series Hands Camera to Someone Else." *New York Times*, September 29, 2009, B17.

———. "ESPN Plays Games with Its Digital Ads." *New York Times*, July 13, 2001, D2.

———. "ESPN Quits Film Project on Concussions in NFL." *New York Times*, August 23, 2013, B13.

———. "ESPN Reaches New Low: Deceit, Catheters and Football." *New York Times*, September 4, 2003, D3.

———. "ESPN the Ring Tone: In the Zone on a Cellphone." *New York Times*, November 9, 2005, D1.

———. "The Games (and Ghosts) of Yesteryear." *New York Times*, February 9, 1997, 90.

———. "Knockout of a Book for the Greatest." *New York Times*, December 10, 2003, E1.

———. "Reality Bites Back: Some at ESPN Assail Bonds Show." *New York Times*, March 31, 2006, 3.

———. "Story behind *Brink* May Be Real Story." *New York Times*, March 12, 2002, D2.

———. "Top Athletes Countdown Is a Big Step Up for ESPN." *New York Times*, December 14, 1999, D6.

Sandomir, Richard, James Miller, and Steve Eder. "To Protect Its Empire, ESPN Stays on Offense." *New York Times*, August 26, 2013, A1.

Sanello, Frank. *Reel v. Real: How Hollywood Turns Fact into Fiction.* New York: Taylor Trade, 2002.

Schaffer, Michael D. "4-Minute Mile, Plus a Girlfriend: In Its TV Movie, ESPN Has Made Roger Bannister a Bit Livelier." *Philly.com*, October 6, 2005. http://articles.philly.com/ 2005-10-06/sports/25442112_1_archie-mason-gerald-w-abrams-love-letter.

Schlosser, Joe. "Lineup Changes for ESPN Classic." *Broadcasting & Cable* (March 1, 1999): 42.

Schmuckler, Eric, and Sidney W. Dean. "The Cable TV Law Hurts the Public." *New York Times*, November 14, 1984, A35.

Schultz, Brad, and Mary Louise Sheffer. "Sports Journalists Who Blog Cling to Traditional Values." *Newspaper Research Journal* 28, no. 4 (2007): 62–76.

Schwartz, Joan M., and Terry Cook. "Archives, Records, and Power: The Making of Modern Memory." *Archival Science* 2 (2002): 1–19.

Scocca, Tom. "Bill Simmons's Internet Tendency Is Going to Be Super Humble." *Slate.com*, April 28, 2011. http://www.slate.com/blogs/scocca/2011/04/28/bill_simmons_internet _tendency_is_going_to_be_super_humble.html.

Sekula, Allan. "Reading an Archive." In *Blasted Allegories: An Anthology of Writings by Contemporary Artists*, edited by Brian Willis, 115–37. Cambridge, Mass.: MIT Press, 1987.

Sepinwall, Alan. "ESPN Scores Big with *30 for 30*." *NJ.com*, October 6, 2009. http://www.nj .com/entertainment/tv/index.ssf/2009/10/review_espn_scores_with_30_for.html.

"Seven Ways to Be an Agency Hero." *Broadcasting* (October 22, 1979): 35.

Shapiro, Leonard. "Coverage of LeBron James's Decision Brings ESPN's Integrity into Question Yet Again." *Washington Post*, July 13, 2010. http://www.washingtonpost.com/wp-dyn/content/article/2010/07/13/AR2010071305908.html?sid=ST2010071306382.

———. "ESPN's *SportsCentury* Goes Back-Back-Back through the Annals of Sports History." *Washington Post*, January 22, 1999, D5.

———. "Say ESPN and You've Said It All." *Washington Post*, December 14, 1980, TV7.

———. "'Son of ESPN' Launches New Satellite 'Enterprise.'" *Washington Post*, March 22, 1981, TV5.

———. "With World Watching, ESPN Is Programmed for Success." *Washington Post*, December 27, 1996, D5.

Shea, Jim. "The King: How ESPN Changes Everything." *Columbia Journalism Review* (January 1, 2000): 45–47.

Sherman, Ed. "Drama On, Off Screen for *Playmakers*." *Chicago Tribune*, October 24, 2003. http://articles.chicagotribune.com/2003–10–24/news/0310250058_1_playmakers-ron-semiao-espn.

———. "Personally-Branded Websites Key to Staying Ahead of the Curve for Sportswriters, Media Outlets." National Sports Journalism Center, July 24, 2013. http://sports journalism.org/sports-media-news/personally-branded-sites-the-key-to-staying-ahead-of-the-curve-for-sportswriters-media-outlets/.

———. "Viewers Lap Up *SportsCentury*, Warts and All." *Chicago Tribune*, December 27, 1999. http://articles.chicagotribune.com/1999–12–27/sports/9912270146_1_espn-brand-dan-patrick-shirley-povich.

Sherry, John F., ed. *Servicescapes: The Concept of Place in Contemporary Markets*. Lincolnwood, Ill.: NTC, 1998.

Shoals, Bethlehem. "Court of Opinion." *New York Magazine*, December 9, 2009. http://nymag.com/arts/books/bookclub/book-of-basketball/index3.html.

———. "A DIY Version of a Large-Scale Project." *Columbia Journalism Review* (December 5, 2011). http://www.cjr.org/the_news_frontier/a_diy_version_of_a_large-scale_project.php.

Siapera, Eugenia, and Lia-Paschalia Spyridou. "The Field of Online Journalism: A Bourdieusian Analysis." In *The Handbook of Global Online Journalism*, edited by Eugenia Siapera and Andreas Vegelis, 77–98. Hoboken, N.J.: Wiley, 2012.

Silver, Dan. "The Growth of Short Content." Presentation at Tribeca Film Festival, New York City, April 26, 2014.

Silverstein, Michael. "Language Structure and Linguistic Ideology." In *The Elements: A Parasession on Linguistic Units and Levels*, edited by Paul Clyne, William Hanks, and Carol Hofbauer, 193–247. Chicago: University of Chicago Press, 1979.

Simmons, Bill. "The Alfred Slote Fan Club." *Grantland.com*, October 25, 2012. http://grantland.com/features/jake/.

———. "Best Sports Book Series." *ESPN.com*, March 30, 2006. http://proxy.espn.go.com/espn/page2/story?page=simmons/booklist.

———. "Bill Simmons on *30 for 30*." *ESPN.com*, August 16, 2010. http://30for30.espn.com/billsimmons-essay.html.

———. *The Book of Basketball: The NBA according to the Sports Guy*. New York: ESPN Books, 2009.

———. "Curious Guy: Chuck Klosterman." *ESPN.com*, September 27, 2005. http://sports.espn.go.com/espn/page2/story?page=simmons/050928&num=0.

———. "The Dr. V Story: A Letter from the Editor." *Grantland.com*, January 20, 2014. http://grantland.com/features/the-dr-v-story-a-letter-from-the-editor/.

———. "Going Toe-to-Toe with 'Ali.'" *ESPN.com*, December 4, 2001. http://proxy.espn.go.com/espn/page2/story?page=simmons/011204.

———. "Interview with Barry Levinson." *"30 for 30" Podcast*, podcast audio, October 13, 2009.

———. "Interview with Brett Morgen." *"30 for 30" Podcast*, podcast audio, June 16, 2010.

———. "Interview with John Dahl and Connor Schell." *"30 for 30" Podcast*, podcast audio, December 10, 2010.

———. "Interview with John Walsh." *B.S. Report*, podcast audio, October 27, 2011.

———. "Interview with Steve James." *"30 for 30" Podcast*, podcast audio, April 9, 2010.

———. "The Mailbag Returns after a Long Summer's Nap." *ESPN.com*, October 10, 2008. http://sports.espn.go.com/espn/print?id=3635493&type=story.

———. *Now I Can Die in Peace*. New York: ESPN Books, 2005.

———. "Now That Jocks Talk to Us Directly, the Press Is Boxed Out." *ESPN.com*, May 4, 2009. http://m.espn.go.com/wireless/story?storyId=8153454&lang=ES&wjb=.

———. "The Sports Book Hall of Fame." *Grantland.com*, July 21, 2011. http://grantland.com/features/the-sports-book-hall-fame/.

———. "The Sports Guy Goes Hollywood." *ESPN.com*, November 1, 2002. http://proxy.espn.go.com/espn/page2/story?page=simmons/021101.

———. "The Sports Guy's Thanksgiving Picks." *Grantland.com*, November 29, 2011. http://grantland.com/features/the-sports-guy-thanksgiving-picks/.

———. "A Tribute to the Ultimate Teacher." *ESPN.com*, April 28, 2014. http://sports.espn.go.com/espn/page2/story?page=simmons/070427.

———. "Welcome to *Grantland*." *Grantland.com*, June 11, 2014. http://grantland.com/features/welcome-grantland/.

Simpson, Jake. "LeBron James and the Rise of Sports Reality TV." *Atlantic.com*, July 8, 2010. http://www.theatlantic.com/entertainment/archive/2010/07/lebron-james-and-the-rise-of-sports-reality-tv/59359/.

Singer, Jane. "Who Are These Guys? The Online Challenge to the Notion of Journalistic Professionalism." *Journalism* 4, no. 2 (2003): 139–63.

Sloan Commission on Cable Communications. *On the Cable: The Television of Abundance*. New York: McGraw-Hill, 1972.

Smith, Anthony A., and Keith Hollihan. *ESPN the Company: The Story and Lessons behind the Most Fanatical Brand in Sports*. Hoboken, N.J.: John Wiley & Sons, 2009.

Smith, Ralph Lee. *The Wired Nation: Cable TV; The Electronic Communications Highway.* New York: Harper, 1972.

Smith, Red. "Cable TV for Sports Junkies." *New York Times*, December 3, 1979, C3.

Smith, Ronald. *Play-by-Play: Radio, Television, and Big-Time College Sport.* Baltimore: Johns Hopkins University Press, 2001.

Solomon, George. "Plan for Bonds Reality Show 'Boggles the Mind.'" *ESPN.com*, January 26, 2006. http://sports.espn.go.com/espn/columns/story?columnist=solomon_george&id=2307658.

Sorlin, Pierre. *The Film in History: Restaging the Past.* Totowa, N.J.: Barnes & Noble Books, 1980.

Spanberg, Erik. "Field of Dreammakers." *Christian Science Monitor*, October 16, 2003, 14.

Spence, Jim, and Dave Diles. *Up Close and Personal: The Inside Story of Network Television Sports.* New York: Atheneum, 1988.

Spencer, Nancy E. "'America's Sweetheart' and 'Czech-Mate': A Discursive Analysis of the Evert-Navratilova Rivalry." *Journal of Sport & Social Issues* 27, no. 1 (2003): 18–37.

Spigel, Lynn. Introduction to *Television after TV: Essays on a Medium in Transition*, edited by Lynn Spigel and Jan Olsson, 1–40. Durham, N.C.: Duke University Press, 2004.

"*SportsCentury* Tour in N.Y." *ESPN.com*, September 2, 1999. http://espn.go.com/sportscentury/features/00016631.html.

St. John, Warren. "The Sports Guy Thrives Online." *New York Times*, November 20, 2005, I1.

Stableford, Dylan. "ESPN Lines Up Big Names—Klosterman, Gladwell, Eggers, Others—for Bill Simmons' *Grantland* Launch." *The Wrap*, April 28, 2011. http://www.thewrap.com/media/column-post/espn-lines-big-names-klosterman-gladwell-eggers-others-bill-simmons-grantland-launch-26/.

Staley, David J. "The Future of the Book in the Digital Age." *Futurist* (September–October 2003): 18–22.

Steinberg, Don. "Philly's Favorite Colt on Another Magazine Cover." *Philadelphia Inquirer*, May 28, 2004, D2.

Stilson, Janet. "A-List Profile: *ESPN the Magazine*." *Advertising Age* (October 20, 2003): S8.

Stinson, Scott. "LeBachelor Gives His Heart to Miami." *National Post*, July 8, 2010. http://sports.nationalpost.com/2010/07/08/scott-stinson-lebachelor-gives-his-heart-to-miami/.

Stoeffel, Kat. "McSweeney's Publishes *Grantland Quarterly*, Blog-to-Print Journal." *New York Observer*, October 3, 2011. http://observer.com/2011/10/mcsweeneys-publishes-grantland-quarterly-blog-to-print-journal/.

Streeter, Thomas. "The Cable Fable Revisited: Discourse, Policy and the Making of Cable Television." *Critical Studies in Mass Communication* 4, no. 2 (1987): 174–200.

———. *Selling the Air: A Critique of the Policy of Commercial Broadcasting in the United States.* Chicago: University of Chicago Press, 1996.

Striphas, Ted. *The Late Age of Print: Everyday Book Culture from Consumerism to Control.* New York: Columbia University Press, 2009.

Strudler, Keith, and Maxwell Schnurer. "Race to the Bottom: The Representation of Race on ESPN's *Playmakers.*" *Ohio Communication Journal* 44 (October 2006): 125–50.

Sugar, Bert. *The 100 Greatest Athletes of All Time: A Sports Editor's Personal Ranking.* New York: Citadel Press, 1995.

———. "Patriots' Turnaround Proves NFL's Map Is Made by Nielsen." *SportsBusiness Daily* (May 10, 1999). http://www.sportsbusinessdaily.com/Journal/Issues/1999/05/19990510/No-Topic-Name/Patriots-Turnaround-Proves-Nfls-Map-Is-Made-By-Nielsen.aspx?hl=San%20Francisco%20Giants&sc=0.

———. *"The Thrill of Victory": The Inside Story of ABC Sports.* New York: Hawthorn, 1978.

Szalai, George. "ESPN Scores Regular Weekend Home on ESPN Classic." *Hollywood Reporter,* June 13, 2011. http://www.hollywoodreporter.com/news/espn-films-scores-regular-weekend-200958.

Taaffe, William. "Hey, DV, Lower the Volume!" *Sports Illustrated,* May 14, 1984, 68.

———. "Legends in Their Own Time." *Sports Illustrated,* November 21, 1988, 67.

Tannenbaum, Rob. "Bill Simmons' Big Score." *Rolling Stone,* May 8, 2014, 22–23.

"Television: The Big Daddy of Nearly All Sports." *New York Times,* December 30, 1979, S7.

Thiel, Art. *"SportsCenter* Proves It Has Legs." *Spokesman-Review* (Spokane, Wash.), May 20, 1998, C5.

Thompson, Hunter S. "The Bush League." *ESPN.com,* September 9, 2003. http://espn.go.com/page2/s/thompson/030909.html.

———. *Hey Rube! Blood Sport, the Bush Doctrine, and the Downward Spiral of Dumbness.* New York: Simon & Schuster, 2004.

———. Introduction to *The Gospel according to ESPN: The Saints, Saviors & Sinners of Sport,* edited by Jay Lovinger, 1–8. New York: ESPN Books, 2002.

———. "A Sad Week in America." *ESPN.com,* April 10, 2003. http://espn.go.com/page2/s/thompson/030410.html.

———. "State of Disgrace." *ESPN.com,* December 11, 2000. http://proxy.espn.go.com/espn/page2/story?id=937848.

Thornton, Sarah. *Club Cultures: Music, Media, and Subcultural Capital.* Cambridge, UK: Polity, 1995.

Toplin, Robert Brent. *Reel History: In Defense of Hollywood.* Lawrence: University Press of Kansas, 2002.

Touré. "Spike Shoots, Kobe Scores." *Daily Beast,* May 6, 2009. http://www.thedailybeast.com/articles/2009/05/06/spike-shoots-kobe-scores.html.

Trachtenberg, Jeffrey A. "ESPN's Next Hurdle: Selling Its Audience on Books." *Wall Street Journal,* February 13, 2007, B10.

Trouillot, Michel-Rolph. *Silencing the Past: Power and the Production of History.* Boston: Beacon Press, 1995.

Tuggle, C. A. "Differences in Television Sports Reporting of Men's and Women's Athletics: ESPN's *SportsCenter* and CNN *Sports Tonight.*" *Journal of Broadcasting & Electronic Media* 41, no. 1 (1997): 14–24.

Turcsik, Richard. "Profiles in Excellence." *Progressive Grocer* 79, no. 4 (April 2000): 22–48.

Turner, Jacob S. "A Longitudinal Analysis of Gender and Ethnicity Portrayals on ESPN's *SportsCenter* from 1999 to 2009." *Journal of Sports Media* 9, no. 1 (2014): 45–70.

"Turner Pondering ESPN Purchase." *Broadcasting* (April 9, 1984): 39.

Turow, Joseph. *Breaking Up America: Advertisers and the New Media World.* Chicago: University of Chicago Press, 1997.

Ulin, David L. "*Grantland* Takes on the Bigger World of Sports." *Los Angeles Times*, January 4, 2012. http://articles.latimes.com/2012/jan/04/entertainment/la-et-grantland-20120104.

Umstead, R. Thomas. "ESPN Makes New Unit for Original Programs." *Multichannel News*, January 15, 2001, 34.

———. "Interview with Ross Greenburg." *The Cable Center*, May 15, 2003. http://www.cablecenter.org/barco-library-hauser-oral-history/item/greenburg-ross.html.

Vecsey, George. "Wilt or Kareem? Chris or Martina?" *New York Times*, January 17, 1999, SP8.

Vitale, Dick, and Dick Weiss. *Living a Dream: Reflections on 25 Years Sitting in the Best Seat in the House.* Champaign, Ill.: Sports, 2003.

Vogan, Travis. "Chronicling Sport, Branding Institutions: The Television Sports Documentary from Broadcast to Cable." In *Routledge Handbook of Sports Communication*, edited by Paul M. Pedersen, 128–36. New York: Routledge, 2013.

———. *Keepers of the Flame: NFL Films and the Rise of Sports Media.* Urbana: University of Illinois Press, 2014.

Wall, Melissa. "Blogs of War: Weblogs as News." *Journalism* 6, no. 2 (2005): 153–72.

Walley, Wayne. "The Colossal Combos." *Electronic Media* (August 7, 1995): 3.

———. "ESPN Gets Chance to Show the Big Boys." *Advertising Age* (July 13, 1987): S14.

———. "Some Clever Taking Buoyed a Listing Net." *Advertising Age* (July 13, 1987): S16.

Wasko, Janet. *Understanding Disney: The Manufacture of Desire.* Malden, Mass.: Polity, 2001.

"Watch the NFL Draft Live Only on ESPN." *New York Times*, April 29, 1980, B23.

Waters, Harry F., and Cynthia H. Wilson. "An All-Sports TV Network." *Newsweek*, November 12, 1979, 124.

Watson, Mary Ann. *The Expanding Vista: American Television in the Kennedy Years.* Oxford: Oxford University Press, 1990.

Webb, Royce. "New Magazine on Sports Culture." Message to H-Arete Listserv, June 9, 1998.

Weinreb, Michael. *Bigger than the Game: Bo, Boz, the Punky QB, and How the 80's Created the Celebrity Athlete.* New York: Gotham, 2011.

"We're #1." *Broadcasting* (May 19, 1980): 55.

Whannel, Garry. *Fields in Vision: Television Sport and Cultural Transformation.* London: Routledge, 1992.

———. "Pregnant with Anticipation: The Pre-history of Television Sport and the Politics of Recycling and Preservation." *International Journal of Cultural Studies* 8, no. 4 (2005): 405–26.

"What's What in the America's Cup." *New York Times*, January 30, 1987, D20.

"What to Look Forward to on Cable." *Broadcasting* (June 10, 1985): 94–95.

White, Gordon S., Jr. "Colleges May Find TV's Golden Egg Is Tarnished." *New York Times*, August 26, 1984, S9.

Whitmire, Tim. "New ESPN Leads Mini-boom of Sports Magazines." Associated Press, February 15, 1998.

Williams, Brien. "The Structure of Televised Football." *Journal of Communication* 25, no. 1 (1977): 133–39.

Williams, Raymond. *Culture*. London: Fontana Press, 1981.

———. *Keywords: A Vocabulary of Culture and Society*. London: Fontana Press, 1976.

———. *Television: Technology and Cultural Form*. New York: Schocken Books, 1975.

Williams, Wenmouth, and Kathleen Mahoney. "Perceived Impact of the Cable Policy Act of 1984." *Journal of Broadcasting & Electronic Media* 31, no. 2 (1987): 193–205.

Windolf, Jim. "With *Black Magic*, Dan Klores Shoots and Scores." *Vanity Fair*, March 13, 2008. http://www.vanityfair.com/online/daily/2008/03/jim-windolf-wit.html.

Winston, Brian. "Rejecting the Jehovah's Witness Gambit." *Intermedia* 18 (1990): 21–25.

Wise, Mike. "X Games: Skateboarders Are Landing in Real World." *New York Times*, August 18, 2002, H2.

Wolf, Mark. "Middle-Aged Need Their Extremes, Too." *Rocky Mountain News*, July 2, 1995, B2.

Wong, Cindy Hing-Yuk. *Film Festivals: Culture, People, and Power on the Global Screen*. New Brunswick, N.J.: Rutgers University Press, 2011.

Wood, Anthony. "Giving Some Heroes a New Look, *Greatest Sports Legends* Become 'Cards.'" *Philadelphia Inquirer*, September 4, 1990, B5.

Woodward, Stanley. *Sports Page*. New York: Simon & Schuster, 1949.

Woolsey, Garth. "Not Your Father's Sports Magazine." *Toronto Star*, April 11, 1998, SA2.

Zeigler, Cyd. "How ESPN and *Grantland* Desperately Failed the Trans Community." *Outsports*, January 19, 2014. http://www.outsports.com/2014/1/19/5326206/espn-grantland-failed-trans-community.

Zeitchik, Steven. "ESPN Films Suits Up Pair of Theatricals." *Hollywood Reporter*, March 6, 2009. http://www.hollywoodreporter.com/news/espn-films-suits-pair-theatricals-80354.

———. "ESPN in Film Festival Game." *Variety*, December 5, 2006. http://variety.com/2006/film/news/espn-in-film-festival-game-1117955159/.

Index

TRAVIS VOGAN is assistant professor of Journalism and Mass Communication and American Studies at the University of Iowa. He is the author of *Keepers of the Flame: NFL Films and the Rise of Sports Media*.

The University of Illinois Press
is a founding member of the
Association of American University Presses.

Composed in 10.75/13 Arno Pro
by Lisa Connery
at the University of Illinois Press
Manufactured by Cushing-Malloy, Inc.

University of Illinois Press
1325 South Oak Street
Champaign, IL 61820-6903
www.press.uillinois.edu